Here is a group of living sermons on biblical characters, including Abraham, Methuselah, Isaac, Amos, Jacob, Jonathan, Paul, Joseph, and ten others. Dr. Bowie has no equal in the art of translating the lives of biblical characters to the problems of contemporary life. In addition to an unusual degree of thought-content, these studies are marked by his gift of poetic imagination and expression, and by deep religious instincts.

This is Dr. Bowie's first volume of sermons on biblical characters, and one which should have an immediate appeal. Joseph Fort Newton has written of him, "He unites spiritual vision with the grace of literary art and a passionate desire to serve the souls of men."

Walter Russell Bowie

GREAT MEN
OF
THE BIBLE

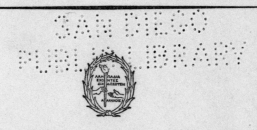

Harper & Brothers Publishers

New York and London

1937

To

AUGUSTUS NOBLE HAND

"Of studie took he most cure and most hede.
Noght o word spak he more than was nede,
And that was seyd in forme and reverence,
And short and quik, and full of hy sentence.
Souninge in moral vertu was his speche,
And gladly wolde he lerne, and gladly teche."

CONTENTS

PREFACE

THE purpose of the sermons which follow in this book is to try to illumine some of the great figures in the long procession of the Bible who rise above the crowd. In thinking of them I have not been too painfully concerned with analytical criticism of the biblical text. I know, of course, that in the opinion of many scholars some of the figures here described are legendary, and that with regard to some of the others also there is an element of legend which has gathered round the central fact. Nevertheless these personalities as the Bible portrays them have lived in the thought of many generations and have powerfully affected the ideals and the judgments of innumerable people. Whether or not objective history can validate the details of some of the lives of which the Bible tells is of secondary importance. The important matter is that these great figures are immortal representatives of the meaning of man. They focus the conceptions of many ages as to what life is in its struggle of good with evil, of courage with cowardice, and of the glory of God entering in through human experience to transform the things of earth.

WALTER RUSSELL BOWIE

Grace Church Rectory
February 6, 1937

GREAT MEN
OF THE BIBLE

I

THE MAN WHO LIVED TOO LONG

*And all the days of Methuselah were nine hundred
and sixty-nine years: and he died.*

GENESIS V:27

IT IS no wonder that one of the old catechisms, in response to
the question, "Who was the oldest man?" answered "Methuselah." According to the enthusiastic traditions which had come
down through the folklore of the people of Israel, Methuselah
lived 969 years, and readers of the Book of Genesis have unanimously assumed that nobody is likely to beat that record. Methuselah has become, not only a legend, but a proverb. He stands
permanently as the world's oldest man.

There is another curious point of interest concerning Methuselah which the Book of Genesis does not expressly state, but
which is revealed by a slight arithmetical calculation. It is stated
that he lived 969 years and thereupon died. But it is also recorded
that Methuselah was 187 years when his son Lamech was born,
that Lamech was 182 years old when his son Noah was born,
and that Noah was 600 years old when the flood came and
drowned everybody on the earth except Noah and his family,
who rode its waters in the ark. Adding together 187, 182, and
600, makes again 969, the total years of Methuselah's life. In other
words, it appears that Methuselah was drowned in the flood. As
I heard a physician point out one day in a delightful address on
"Keeping Fit and Living Long," nearly all people might live
longer than they do. Even Methuselah died prematurely. For all
we know, if it had not been for the flood, he might have been
living yet.

As it is, however, Methuselah's age of 969 is a respectable enough
term to make him the patron saint of longevity. If anyone wants
to live a long time, he might well contemplate Methuselah as his
standard and his ideal.

I

Most people do want to live a long time. Life unquestionably
has its difficulties and its disappointments, but in the main it
seems sufficiently desirable to hold on to. In our best and most
exultant moods, it seems much more than that. It is a gay and
gallant adventure, here on this planet swung in the spaces between
the mighty stars, warmed by the sun, lit by the languorous silver
of the moon, sweet with the winds of spring that blow through
budding orchards and over the open fields, and beautiful with
the glistening mantle of the winter snow. As the seasons come
and go, we may well think

> this earth our heritage
> A cheerful and a changeful page.

And when to the outward fascination which the world presents
to the awakened senses there are added those subtler and more
distinctly human interests,—work and play, the grappling with
responsibility, friendship and love, and great aims pursued together,—then life does come to have a zest which makes man re-
luctant to lay it down. In the Ten Commandments, the one
promise which is held out as a reward from God is a promise
which obviously it was assumed that all men would kindle to—
"that thy days may be long in the land which the Lord thy God
giveth thee." In the Psalms the note of that promise rings again—
"With long life will I satisfy thee and show thee my salvation."
From the times of the Old Testament down to the present, men
have not instinctively changed. Long life is still a hope, sometimes eager, sometimes wistful and almost overborne, but seldom
altogether quenched.

It will be possible, therefore, for us today to direct our thought
to this matter of the desirability of living long and to the question as to how the desire might come true. We are, of course,
under certain handicaps which Methuselah did not have to reckon
with. He did not have to listen through his office window all day
to compressed air riveters hammering on steel skyscrapers, and
presumably he did not even have an office. He did not have to

keep up with the pace of automobiles, nor hear telephones ringing in his ears, nor try to scatter over ten people and twenty things the amount of intelligent attention which might be sufficient for one. He lived in a large and pleasantly empty earth where he could walk abroad without remembering traffic signals and without being run over in the streets. What with the noise and hurry of our modern civilization, we are certainly not likely to keep going as long as Methuselah. Nevertheless, as the doctor to whom I referred just now would remind us, we could actually live longer than we do if we took some intelligent pains about the matter. We could avoid some of the unnecessary fret and frenzy of our present habits. We could discipline ourselves into a steadier effort to keep physically fit and treat our bodies with some fraction at least of the rational concern which we give to the machinery of an automobile. To some extent then we might approximate Methuselah's one achievement and live out the years that rightly belong to us without allowing friction and foolishness to throw our bodies and minds upon the scrap-heap before their time.

Thus far, I hope, I have paid due recognition to Methuselah's solitary virtue, if it can be called so—that he did at least, like "Ole Man River," just keep rolling along. But when that is said, all that can be recorded to Methuselah's credit comes to an abrupt end. All the days of Methuselah were nine hundred and sixty-nine years: and he died. That, with the exception of the statement that he was the father of various children, is absolutely everything that was remembered as worth mentioning about his life. He stretched out his existence over a prodigiously long period, and, when he got through existing, he and all that his life had amounted to simply stopped. He had been in this world longer than anyone else who has ever been heard of; but, so far as the record goes, the world did not feel the slightest inconvenience when he went away.

In other words, Methuselah's life had length, and that was the only dimension it did have. This brings us directly to the real question which I ask that we shall propose to ourselves today. We often think and say that our lives are not long enough, and that we want to live longer. In certain specific instances, and in particular ways that may be importantly true, as we have already recognized. But, on the other hand, it is quite as apt to be true, and it is even more important, that considered in proportion, many of our lives are too long already. They have duration and nothing else. They are spun out like threads, thin and trivial, and, when they snap, no real loss has happened to our world.

II

We do need, therefore, to extend life, but this does not mean merely that we need to lengthen it. A life which is always bent upon prolonging itself may be as unwholesome a freak as the tall man in the circus. And with all due recognition of the fact we have already noted, namely, that many lives which are essentially valuable are cut short because of carelessness in their physical safeguarding, it is equally true that many men and more women are thinning their lives into ugly abnormality because they are always running here and there, with pathological obsession, to this new doctor and that new treatment in order that they may spin out an existence which, when all is said and done, has no impressive reason for existing. Now and then I read in the papers the advertisement of an organization called "The Life Extension Institute." So far, so good. But, when you think about it, what kind of life extension is it that ought to concern us? Does life extension mean merely adding to us more days that we do not know what to do with, more months and years which we tear off and throw away like crumpled leaves of the calendar? It does not. The true thought of life extension ought to mean, not length only, but also breadth and depth. And it is of these latter dimensions that I am asking you definitely to think. Begin with the matter of your most ordinary occupations—the plain reality of the daily job. It is possible for this to drag itself out through the endlessly monotonous days like a hateful track of routine which you must follow. But the man or woman who understands the possibilities of life will not let this happen. Business can have something more than length. It can have breadth too. Nor is it necessary for this that one should be some peculiar genius, endowed above the ordinary with large and remarkable ideas. The one thing necessary is that a man or woman should be alert to notice, and industrious to follow, those natural lines of suggested interest along which the narrowest task can reach out into contact with the great realities of our world, The public career of Alfred E. Smith may have come now to an end, and the latter years of it will seem to most people to have been clouded by failure and frustration. Nevertheless, no thoughtful person can forget the extraordinary career which began in tenements and among the city streets under the shadow of Brooklyn Bridge, and rose to a brilliant period of executive efficiency in the four-time governorship of the State of New York. And in a recent biography of Alfred E. Smith there is this curious and revealing statement. Referring to his uncanny mastery, acknowledged by political friends and opponents alike, of the details of the State's business, his biographer wrote: "He craved education, but he was so built that he had to get it in his own way. This is perhaps connected with the singular concreteness of his mind. He does not start from an interest in general principles and proceed to an interest in detail. He starts with the problem in front of him, and the mastery of that special concrete problem is what leads him to his general principles."

There is no one of us who does not have his special concrete problem. The difference which makes some men remain hackworkers all their lives and makes other men rise to mastery is this: that the hack-worker goes dully along the narrow groove of his immediate responsibility, giving no more than he is paid for, taking no interest in anything beyond what he is obliged to do, and never turning an intelligent and inquiring thought toward what might be a better relationship of the thing he is doing to the larger work of which that thing is part. But the man who is marked out for mastery has a ranging mind. He sees the next thing beyond that which he knows already, which it would be worth-while to learn, and he is not too lazy to make the extra effort to learn it. One of the great industrial captains of our time was a telegrapher in a railroad dispatcher's office. By alert observation he learned what the dispatcher did, and one day, when the dispatcher was suddenly taken ill, he stepped quietly into his place. That was the beginning of his rise, and other prominent men in the business world have risen from obscure beginnings through exactly the same ability to let the narrow job broaden out through an intelligent interest toward a wider mastery. Nor is this truth merely applicable to business advance. That is only one aspect of a man's real broadening. It is possible for one to cover the full range of business detail and still be narrow. The great man is the man who goes on broadening far beyond the ground of his material responsibilities. He is linking his business or his profession with his citizenship. He is trying to translate practical affairs into their human values, to become constantly a wiser, gentler, and more humane student of his world, and to relate what he is doing to the genuine welfare of his community and of his time. From "special concrete problems," he is being led on to "general principles." He has learned that the only real way to do the little task with zest and to fit himself for the next larger one is to illumine the thing that might seem small with a large imagination of its relationship to bigger ends.

If I have shaped illustrations thus with apparent reference to men, it would be equally possible to shape them with reference to women. The woman's life needs broadening as well as the man's, and her ability to win that broadening depends upon exactly the same requirements—an alertness to look beyond the boundaries of the immediate task, and a willingness to take the trouble to extend those boundaries until they include the interests which she has seen on the other side. The woman in industry, or in organization, will make herself indispensable just so far as her intelligence has concerned itself with the larger aspects of the thing she does until it is evident that they are increasing the ranges of accomplishment within which she walks with mastery. The teacher in a school may doom herself to becoming nothing more than a human phonograph, her mind grinding out year by year the same mechanical text-book records under the needlepoint of her pathetic concentration; or, on the other hand, her interest may be challenged by the living fascination of the boys and girls before her, and through the beckoning doors of the problems they present her eager intelligence may go forth to a wide understanding of child psychology as the scholars have discovered it, and the actual facts about American homes and American children as she discovers them for herself. And the woman whose practical responsibility does not take her beyond the walls of her own home, the woman who is keeping house and rearing children of her own, in this amazing age of ours when books are plentiful, and when current magazines, in the midst of much chaff, will bring also the brilliant wisdom of this creative century to her disposal; when there are voices to speak to her over the radio, and lecturers at the museum or town hall around the corner,—this woman has no longer any reason why the wheels of her mind, instead of sinking into ruts, cannot go instead on wide highways of adventuring curiosity and joyously fruitful knowledge of things which will enrich her life. She can prove that delightful definition which Professor William Lyon Phelps has given—that the happiest person is the one who has the most interesting thoughts.

Let us by all means then see to it that our minds attain to breadth in the realm of their daily work. Let us see to it that they attain the same thing in the realm of our religion.

I do not mean, of course, to suggest that religion is a separate thing from the daily task. The two are co-terminous and belong together as the earth on which men walk and the atmosphere above it which they breathe. But though these two do thus belong together, it will sharpen our understanding to focus attention on the second element of our living, as we have already focussed it on the first.

Religious ideas, like those dull, unfettered habits which may cramp the daily task, can become too much the devotee of St. Methuselah. We can fall into the error of supposing that the long life of any particular notion makes it into a virtue, when it may only make it into a curio for a museum. It is quite imaginable that Methuselah, as his life went triumphantly past one century mark after the other, may have walked among his neighbors somewhat haughtily. "Look at me," he may have said. "I was nine hundred and sixty-eight years old my last birthday. What does anything that you know matter in comparison with what I know? And what do you amount to in comparison with me?" This same not unnatural delusion of

Methuselah's, that anything which has been here very long becomes thereby entitled to lay down the law, did not cease when the disrespectful waters of the flood took Methuselah away. We still tend to suppose that if we have thought anything long enough, it must be so. "I have been going to this Church all my life," a man will say. "My grandfather had a pew here. I was baptized here, and I expect to be buried here. I know what I think, and I expect to go on thinking this way until I die."

Very well. So presumably did Methuselah. But the unhappy difficulty is that there is no record that all the things he may have kept on thinking, even for nine hundred and sixty-nine years, were ever particularly worth being thought. That is the danger with many of our own inveterate ideas, more especially our religious ideas, for there is no guarantee that duration means desirability. Often the reverse is true. In the ground of the Church's thought, and of the thought of the individual, false conceptions may take root like weeds. Year after year they persist and occupy more of that ground which ought to blossom with fairer things. They do not broaden the aspect of the individual, or the collective thought. They only make it narrow with an ugly monotony. Take, for example, the theory of apostolic succession. That, allowed to run wild, can become a weed in the garden of religious truth. It can crowd out of men's minds all varied and fragrant conceptions of the many ways in which the spirit of God may blossom, until the whole field of thinking is filled with a drab intolerance. Or take the extreme Roman Catholic or Anglo-Catholic conception of the sacraments. That also, lovely as it is in origin, can degenerate until it is a destroying and relentless weed. Take any of those stubborn prejudices which you or I may cherish, prejudices which push out their hostile roots to stifle any thinking in the Church which is different from our own, and these things also may be deadly weeds. They do not deserve to go on living simply because they have lived a long time. Their very duration and deep-rootedness is the thing that makes them least desirable. They would condemn the mind and soul of religion to a sterile uniformity. They would kill all that broad variety in which religious experience is meant to flower.

I plead, therefore, for that spirit in religion and in life which has not only length of precedent behind it, but breadth of appreciation now. It is a pitiable thing when men's minds become like so many little Methuselahs, having nothing to boast of or rejoice in except that they have gone on existing exactly as they are for nobody knows how long. Round us are the great widenesses of the unlimited grace of God. If only we are teachable, thoughtful, and outgoing, the true ideas and the deep loyalties we already have will not be sacrificed, but only made more beautiful with a larger understanding. Has not the time come when we can cease our pathetic quibblings about the things that make us into Episcopalians or Presbyterians, or one and another of a hundred exclusive kinds of would-be Christians, and begin to understand that God's recognition is more catholic than we have dreamed? Within the fullness of men's worship, must there not be many flowers round the feet of Him who perhaps will come to walk in the garden in the cool of the day, and, among the differences, does God desire any stricter oneness than this—that all in their various ways should alike be fragrant with desire for Him?

III

We have spoken of length of life, and we have spoken of its breadth. One further and final quality needs to be remembered. It must also have depth.

There is a kind of breadth which has no depth, and its result is shallowness and stagnation. Some men and women have wide-ranging curiosities, insatiable and unresting interests, but all those interests are selfish. They spread their desires here and there, in order that they may occupy the ground of life for their own enjoyment. The current of their life is like a stream of water flattening out into a marsh. It possesses everything and produces nothing. It takes wide spaces of the world away from those who might use them, and turns them into a sluggish pool. In our world today, with its thousand channels of attraction, it is not difficult for the tastes of men to flow over wide areas of learning or of beauty. But the danger is that many of

those who have great privilege and broad personal culture may
lack any sense of their responsibility. Like the marsh, they have
a glittering surface, but they are passive and inert. Their energies
never flow into some deep channel as of a river on which the
great ships of the world's need go up and down.

Yet this is the ultimate question with which all true souls
must some day reckon: how shall life attain those right dimensions which make it deep as well as broad and long? It is not
enough to have an existence merely lengthened out beyond
the normal years. It is not enough to have it widened out like a
sheet of lazy waters mirroring the beauty of the world which
it has done nothing to create. In that incisive satire of Eugene
O'Neill's called *Marco Millions,* the great khan of China says
of this incarnation of much modern selfishness:

Marco's spiritual hump begins to disgust me. He is not even a
mortal soul; he is only an acquisitive instinct. We have given him
every opportunity to learn, and he has memorized everything and
learned nothing. He has looked at everything and seen nothing. He
has lusted for everything and loved nothing. He is only a shrewd
and crafty greed.

But the perpendicular dimensions of a life may be thought
of not only as depth but also as height. When man stopped
going upon all fours, like the brutes, and rose upright as a human being, something happened not only to his body but to
his spirit. He began to look at the sun and the moon and the
quiet spaces between the stars. He began to see those things
which are on high, and ever since then something within our
human nature has responded to the calling of the heights.

In the old prisons of the Inquisition and of other ancient
tyrannies no forms of torture seemed more horrible than those
cells deliberately made too low for a man to stand at his full
height. Thrust into that cell a man might sit down, or lie down,
or crawl about. His life was not necessarily endangered, nevertheless it was made hideous; for all his man's instinct to lift
himself, to breathe freely and to hold his head high was smothered. So also, to our human spirits as to our human bodies, there
is something intolerable in conditions which do not give us

height enough to stand, and under conditions such as these thousands of men and women are actually suffering now. When people have forgotten God, they have made existence like a cell with iron ceiling that shuts down above their heads: and if the cell were a thousand miles long and a thousand miles wide, none the less would they be in torment through this one fact that it is too low for their souls to stand up straight.

That is what is the matter with the spirit of our time. We have imagined that all we needed to give to life was length and breadth, and we have forgotten that we also needed to give it height. Lacking this sense of life as something high, we have made it seem so mean and cheap that even boys and girls who ought to feel life beautiful are sometimes sick of bearing it. What is the reason for that joyless mood of cynicism which so many even of our more normal young people show? Is not *this* the reason? They have never been taught to understand the real dimensions in which life ought to move: and the very instinct in them which might make their living high and fine, being smothered and frustrated, turns into the poison of blind discontent. We have taught our young people, and we have told ourselves, that life is long—at least in one direction. We see it leading back through the ages to its rude origins among the brutes, and sometimes we have encouraged that poor half-knowledge which interprets all the meaning of life not in terms of the levels to which it ought to climb but in terms of the jungle where it began. We have said also that life is wide—full of ten thousand interests and pleasures and imagined profits which we must be possessing on every side. And when we have taken this description of life as though it were the truth and all the truth, we have produced the kind of living in which so many now pathetically grope—a sprawling search for shallow excitements, a following of instincts with no clear guidance of ideals, a blind commotion undignified by any character.

So then we turn back to the words with which we began. "The days of Methuselah were nine hundred and sixty-nine years: and he died." And he died. That is all there is to say of mere lengthened existence. That is all there is to say at the end of diffused and shallow selfishness, no matter how bright its glittering opportunity. But there was a life once which not even death itself could cause to die. It extended at the most over only thirty-three years; but it has shown the secret of the kind of living which is eternal in its power. Though its years were short, it is as vast as eternity, for it was as broad as the heart of man, and it was deep with the passion of the purposes of God, and high as the stars of heaven. From the failure of Methuselah, we turn our eyes to the fullness of Jesus, and we know that only as we come back and back again to learn of him can we understand the dignity of life.

II

THE MAN WHO LIVED FOR TOMORROW

*By faith Abraham, when he was called to go out
into a place which he should after receive for an inheritance, obeyed: and he went out, not knowing
whither he went.* HEBREWS xi:8

THAT seems a strange description for a man who was considered to be great. That he *was* considered to be great,
every one who has read history knows. The people of Israel
have made a supreme contribution to the spiritual life of the human race, and Abraham was regarded as the founder of that people. He was "the father of the faithful." The story of Abraham
comes down from ancient times; and how much of it is fact and
how much of it is legend, no one can positively tell. But for
the spiritual value of his figure this is unimportant. It was such
a man as he is portrayed to have been that men afterwards believed to have existed. It was such a man as he that they *wanted*
to exist. He stands as the ideal which successive generations
claimed. In him men recognized the spirit which seemed to
them to make life great.

But how could a man be great who could be described in
such words as those which I read just now? "He went out, not
knowing whither he went." Is that not rather the antithesis of
greatness? What can be great in a man who gropes? What
sort of leadership can we look for from one who, when he starts
out, does not know where he is going? We tend to think that
consequential men are of a very different sort. The big man is the
hard-headed practical man who, before he attempts anything,
knows exactly what he is doing. The successful man is the
shrewd man who has all his plans ready in advance and will
undertake only those things which are within his grasp. Abraham was not like that. His story is the story of a man who went
out from his own surroundings into a country he had never
seen, following an inward moving which as yet had no suffi-

cient proof, entering upon an experience which had in it very little which other men of his time might have envied, attaining no great visible success, and yet at the end himself so vast a success that all history is ennobled by his name. It is of this man then, and of this kind of man, that we are to think today. He is the kind of man who cannot fully know the road on which he adventures because the road he chooses is too high a one for its end to be visible from the levels where men start. He is a man who cannot fully know where he is going because he lives in the strength of tomorrow and not only within the limits of today.

Let us take up, therefore, these three considerations as to Abraham: first, the impulse which moved him; second, the experience through which he went; and third, the result he reached.

I

The impulse which moved him. The story of his life begins in Ur of the Chaldees. Only a few mounds in the midst of the drifting dust of the desert mark now where Ur of the Chaldees used to be; but in its day it was an important city situated on the west bank of the Euphrates near its junction with the Tigris, in the midst of the richest and most advanced civilization of its age. There were many obvious reasons why a man born in Ur should stay there. Ur was comfortable; it was familiar; it was safe. But something moved Abraham not to stay. The old story in the book of Genesis puts it in vivid fashion. It says that the voice of God spoke to Abraham and said to him: "Get thee out of thy country, and from thy kindred, and from thy father's house, unto a land that I will show thee."

"Get thee out!" What a pageant down through all the avenues of time begins to move again at the echo of those words! From the beginning there has come to men, sometimes singly, and sometimes in larger groups, the urge which has made them rise and go. Against the dark background of the common crowd moves out this endless procession of the pioneers. Tribesmen in the dim beginnings of history migrating from old lands to new; vikings launching their curved ships into the perilous northern seas; Columbus setting sail from the ports of Spain, while the eyes that watched him saw his ships melt into the unknown horizon; colonists from England landing at Jamestown and the Pilgrims coming ashore in the desolate winter of New England; the western tide of emigration flowing over mountains and rivers and unbounded plains, adventurers into new worlds, their deep eyes mirroring the far distances of their unsatisfied desire. This impulse of the pioneer is the creative force of human history. Sometimes it has seemed only a half-conscious instinct. It has been the spur which made the bolder spirits grow restless where they were. It has been a vague hunger for new lands, new experiences, new expansion for energies which were cramped. But at its highest this spirit of the pioneer has been conscious of a larger guiding. Men have felt that a Voice spoke within their spirits to which they could not choose but listen. They might call it necessity; they might call it instinct; but the greatest souls have called it—God. That was true of Abraham. He is the exemplar of man's great consciousness that life has its divine meanings, and that a divine urge wakes within it and tells it the road on which it must begin to go.

Abraham left the land of his birth to seek what he called "the land of promise." He moved out beyond the inherited associations, ideas, and satisfactions. He was in pursuit of an ideal for his life and his life's service which he felt to exist though he could not yet define it. In that choice he becomes more than an individual. He became an exemplar of the spirit which some men in every generation have followed, and to which something in every man responds. Always there are two alternatives. We may make terms with our world and make terms with our easier and more complacent self. Or we may hear a Voice that calls us to seek the "land of promise" of a wider spiritual venturing, and we may follow that. We may hear something authoritative say to us "Get thee out," when the less effortful impulses tell us to stay in.

We can observe this difference, in the first place, in regard to our physical inclinations. Very few of us live at the full stretch of our powers. It is true that in the rush and hurry of our modern civilization this fact may be disguised. We think that we are taxing our physical energies not too little but too much. We say that we are strained and tense and over-driven. So, indeed, we are; but the reason is, not that we are using too much strength, but that what we do use is used in the wrong way. We are the creatures of our surroundings instead of their masters. We are distracted by a thousand irrelevant demands. We are tired and harassed not by any great things we do but by the irritation caused through a thousand petty and non-essential things which we allow ourselves to be drawn into because we have no controlling aim. And the still graver lack may be that life for so many of us has no reliance in religion; and that consequently, when we come to the end of our immediate resources, we have no steadying sense of something which carries on, and carries us with it, past the point where we are halting. The result is that our society is full of despondent men and neurotic women who are failing, not because their real strength is exhausted, but because it is not mobilized in any happy unity. Under these conditions, people grow nervous about themselves. They think that they must be constantly resting and sparing their vital force when what they really need is to get it mightily released. I am not indulging now in any silly exaggeration, and I am not forgetting people who really are physically crippled, so that they must live their lives—and it takes high courage to do it—within limits which they must accept, and fight their battle with a broken weapon. But I am thinking of the far greater number who are making an unconscious laziness the excuse for their narrow interests and their aloofness from the larger possibilities of service in their world. It is so easy to grow comfortable, so easy to fall into relaxed habits, so easy to fence off increasing areas of our time and energy as our own preserves within which we shall be at ease, and to give ourselves plausible excuses why we do so. But as William James wrote in one of his unforgettable essays: "The human individual lives usually far within his limits; he energizes below his maximum, and he behaves below his *optimum*. Men habitually use only a small part of the powers which they actually possess and which they might use under appropriate conditions." We have, as James goes on to say, the "habit of inferiority to our full self," and this is a corroding.

thing. Most of us need to feel that there are larger things we ought to be doing and can be doing when we follow one central purpose with all our might. From our little reservations and inhibitions, we need to hear such a voice as Abraham heard, saying, "get thee out."

The choice which Abraham had to make, and which we likewise must make, exists not only in that realm of physical effort concerning which we have spoken, but also in the realm of our ideas. It is sometimes less difficult to put our bodies in motion than it is to put our minds in motion. If Abraham's neighbors were never moved to seek for any "land of promise," the reason was not so much that they flinched from the effort of the journey as that they were not interested in making any journey at all. They were entirely satisfied to stay where they were. It did not occur to them that there was anything which could allure them in the new and undiscovered. They clung to their old ideas and to the conventional ideas of the crowd among whom they moved. What was the use of going after a new kind of world when the world they were in the midst of suited them well enough already? What was the use of thinking new thoughts when they were contented with old thoughts, and better still, were satisfied with not thinking at all? In every civilization, from Ur of the Chaldees down to our own time, men are prone to do just this. They accept what they find. They let their mental processes travel in old grooves. They repel the suggestion that they should climb out of these and follow some new and uneven path which the intellectual pioneers have begun to blaze. There is a quaint illustration of this which involves the name of Dr. William R. Huntington, one-time rector of Grace Church, New York. When he was making his brilliant effort to enrich and beautify the Book of Common Prayer, one who was then a young clergyman said to his father, old Bishop Davies of Michigan, "Father, why don't you use in the service some of the beautiful new opening sentences which Dr. Huntington has in his revision?" And the elderly Bishop answered, "Son, I am too old to be following after Willie Huntington's notions." In the *Gloria in Excelsis* at the end of the service of Holy Communion, there used to be in the Prayer Book a repetition of the words, "Thou that takest away the sins of the world, have mercy upon us." They were an accidental duplication caused originally by a printer's error; but when it was proposed to omit these repetitious words, a dear old clergyman of the Church argued vehemently against it for no other reason than that during all his lifetime the words had been there. He did not want to move beyond the things to which he had been accustomed. Let things, no matter how conventional, remain as they were.

These are instances at which we may smile; but we know that there are instances of this same tendency which are far more serious. We live today in a civilization which is confronting the possibilities of great change. Nobody knows what the future will be. Few persons are as confident as they once were that our future is secure. It may be that much of our colossal material achievement here in the West may some day be as desolate as the desert mounds under which long since the civilization of Ur of the Chaldees was buried. Certainly we know that we need the play of quick and living ideas if we are to adjust ourselves to these fateful times. There lie beyond our old acceptances wider things which are like the land of promise which Abraham glimpsed. That land of promise, which may mean for us a social order more just and generous than we have hitherto accomplished and a world set free from old hatreds and wars into a new cooperation, can never be inherited by men whose ideas refuse to move out beyond the circle of yesterday. We cannot seize our better future by clinging to old prejudices and reciting outworn shibboleths in regard either to our political, economic, or religious life. We cannot hide ourselves behind the walls of our complacency. Greatly in many men, and in some measure in all men, there must stir today the spirit of the pioneer if we are to fulfill our higher destiny. For all our thinking we must hear again the ancient but never antiquated words, "get thee out."

There is another aspect also under which we must consider the choice which Abraham made, and which we also are called upon to make. We may consider it also in reference to what I may perhaps best call our *devotion*.

A man's first instinct is to be devoted only to that with which he is already familiar. For most of Abraham's neighbors, Ur of the Chaldees was all sufficient. They had no concern for anything beyond its borders. They saw no vision of purposes for human life which operated on a larger field. And that is true with many people always. There are men and women who are interested in their own families and have no sense of civic responsibility for their neighborhood or for the whole city in which they live. There are multitudes of people who are social parasites upon their community. They take advantage of all it furnishes; but they will scarcely take the trouble to vote, and never take the trouble for any patient and steady effort in the direction of cleaner politics which would make their city a better place for all the people who live in it. There are people who like the kind of values which the Church puts into a community. They would prefer to have neighbors who are morally clean and high-minded and possessed of some ideals; but it never occurs to them that they owe a responsibility to the maintenance of the Church and to the stimulus of its spirit. They will stay at home in their apartments on Sunday morning and read the newspaper, or go out and play golf, nor ever make the Church aware of their existence until they want to use it for a baptism or a marriage or a funeral. Similarly there are men who pursue their class advantage in business, regardless of its effect on other groups. And there are vast bodies of public opinion which suppose that our own national welfare, short-sightedly pursued by provocative tariffs and by competitive armaments, is the one thing we need to be concerned with, regardless of what happens to the other peoples of the earth. All this is the spirit of Ur of the Chaldees. It is the kind of devotion to our own narrow advantage which presently turns stagnant and breeds a spiritual miasma from which individuals and nations die. And on the other hand, there is the larger devotion which was typified by Abraham, a devotion to something beyond the borders of one's own immediate profit, a devotion to those far hopes for humanity which the spirit of God Himself kindles in great souls and makes them follow. Abraham stands in the Bible as the first of the cosmopolitans. Something in him made him want to live, not merely upon what he had received, but for what he could give. God made him willing to devote himself, not to the things of yesterday, but to the looming promise of tomorrow. God called him out from the place where he might have pursued his own interests to a vaster field where he should achieve not many immediate advantages of his own, but where he should be the creator of great hopes which the future should inherit. To that same sort of devotion God calls men today, if they will be still to listen. He calls us out to that kind of imagination and of sympathy which may make some lasting contribution, not only to our world that is, but to our world that ought to be.

II

The experience through which he went. From Ur of the Chaldees Abraham went toward the west. He was to cross the deserts before he reached the land he sought. It was a long journey and an arduous one. It led into a region as yet unknown, where Abraham had no friends. His one personality was matched against a vast indifference. Somewhere once I read a description, written I do not remember now by whom, of the loneliness of the desert, a loneliness which Abraham encountered then and which travellers can encounter still. "The four tents and the animated group by the well were infinitesimal specks on the desolate, limitless waste, silvered by moonlight into an unbroken sea without ripple or bourne. It was the aching solitude of nature pitted against the pathetic energy of man, and nature had no need to fight. She could leave the struggle and the stress to the human midges who would traverse her trackless silences, and when their pitiful vitality and forces were spent battling with her winds and her droughts, she could bury them noiselessly in her fathomless drifts beneath the white serenity of her moons."

Through that sort of desolation Abraham went until he came to the land of Canaan, and there in the land of Canaan he lived for the rest of his career. As you will see by reading the narrative in the book of Genesis, he never gathered to himself what seemed to be any very conspicuous or permanent possessions. He had his flocks and herds, it is true; but he was still a nomad. He moved here and there across the land wherever he could find pasturage and water for his flocks. He was not seeking the best things for himself. Once when there was a division and a dispute between their herdsmen, he gave the most fertile region to his nephew Lot, and he himself went on a more arduous way. When the end came, he did not own any land except one field and a cave in a hill. He bought that for a burial place. The only thing he possessed in this region of his adventuring was a sepulchre. He had gone to the land of promise, and he lived there, and at last he died there; but not in any obvious way did he inherit it, nor did the land of promise seem much different when he died from what it seemed on the day when he came. He had to trust to the future still.

In the Epistle to the Hebrews, there is one vivid sentence which describes this experience of Abraham's in the land to which he believed that God had called him. "He sojourned in the land of promise as in a strange country, dwelling in tents." That is to say, his vision seemed to lead to no certain stopping place. He had gone on a quest, and that quest was unfinished to his life's end. He was like a pilgrim who never fully reaches his goal, but always sees it shining at the end of a longer road. He had gone out; and, in the sense of a completed task, he was never to come in.

Is not this always the way with men's great hazards in pursuit of their ideals? Life seems to be all road, and no arriving. It is like the search for the end of the rainbow, which always melts beyond the horizon where it seems to rest. Those souls in every generation who have in them any quality of the spiritual prophet and pioneer know what this means. Like Abraham, they have not been able to rest in the narrow and complacent conditions to which they were born. They seek a more heavenly country somewhere on this earth. They want to find or to create a kind of life more true, more righteous, more beautiful than that with which most of their neighbors are content. They want more generous relationships among individuals. They want a social and economic order which is more just and kind. They want to see old, narrow nationalisms melt into a new unity of the nations. They want to see the pitiful divisions of our several churches broken down in the new inclusiveness of a great Church obedient to the living will of God. But the ideal is seldom realized in their day. They are pilgrims and sojourners on the fields of their devotion. Like Abraham, they dwell in tents, establishing their venture here today, moving on to something else tomorrow, never reaching that which they could rest in as their final vindication. Ordinary men looking at them, think that they have failed. The world usually thinks that the pioneers of its own generation have failed, for the world wants results, and the results which pioneers have desired are a long time coming. Joan of Arc, who followed her voices to deliver France, died at the stake in the market-place of Rouen, and France was not yet free. Savonarola, prophet of a new moral reformation in the corrupt last days of the medieval Church, was burned in Florence, and the city which he died for seemed as wicked as it had ever been. William Tyndale, who brought the Bible to the English people in their own tongue, had his body brutally dishonored and his ashes thrown into the sea. John Bunyan, whose soul was bright with the vision of Pilgrim's Progress, was kept for twelve years in Bedford jail. Woodrow Wilson, hazarding all his leadership upon the creation of the League of Nations, was rejected by his country. The stodgy men, the safe and sane men, the men who always want to keep their world as they found it, because it is more familiar and more comfortable thus, can never appreciate the pioneer. They do not believe in his success because to them success must be measured by the here and now. They do not understand the kind of spiritual victory whose fulfilment will be tomorrow, but not today.

But the man who has in his soul some spark of the pioneer goes on. It does not dismay him if he cannot do all that he would like to do. It does not dismay him if the ideals he believes in, ideals for private life and for public life, are flouted and post-poned. He knows that any man who sets out to be the advance guard for human opinion and human choice has adventured upon a long road. He does not need to have assurance of quick results if only he is satisfied that his direction is right. He does not have to know altogether *where* his path leads if he knows *why* it leads. He does not have to perceive the end from the beginning, if only he is confident that beside him and above him is the reality of God, who sees what he cannot see. It is enough that he hears a Voice telling him to go forward and to keep on, for in his heart are sounding the sufficient words, " 'I am the beginning and the ending,' saith the Lord."

III

The result he reached. We have said that Abraham did not reach any clear result. That is true so far as immediate judgments are concerned. He was a wanderer, dwelling in tents. He never built a city. Ah, so we think; but in so thinking we are wrong. He did help to build a city which is invisible, and which outlasts all time. For as another verse in this Epistle to the Hebrews goes on to say: "He looked for a city which hath foundations, whose builder and maker is God."

Abraham did not know what was going to happen in that region which he called "the land of promise." He could not look through the veils of the future. He could only follow his life's best leading, and be faithful, and trust to God for what should come. And what did come? Out of him there rose a family, and out of the family a clan, and out of the clan a nation which was to be called henceforth "the chosen people." It was to be the nation which, more than all others in the history of this earth, has stood for the emphasis of the spirit. In the midst of that nation, as its capital, rose Jerusalem; and through the streets of Jerusalem at length should walk the feet of Jesus. That city in its material fact should fall, and did fall. Its walls and towers should crumble into dust. But its religious significance should stand as the supreme symbol in our world for the presence of God in the midst of human life. In all the poetry of the soul, Jerusalem means something more than a place. It means the holy city that belongs to every man. It means the imperishable ideal of human life fashioned according to the purposes of God.

To the building of that city every man who moves out beyond the commonplace along the way of some inconvenient spiritual effort is contributing. In the building of that city all those have a part who are quarrying out of life's common ground stones of truth and honor and righteousness. Great is the inspiration

A few paragraphs from this sermon were included in *The Renewing Gospel*, published in 1935, and are reproduced here through the courtesy of Charles Scribner's Sons.

which this truth can bring to all our life. Other ambitions may succeed, or they may fail. A man may construct a business, and some disastrous turn of affairs may tumble it into ruin. A woman may give her life to some fine enterprise in her community and see it frustrated. The organizations we have assembled may melt away. The possessions we thought we would use for great purposes are scattered. What then? Is nothing left? Is nothing left when men and women seem to be, like Abraham, pilgrims and strangers in a land which defeats the things they have tried to do? Not so! A thousand times not so! For every clean ideal once set to work in this world becomes part of the spiritual energy which is never destroyed. Every right word spoken, every brave deed done, goes on reverberating in the souls of men beyond our reckoning. Every living stone fashioned by faithful service is a part of the invisible city of that presence of God within the walls of which the spirits of unborn generations shall rally and take courage. Through the difficult days, believe in that unseen city, the city "which hath the foundations, whose builder and maker is God!"

"He went out, not knowing whither he went." Is there anything foolish in that now? Is there anything futile in that now? Do you not know rather that the only great paths of life are those of which we can never know fully at the beginning where they go? Our little shrewdnesses can know where *their* paths lead. Our little cautions and our calculations know. For the paths *these* choose never go beyond our narrow sight. But the great roads which make us follow the quest of some ideal, and make us venture upon convictions about our personal and public life which only the future can prove—*these* roads lead farther than any immediate understanding can perceive. These are the roads on which the pioneers have always gone, and they are the only roads which the best in us must want to follow. They lead us out from small satisfactions and cramped ideas and petty loyalties toward great devotions which will not give us any easy abiding place. But at the end of the road we shall see and know that we have helped create the spiritual city built on the eternal foundations of God where all that is finest in our human life can find its home.

III

THE MAN WHO DIGGED OLD WELLS

*And Isaac digged again the wells of water which
they had digged in the days of Abraham his father;
for the Philistines had stopped them after the death
of Abraham: and he called their names after the
names by which his father had called them.*

GENESIS XXVI:18

HERE is a very natural and understandable act. Isaac is
moving here and there in Canaan, pitching his nomadic
tents where he can find sustenance for his people and for the
flocks which he carries with him. Most vitally of all, of course,
he needs water. Through the dry lands on the edges of the
southern desert he seeks for those scattered oases where there
is life for man and beast. He remembers how as a child he had
gone that way with his father, Abraham, and he remembers how
Abraham had dug wells in the valleys where the waters gathered.
He will find again the wells of his father. One by one, he does
discover them, but they have been filled by the hostile Philistines
who resented this intrusion into their land by the newcomers from
the East. So he sets to work to dig again the former wells. He
will recover what the foe has destroyed, and drink once more
of the waters of which his father drank.

I

The motives which moved him to seek his father's wells
instead of trying to dig new ones were the simple ones which
a moment's reflection will suggest.

In the first place, Abraham had sunk his wells in places which
had already been proven. It was no venture in the dark to go
seek water there. Since water had been drawn thence before, it
could be drawn thence again.

In the second place, it was easier to clear the shaft of a well that had once been dug than it was to sink a new one in the unbroken earth. True, the Philistines had filled up the wells, but they could not obliterate their sites, and the earth which they had flung into them had not hardened like virgin soil.

In the third place, there must have been a sentiment for Isaac in drinking from these wells where he had drunk beside his father. The thought of them was linked with far reflections of his childhood, which came back to him like distant music there by the familiar waters, sweet with old associations of days and faces that were gone. Who is there of us that does not recognize the values which gather round things in themselves not inherently better than something else of their same kind, but invested with that glamour of memory which lifts them up and sets them apart? Wearied in his flight from the pursuit by Saul, David looks from the covert of the hills toward Bethlehem, the little village in whose serene pastures he had kept his father's sheep, and yearns for a drink of the waters of the well beside the gates. Two stalwart men of the band that gathered round him took their lives in their hands and went through the lines of Saul to bring David a cup of this water from the one well which spirit, as well as flesh, was yearning for. With quick and generous intuition they understood what David longed for; for in the well of water by Bethlehem's gate, there was not only a draught to quench his thirst; there were youth, and love, and life, and dear remembered laughter. Rupert Brooke, at Gallipoli, surrounded by the blood and horror of the tragic peninsula upon which the tens of thousands were to lay down their lives in vain, thinks of England, and of that land which is

Washed by the rivers, warmed by suns of home.

Water might be brought to the trenches—water in the great containers that men toiled up the hillside in the face of Turkish fire to bring, water that was desperately welcome—but it only made more poignant the remembered taste of the waters that ran in English rills, or gathered in its springs beneath the quiet trees and down the fragrant meadows of that serene and hallowed land. All our childish recitations, and all the familiarity that would make most things grow trivial, cannot rob of their immortal suggestion the old verses that sing of

> The old oaken bucket
> That hung in the well.

Who is there that does not think at this moment of some well which is played upon by the golden sun and the sweet still shade of childhood, the well under the great, wide tree to which the paths lead from the hot fields and the dusty roads, the clear water coming cool from the dim depths, the pure sparkle and the freshness like the morning dew? The water from wells like these is more than water. It is magic potion for the spirit. It quickens into life the romance of lovely memories, and sets to ringing again the bells of old, forgotten happiness, like the bells of Ys which the fisher-folk of Brittany will tell you ring from the buried city that sleeps beneath the sea.

For those three reasons, then—because he was sure he should not fail, because these wells were easier to dig, and because they carried a value for his spirit that no other water could match—Isaac dug again the wells of his father Abraham.

Herein, we say, we find a most natural and simple act. Yet here is also something more. It is the parable of a spiritual truth which we may well ponder and appropriate.

There is in all life the instinct to go back and dig again the wells of our fathers. Sometimes we call it conservatism. Sometimes we call it reverence. It is not so much in fashion today as it was. Our time is a restless one. It is full of the smartness of an often raw revolt. It does not want the wells of the fathers. It wants to go and scratch new reservoirs of its own.

But we today may well remember that the same motives which impelled Isaac will impel us, if we are wise. The wells of our fathers, to begin with, are proven wells. At our peril we cast aside the ripe experience of many generations. The newest things are not of necessity the truest. As Jowett of Balliol quaintly said, "We are none of us infallible, not even the youngest." From the successes and the failures of those who have gone before we can learn inestimably much.

Indeed, is not this the very central message of the whole evolutionary process of the human race? What is it that makes us superior in knowledge and skill to the men of many centuries ago? The archaeologists who have read for us the stories written in the remains left in the caves that men used in the stone age make plain that the men of today are in their brain-capacity not the superior, and, in some respects scarcely the equal, of the men whose bones are found in the Cro-magnon grottoes. It is doubtful if the average intellectual abilities of our generation equal those of the Greeks in the age of Pericles. What is it then that makes our civilization a so much richer thing than theirs? It is because we inherit generation by generation the best that those who have gone before us have learned. We take up the race not where they began it, but at the end of the relay where they passed on the torch. We take from them the grain winnowed from the chaff of their mistakes. Or at least, if that is too broad a statement, that is what each age *can* do, and that is what, on the whole, in spite of mistakes and stupidities, the race has done. In technical control over the forces of nature, in better knowledge of our own mysterious selves, and in the slow mastery of morality and religion over the brute in us—in knowledge, in ideals, in faith—we can drink from the wells which the fathers have dug, knowing that whatever adventure of our own may fail us, there at least we shall find something that gives us life.

Apply this thought to some of the facts of today. Take, for example, the matter of our social standards. There are many who are deliberately in rebellion against old conventions which used to seem a matter of course. The liberty wherewith we have been made free becomes a cloak of license. Young people want to have their own way and resent the advice of their elders. They imagine that the freedom of their own personalities can only be expressed by repudiating the guidance of those who have learned by experience. "I shall do as I please, for the age is new," says some young person, "and I turn my back on yesterday. The former generation may have thought they knew where the wells of clearest pleasure were, but we will go make ours in other ground."

Take also the matter of our religious faith. The world is full of new cults. Christian Science, with its ray of truth concentrated in one strained emphasis, has fascinated many people, like the bull's-eye of the hunter in the forest fascinating the deer, which sees the light and does not know the dangers that move behind it. In some of the great cities, people are deserting avowedly Christian organizations and flocking into the so-called Community Church which meets in a theatre and professes no creed. Restlessly they hunt for a place from which they can draw water for their spirit which they think will be more satisfying than their fathers' wells. It is quite possible—and of this we shall speak presently—that some men seem to succeed. They may sink their shafts of the quest for truth into deeper and richer springs of God than they had known before. Yet always this fact remains: the wells of the fathers are proven wells. Out of the worship, out of the fellowship, out of the faith from which they drew, we know that water has come, and can come again. We must needs be very sure that God has guided us to a better place before the Isaac of today turns his back upon the wells of Abraham.

In the second place, the wells of the fathers are easier to draw from than are new wells. This, of course, is no decisive consideration, but the weight which it does have deserves to be taken into account. When Isaac went to the wells of Abraham he found that the Philistines had filled them up, but, as we have said already, it is a simpler matter to clear the old shafts than to create new ones. And here is surely a truth which the impatient temper of our time needs to recognize. The reason many people are estranged from the wells of their fathers, whether it be in the social code of pleasures, or in the deeper matters of all-embracing religious conviction, is because they are angered to find that the wells which they thought would flow with full, sweet streams of water are all but choked with rubbish. The facts may seem to give them cause for this estrangement. Some real conviction concerning human life and the place from which to draw its satisfaction digs a well, and then, little by little, hostile or stupid forces will begin to fill it in. Some sour critic, or some harsh and clumsy would-be reformer, may pour such bitterness into the wells of natural social pleasures that young people may revolt entirely from what they think to be the ideas of their elders, and go off to fashion some new conception of their own. Theologians may fill the wells of truth with the lumber of their unprofitable dogmas. The sweet naturalness of the religion of Jesus may be buried beneath the drift of formalism, so that people, impatient at all the wretched accumulation which blocks the life-giving draught they hoped to drink, turn indignant and disillusioned away from the Church to seek elsewhere some water for their spirit. It is easy to understand that impulse; yet, nevertheless, that impulse needs patiently to learn its own mistake. Difficult though it may seem, yet, nevertheless, it is easier to free the old wells from their accumulations than to try to dig wells, and to try to find water, where perhaps no water is. There is a task today for all those open-eyed people who see the faults of the Church and the errors of a sometimes stereotyped religion, to put their hands deliberately to the task of clearing away false things and making an outlet for the truth. There is need for those whose intellectual questioning sees the inconsistency of some of the theological expressions of other ages to try to shape anew by their constructive interpretation those things which, though they were meant to be channels for the living waters in their day, are now only the broken conduits whose ruins obstruct the living flow. There is need in the Church for those who see the stodginess of accepted ideas, and the inconsistencies of life which hide the deep things of God that are supposed to underlie the Church, to bring such sympathetic and patient love for that which they know to be the reality of Christian experience as shall broaden the rivers through which these realities may pour.

And, in the third place, there is that other motive which we ascribed to Isaac. We cannot cast out of any life, save to its infinite impoverishment, that immeasurable thing which we call sentiment. Like the wells of Abraham, like the waters that David thirsted for by the gates of Bethlehem, like the springs in the sweet lands of England to which the thoughts of Rupert Brooke went back from Gallipoli, there are waters which refresh our souls beyond those of all other imaginable sources because of the memories to which their taste is as a secret spring. No objects, and no experiences in their plain, stark outline have any magic for our spirit. It is that intangible something called atmosphere which makes them full of the hovering of immortal wings. Go look at the so-called portrait painted by the clumsy, would-be artist. There may be the labored representation of the features of the man we knew. All its measurements may be exact, its proportions as true as any photograph could have given them; but nevertheless we say the picture is not true if its stiff exactitude carries no suggestion of the deep background of the man's personality—his brooding memories, his thoughts and his convictions. In one of the museums at Harvard University is a famous collection of botanical models, and thousands of people go every year to see these glass flowers. In form, in color, and, as far as the eye can see, in minutest construction they are indistinguishable from the flowers they represent. And yet how infinite is the difference!—for the fragrance, the delicate fragility, and all the elusive wonder of the living thing is lost. Much the skill of men can do, but no human skill can duplicate the magic legacy of sun and rain and all the quiet miracle of growth beneath the skies of God. And so men go and formulate their hasty new convictions in morality and religion. They go and construct new organizations and call them the Church, but the rich wealth of long association and sentiment is lacking, and because of that lack something very deep in the human spirit must go unsatisfied. On the heights in New York men may build the mighty cathedral of tomorrow. Very wonderful will it be as the shrine of the Church's life, but how can men give to it the mighty awe, the holy hush of immemorial meaning which puts its spell upon our spirits as we go beneath the ancient trees into the long vista of Winchester where the footsteps of the centuries are trodden deep into the stones, or pass into the shadowed sublimity of the Abbey at Westminster?

We in America are in danger of forgetting the incomparable loveliness of ancient things. We live, so many of us, in cheap houses and pretentious apartments knocked together out of shoddy stuff by speculators who built them for today's profits, regardless either of yesterday or tomorrow. The old homes in which families dwelt for generations are growing scarcer. Old churches are abandoned to build some new one convenient to the people. In the same way the thoughts, the ideals, and the principles which have been the homes of human spirits, full of strong and sweet suggestion, are lightly abandoned, that we may move into some new and gaudy-fronted thing. Yet, when we search our souls, we know that the hunger and thirst for the old loveliness of association is still there. In the midst of what he calls his modern conveniences a man's soul may be wistful in his deep-regarding moments for the simplicities of his childhood's days. And in the modern convenience of these hasty expedients which sometimes our souls set up in place of the slowly built and richly furnished convictions of our fathers, we know that there is an emptiness. The waters may flow from our modern faucets, but the taste of life is not there. We must go to the brink of the old sweet wells. We must taste again the waters which are athrill with the best that our fathers knew.

Such, then, it seems to me, is the message that comes to us from Isaac digging again the wells of Abraham, calling them after the names by which his father had called them before.

II

It would be simple, and it is tempting, to leave the message here. It is always tempting to set forth truth with a simplicity that obviates those seeming contradictions which are so often a part of actual life. Yet truth is never truth when it is looked at from one side only. We speak of truth full-orbed when we want to express the truth as it really is. And so as we think of Isaac, who represents in this instance which we have selected the best there is in the conservative spirit, we must turn and look also at the spirit of the man who dug those wells which he should dig again. Isaac was the conservative; yet the man whose work he was making precious by his conservatism had been a radical and a pioneer. Isaac cleared again his father's wells, but that father of his dug those wells in a land far beyond the horizon which his fathers had ever dreamed.

Once, some years ago, I was on a train going into the West. There I met a pleasant gentleman who turned out to be a minister going to the bi-ennial national convention of his Church.

He was telling some of the matters most interesting to him which were to arise in that convention, and he described particularly, with much enthusiasm, the program of those whom he called the "fundamentalists." It seemed that the convention was likely to see the issue fought between the men of modern scholarship who represented the liberty of religious inquiry and those who were determined to lay down certain fixed and unalterable definitions which they called the fundamentals, beyond which no one should be allowed to range without being proclaimed a heretic. This minister on the train was an ardent supporter of these so-called "fundamentalists," and he told how on the previous Sunday he had preached to his congregation on this same text which is ours today. He made it the basis of a plea for conservatism which should be absolute. Isaac drank from his father's wells; so the Church ought to drink from the words of the teachers of yesterday and never dare to sink its shafts of thought or questioning anywhere beyond the borders of their imaginings. He seemed surprised when, after as hearty an appreciation of his sermon as I could in politeness express, I asked him if it had occurred to him that Isaac, whose act he took as his pattern, was, after all, a very second-rate figure in the history of Israel, and Abraham, who had not dug again his father's wells, but had dug new wells, was the creator of that great religious experience which all the rest of the Old Testament goes on to expand.

Yet this is a fact, and this is what we must take into account— side by side with all that we recognize to be noble in the spirit of Isaac, if we would see the rounded truth. Life cannot be made up all of conservatism. There are times when the radical has his incomparable place. There are mighty tidal movements in the affairs of God and men when human souls must launch out beyond the utmost borders of their accustomed seas. There are times when with heroic adventure they must turn their backs upon the familiar wells, and across the desert seek the mightier promised land where they shall dig new wells for the thirst of the souls of men.

Out into Canaan Abraham went, moved by such an impulse of the spirit as has moved the pioneers in all great chapters of human change. We cannot analyze that impulse. The great creative souls themselves who feel it can never analyze it. They know only that the urge of God is within them. The compulsion of an irresistible command brings them into the path that leads ahead. By faith Abraham went out, not knowing whither he went. By faith he looked for the city which as yet had no foundation save in his dreams—the city of a new civilization, a new religious experience for the human race, a city whose builder and maker is God.

So in after ages other souls have felt this same divine compulsion. So out of the religion of Israel, conformed to the profitable superstitions of the heathen round them, came the prophets, abandoning the wells from which their fathers had drunk, denouncing the corrupted altars, the dead, unprofitable shrines of an established worship, digging new wells of the truth of God from the naked rock of human righteousness to which they appealed. So also in the far later day came Martin Luther, not at first intending, but driven at the last by the strong necessity of events, to turn aside from the wells of the Catholic Church, fenced around with its stubborn corruptions, and dig new wells of immediate access to the thought and life of God. So John Wesley and the Methodists were reluctantly separated from the wells of the established Church because only by new shafts sunk into new ground could they uncover the fountains of evangelical fervor which the formalism of the Church had buried deep. And, above all, to name the greatest Name, there stood the Master himself, proclaiming that the wells of the ancient teaching, filled as they were with the trivial litter of the teaching of Scribes and Pharisees, could no longer pour forth the water that quenched religious thirst, sinking through his own life the wells of the grace of God, from which henceforth the soul of the race should drink.

Therefore, even as we value all that is beautiful in the conservative spirit, let us keep clear of that intolerant blindness of determined prejudice which makes men unable to recognize the hour when, for the reconstituting of our industrial relations, for the reinterpreting of religious truth in terms of modern science and modern scholarship, for the refashioning of the Church to meet more vitally the needs of today, the signal strikes for the pioneers. The wells of the fathers are precious wells, but he who knows best how precious they are as channels of ancient truth will be most swift to confess when the time has come to sink shafts elsewhere, if the teachings of the fathers do not satisfy the thirst of life.

Here, then, it would seem, there is a plain contradiction. First we advocated one attitude toward life, and now we seem to advocate another. First we commended Isaac who dug again the wells of his father. Now we glorify Abraham who went out from all his father's lands to dig his wells and live his life beyond the horizon of new dreamt-of days.

Is there any harmony between these two seemingly opposite suggestions? I think there is. It is the sort of harmony which life often presents—the harmony which does not consist in fixed definitions laid down in advance, but in a sort of living balance which, in a soul sensitive to the touch of God, inclines according to an instinctive perception of the immediate purpose of God. For ordinary times and over great stretches of our experience, the natural act is that of Isaac. We dig again the fathers' wells. We do it because there, surely and most easily on the whole, and with all the sweet values of sentiment and association, we find in what other lives have left in store for us the values our spirits need. Yet we too may need to go beyond those wells, nor shall we be troubled, if only we can find the principle to guide us in recognizing the moment when this larger appeal of the spirit calls. Though we cannot predict the answer in advance, we can at least set up this sure test. When we are moved to turn away from the wells of yesterday and dig new ones for today, do we stop to make sure that the motive which rules us is clearly and wholly the motive of the soul that looks to God for guidance and looks to God alone? When we know that it is merely some irritation of our intellectual pride, and some impatience with the slow blunders of our fellows, which sends us forth to a self-assertion which casts off our sense of responsibility for others, then we may well be afraid of that which recklessly we dare. Our place is by the wells of our fathers until there comes within us, as there came within Abraham, such a conviction of God's consecration for a new adventure, and such a sense of compulsion of a new truth, as lays hold upon us with a power which it would be treason to deny. When we have truly cast self out of the calculation, and have settled with our conscience that the new truth we must try to speak and the new formulation of faith we must defend, are the very truths of God than which we can speak no other, then, but only then, are we like Abraham, bidden beyond all reservation to go forth.

For, last of all, and linking our second message in some deep sense with the first, let us remember that no man can dig new wells which will really flow save as he links his life in pure intent and whole-hearted plan with the unchanging facts of God. Abraham went out beyond the land of his fathers. He went on a way by which he dug new wells. Wherever he might have gone, he never could have dug those wells nor drawn water from them except in such spots of the earth as had been prepared by God before. If by some freak of wilfulness he had determined to dig his wells on barren slopes, he might have dug forever and his wells would forever have been dry. He must seek the valleys where rains long since fallen and the slow accumulation of hidden springs had gathered the hidden waters for his finding. There and there alone, where God's forces had made wells possible, could he sink his shafts and find water. He could not make a well; he could only open the wells which God had made already. So is it also with the facts of the spirit. The normal place for most human lives in most of their experience is by the wells of their fathers. When we are moved to go from these, as sometimes souls are moved so mightily that it would be spiritual betrayal to disobey, let us be sure that this desire by which we are moved is consistent with the deepest that we know of God and of His ways of revelation. When we separate from the wells of the fathers, let it be to dig new wells only where we believe that God's truth has gathered itself in a fullness which is His larger answer to our thirst.

IV

WHEN MEN GO LAME

And he halted upon his thigh.—GENESIS XXXII:31

H ERE was a man who had thought he could stride ahead at
his own will, and now he had to waver. He had supposed
that every energy in him must always be alive, but now he had
to limp. The confidence he had had before could not hide the
fact that he was crippled now. "He halted on his thigh."

How wonderful the Bible is in its picture of experiences that
repeat themselves in every generation! The man of whom these
words were written belongs to a time so long ago that it is
uncertain whether its records are history or legend; but the
reality of the picture is as fresh as life today. For all round us
now are those who suddenly "halted upon his thigh." That is to
say, the expectations with which they walked so confidently have
suddenly gone lame. Something has happened to break their
stride. They have been accustomed to feeling free from any limitation; but now they are moving heavily along.

What is the message for spirits such as these—for those who
for the first time in their lives have to go haltingly, for those who
have always been eager and alert and now have begun to limp?
Is there a word from God for them? That is what we want to ask.

We begin by considering more fully the story out of which
the whole suggestion grows. This story of the halting thigh is in
the story of Jacob; and there are few characters in the Old Testament which are portrayed as completely as he. He is the younger
and physically the less favored of two brothers, but there is much
which from the beginning turns in his favor. His mother prefers
him. He is quicker-witted than his brother, more imaginative,
and with a larger consciousness of the things that do not belong
to today but to tomorrow, and are worth waiting for. He sees
ahead and he chooses ahead. He wins from his brother Esau
the elder son's birthright which Esau negligently lets go. He has
the better of Esau and the better of his father who preferred

Esau but had to yield to Jacob. He has to leave home presently because of Esau's anger; but that too turns out ultimately to his benefit. He comes into contact with a hard-bargaining kinsman, but he out-thinks and outlasts this Laban who supposed he could out-maneuver him. He gains most of the objectives he had set before his purpose. He had gone on difficult roads, but he had walked like a man who was more and more certain of his goal. Now, however, he collides with a different influence. He who had begun to think that he could not be blocked is blocked. He who had been erect and self-assured so long has begun to limp.

What caused that? The answer is there in the wonderful old story in the thirty-second chapter of the Book of Genesis. At least it is partly there, veiled and cryptic, but inviting us to read its meaning. Jacob is coming home from years of absence. He has prospered greatly, and he reappears as a man of consequence. He had gone out long before in flight from the indignant Esau: but now he is returning apparently more successful than Esau will ever be. Then at that point in his career, on the night before he is to see Esau again face to face, as he is walking out under the sky in the darkness, suddenly something leaps upon him, seizes him, pins him in its grip. With this unrecognized antagonist Jacob wrestles desperately. He will not surrender and he will not cry for mercy. But his frame is wrenched by the power that holds him now. In spite of his pain he cries, "I will not let thee go except thou bless me"; and he does win a blessing. But also he has to pay a price: he knows that henceforth he is crippled. "He halted upon his thigh."

What was this antagonist with whom Jacob wrestled? At first, doubtless, he supposed that he was in the grip of some human enemy. But as the story unfolds its meaning, it is evident that it was no human form with which he had to deal. The one who wrestled with him was a messenger of God. That is to say, Jacob was being seized now by that which represented a Reality which too long he had supposed he might escape. He must face the consequences of his own past life. Years before he had done an evil thing to his brother. In the intervening time, while life in the main ran prosperously, he could bury that out of recollection; but now he could not do so any more. Tomorrow he must face this brother of his. He must admit to himself his own old fault, his need for forgiveness, the sudden inescapable realization that the facts of yesterday had caught up with him and would not let him go without a reckoning. This, I think, is the meaning of the superb symbolic story of the wrestling with the awful figure in the dark. And the supreme significance of it is this: that Jacob received his blessing and realized that he was lame in one and the same act. His strength was that when he was seized he did not flinch nor avoid the struggle. So heroically did he endure that the dark figure said to him at last, "Thy name shall be called no more Jacob, but Israel: for as a prince hast thou power with God and with men, and hast prevailed." But how had he prevailed? He had prevailed by recognizing now that he was lame, and by the will to win a blessing even from his lameness. For the first time he had wrestled with the whole fact of God's force in his life and both in its help and in its hurt had admitted and accepted it.

Is there not many a human soul which sees itself reflected in this picture? To many a man there comes some day a crisis when suddenly out of the dark he is seized by a realization which for a long time he has ignored. He knows now that he must deal with the inexorable consequences of old faults. He must admit limitations which he had thought he could hide under a superficial success. He must grapple with the full truth of God as this applies to his own life. If he shuns that conflict, then his soul will drift back in some way or other into failure. But if he measures up to it with all the truthfulness and strength he has, then out of it he can win a blessing. He wins it not by imagining any more that he is whole. He wins it by admitting that he is lame— and that, nevertheless, with a lamed gait he can go forward in a new steadiness and splendor of assurance which comes now not from himself but from God.

Let us think then of some of the specific ways in which this experience may manifest itself.

I

In the first place, it may be, as it particularly was with Jacob, a matter of admitting and adjusting the inescapable consequences of old wrongs.

Jacob had had a very mingled career. There had been much in it that was noble as well as elements which were base. There were yearnings in his soul which belong only to the man who is fundamentally sensitive to God. It was to him that there came one of the most exalted visions which religious literature records, the vision of the ladder set up from earth to heaven with the angels of God ascending and descending upon it. From the beginning to the end, Jacob believed that human life is not itself until it has reached up to make its heavenly contact. Even his desire to get the birthright from his brother Esau had a spiritual significance, for the birthright among those early oriental peoples was not a matter of land and property but a matter of leadership as the priest and spokesman to God for the family group. Yet it was true that Jacob had tried to satisfy his ambitions through unscrupulous means. It was by an ugly deception that he had got the birthright from his brother. He was sorry for that old breach of honor now. He knew that he could not be at ease within himself as he came again to face Esau. He did not have within himself the unassailable integrity which alone could have supported him in this hour. Despite all the outward seeming of success which he had brought back with him, he was not the man he wished he were. He could not walk erect into Esau's presence. Morally he was lame, and he had to see that and feel that before he could go forward.

Here is where the courage of men too often breaks down. How many are there of us who can search our inner selves without admitting the need for this most difficult kind of courage? Somewhere in our lives there may be an act which has destroyed or imperilled some human relationship. Perhaps we have tried to act as though it did not matter. We have gone on placating ourselves with the suggestion that all the general average of our life's achievement could cover up and permanently conceal that old wrong. A false pride makes us unwilling to stoop to the difficult, and, as we think, humiliating process of undoing the harm that once was done. We would rather pretend that it never existed, that it was not our fault, or that in any case so much time has gone by that now it does not matter. It is even possible for a man to seem to succeed in affirming that. He can keep the old uneasiness buried so that it does not obviously disturb him. But if he does succeed thus, he succeeds at a cost greater than he knows. He may be a self-satisfied man; but he will never be a great man. He will be as Jacob would have been if he had fled like a coward from the dark antagonist and had refused the agonizing wrestle. He will never be what Jacob did become, namely, a prince with men and God because through his bitter wrestling he had let the magnificent though agonizing truth prevail. The great souls are only those who in some critical moment of life's awareness are willing to limp, willing to go on, that is, to the confession, to the repentance, to the reconciliation, which may bow their unreal dignity down to the ground, but will let them rise up again to greet the dawn as Jacob did, with a new light shining in their eyes.

II

That, then, is one type of experience which is pictured in the story of Jacob, the experience of the need for correction of some remembered wrong. We pass on to a second experience which is suggested there. It is that of the man who must learn to adjust himself not so much to the fact of an error which must be corrected, but to a limitation not due to any direct wrong of his with which, nevertheless, he must inescapably live.

No more vivid exemplification of this could be desired than that which is embodied in the glimpse into his own life given by William Seabrook in two articles originally printed in *The Atlantic Monthly* and later enlarged into a book. Here is a man who with extraordinary directness revealed the inner truth about himself. He had gone to what he bluntly calls an asylum, which was a private hospital for the treatment of all sorts of nervous, mental, and character break-downs. He had been going from one alcoholic excess to another until he had got to the point where he himself knew that his case was desperate. Then he describes what happened to him in the hospital, and what it was that he learned about himself. He came to discover that he had been engaged in a continual process of trying to escape the acceptance of his own reality. Nothing that he ever did satisfied him, because he was always following the fantasy of something more stimulating or more showy which perhaps he might do. He had had wide and interesting experiences in many parts of the world. He had been a successful writer. He had earned a sufficient income to live comfortably. But he was always comparing himself with imaginary achievements that he could not reach. What was the use of writing as well as he did when he would never be a Goethe or a Shakespeare? What was the use of doing the things that seemed next at hand when conceivably there might be things so much more interesting if he could think of them? So in order to keep himself from grappling with the actual facts of every day and to indulge his dream world a little longer, he would turn to drink. And what he learned in the hospital was that at last he had to face and accept himself. He had to take his own abilities as they were and to use these with steady and courageous self-respect. He had to stop thinking and living in the fantasy that life was worth-while only if he could walk its roads with giant strides. He had to see that, compared with geniuses, he might be making only a limping progress, and then to accept the limp and go on regardless.

The face of the author of *Asylum* is reflected in the faces of hundreds of men and women all round us in this day. Their history, of course, is not identical with his; but their essential problem is the same. They do not want to take life as the imperfect but nevertheless worth-while adventure which it is. They are always wishing that it were something else, and retreating into weak evasion of its present facts. If only they were someone else, they say to themselves, better endowed personalities, more cheerful, more easily liked, more adaptable to people and to circumstances, then they could manage their place in the world. Or if only it were not too late. If only they had not been so indifferent and ineffective last year or the year before. If they did not have so much to be sorry for, and were starting fresh today, then they might make a great effort and begin; but with things as they are, they could never achieve more than a fragment of a worth-while life; and so why start on a belated and unavailing effort? This mood may begin in very small ways. It may begin with a shyness yielded to which makes one turn away from the wholesome contacts that ordinary life presents. It may begin in the unwillingness to help in some plain duty because the man or woman is thinking that he or she cannot be a shining success. It may go on through a disinclination ever to join any courageous pilgrimage of human effort if anybody in the crowd is likely to be walking more conspicuously than ourselves. And at last it may break down into a neurosis which threatens to disintegrate the personality altogether and leave us plaintive moral invalids spinning out our perpetual rationalizations as to why there is no use trying to do what we ought to do because we cannot do it superlatively well.

Or consider that multitude of folk who refuse to go forward in the real ways of life which belong to them because the state of the road itself has changed. Look, for example, at all the elderly women pathetically pretending that they are young. Theirs could be the quiet poise and grace of unashamed maturity. They could give to the world, as many of their contemporaries do, the evidence of personalities so sure and clear in their inner worth that all they need to do is to be what they are and not to put on some pitiful veneer of what they are not. Suppose it be true that the look of youth has gone out of their faces. Why should they think that they gain anything but pity when they try to varnish it on? And suppose they cannot keep up with the exuberant amusements of boys and girls in their 'teens. Suppose they are not adjusted either in physique or in temperament to the tempo of the jazz age. Why not accept these so-called limitations and turn them into finer and more prevailing strength? Why say of every stage in life's advancing and changing course, "If only I were back earlier in the journey!"? Why not say rather of the vital present, "I will not let thee go except thou bless me."?

III

For mark—and here we pass to a third consideration—that the experience of being lame is not necessarily a loss. Jacob's career did not stop when he began to halt upon his thigh. There were long years after that of expanding experience which reached at last the ripeness of understanding and of spiritual growth which

his earlier years had not arrived at. It may be the fact of a man's
discovery of his lameness that for the first time lifts him into
greatness, because he may then begin to turn his reliance away
from his own shallow resources and to throw himself instead
upon the illimitable richness of God.

We can see how this is so both in the great figures of religious
history and also in the average men and women round us in any
living time.

To turn to the Bible, look at one figure in the Old Testament
and one in the New. There was, to begin with, Moses. In the
beginning everything belonged to him. He was the adopted son
of Pharaoh's daughter. He lived as a prince of the royal court.
He might have walked erect on a highroad of the ease and
splendor of his world. But the necessity of serving a harder purpose came upon him like the dark angel wrestling with Jacob
in the night. He had to serve God's work and not his own
advancement; and when we next see him, driven by the inexorable compulsion of his own more difficult loyalties, he has
fled from Egypt to the wilderness. There the voice of God comes
to him and bids him go back to Egypt and deliver his people
Israel from the tyranny of Pharaoh. Moses is appalled at the
thought of his own inadequacy for such a task. He is not elo-
quent, he says. He is of slow speech and a stammering tongue.
But God sends him, nevertheless. And presently, when he has led
Israel out of Egypt and the whole people are on the weary and
dangerous way to the promised land, God is still with Moses
when Moses almost thought the way ahead was hopeless. He
was buffeted by the complaints and recriminations of the people.
He could lead them only little by little along any steady way of
progress. He was like a man who in all his natural energies and
ideal abilities had cruelly been made lame. But in that lameness
was his strength. The old New England catechism picks out
Moses and gives his name in answer to the question, "Who was
the meekest man?" He was not a meek man in the sense that
he was dumb or passive. He was not meek with anything of
that false suggestion which we sometimes give to the word, the
suggestion of yieldingness and weakness; but he was meek in
the sense that he had conquered all stubborn selfishness of pride.

He was not thinking of his own eminence. He was thinking of the people he had to help. He could not go his own gait of independent greatness; but he could learn the diviner greatness of shortening his step and stooping to their needs until he seemed to limp with them. Out of that sort of willing lameness he prevailed both over himself and over life. He became one of God's princes, glorifying history forever with the grandeur of the life he lived amidst accepted limitations.

Then, turning to the New Testament, consider the Apostle Paul. Again and again in his letters there sounds a tragic note. He refers to what he calls "a thorn in the flesh" which he had to endure. What it exactly was, nobody today knows; but evidently it was some acute cause of suffering which Paul carried with him in his body and which crippled the full and joyous energy that otherwise he might have had. It was so critical that he says he prayed repeatedly to the Lord to take it away; but this cross laid on him was not removed. He had to bear it to the end. The result was that others were sometimes far more impressive figures to the crowd than he. His enemies even said that his personal appearance was insignificant and mean. The knowledge of his limitation, whatever it was, must have been gall and wormwood to his passionate and tremendous spirit. He knew that he did not command admiration in the crowd. He knew that, when he went by, men's attention was not caught by the dignity of his stride. In comparison with the bearing of those whom the world considered great, he seemed to have the halting step of the lame. But did that work disaster in his spirit? On the contrary, it brought him to his heights. What did it matter if in his human equipment he was as one lame? He reached up to God, and God gave him wings. The more he recognized that there was something in him that limped, the more he drew to himself the power that lifted him above the dusty road. To his prayer that the limitation might be taken away, God answered, "My grace is sufficient for thee: for my strength is made perfect in weakness." And Paul's rejoicing spirit cried, "Most gladly therefore will I rather glory in my infirmities, that the power of Christ may rest upon me . . . for when I am weak, then am I strong."

But it is not only from the pages of the Bible that we can draw our illustrations of the souls whose limitations have become their glory, and who in the very act of discovering that they were lame have found the power of God for heroic progress. It may be that a man's lameness is not irrevocable. It may be that it has come upon him as a temporary hurt meant to summon all his courage to overcome it. There are those known to every one of us who have thus dealt with what proved to be temporary disasters and have won a confidence and power such as they would never otherwise have had by overcoming the difficulties with which they were forced to grapple. But there are others who have had to make friends with difficulty itself, and like Jacob, find their blessing in the very moment and fact of finding that figuratively speaking they must always be lame. There are men still living in New York City who knew a great-hearted young clergyman named Alexis Stein, whose brilliant career was cut short by illness and who died a young man. He who had tasted the bitterness of what seemed frustration learned by spiritual courage to make it into triumph. Pondering upon his own experience, he wrote:

To make his fate his friend! thus man has won his kingdom in the world: thus men win kingdoms in their private souls. For in each fate of men, as in the fate of man there is hidden a rule, to know that, what it is, to make his peace with it, to fit his will to it, to learn to see such beauty as it has, such worth, to joy in it, to find one's self anew in it—this is to find life good and on one's side. . . They conquer best by peace.

Let this message come to you today, and through you to all whose experience is like yours—you who come to the moment in your life when you realize that in some aspect or other you are and must be lame. Do not imagine that this means for you defeat. Do not imagine that it means any ultimate disaster. It may be the sudden dawn of your opportunity to find for your own life the fulness of the meaning of God. And when you have found it, and you go ahead upon your road of a higher and more understanding courage, it is not a lonely road. By the very fact that you walk bravely in your lameness you are helping to brighten the whole way of human life. Something nobler has come to you than the easy lot of unhindered progress. In the great words of one who knew whereof he spoke:

Your task is nobler yet. You are a burden bearer of mankind. There is the burden of the race, the burden of its folly and its wrong, its ignorance, its stupid prejudice, its sin, its wilful violation of the law, its innocent transgression of the rule. Some one must carry that—must carry that great sadness and great pain, that ineptitude, that care—must carry it that others should go free, that mankind should go forward and go up.

"That mankind should go forward and go up." How all the bugles of the spirit are blowing in those words! Whatever its seeming defeat, the courageous life never goes down into any abiding darkness. Through the darkness it moves onward into light. In the story of Jacob which we have been following, the text from which we have drawn our particular thought contains also this supreme suggestion which we have left till this climactic moment. As Jacob passed over Peniel he halted upon his thigh. But that is not all of the sentence. As he passed over Peniel, halting upon his thigh, "the sun rose upon him." The night was gone. The day was dawning. The dark shadows of his agony lay behind him. The splendor of the sunrise shone upon his face. So it shall be ever for this life and the life to come! If a man has struggled bravely with all the hard things with which he has to wrestle, if he, like Jacob, caught in the grip of his spiritual testing, has said, "I will not let thee go, except thou bless me," then for that man the night of his humiliation is over, and he faces forward to the dawn.

V

THE DREAMER

Behold, this dreamer cometh.—GENESIS XXXVII:19

HERE we have to do with one of the most brilliant men whom the Old Testament portrays. Like the central figure in some well-ordered drama we hear him announced by those already on the stage before he himself moves out of the background. Scowling faces are turned toward the direction from which he enters. "Behold," their scornful voices say, "this dreamer cometh!"

"This dreamer cometh!" Let us watch him as he comes and see the part he has to play in that life of Israel which concerns so greatly the spiritual life of all the world. Those who called him a dreamer did so in contempt, but it was the quality that lay back of those dreams that made him great.

We know the features of the story—this story of Joseph; for it is he, of course, with whom we have to do. It is divided into three chapters. The chapter of early ambitions; the chapter of darkness; the chapter of final success. We shall trace them as they come.

I

In Canaan, settled at last after his long exile, is Jacob, with twelve sons. Grown men they were, with the exception of the two youngest, both of them the sons of Rachel, for whom Jacob so long had served. To Joseph, the first-born of these, the father's love went out with a peculiar devotion. There was something about him different from the group of his fierce and intractable elder brothers—a kind of sensitive spirit and wide imagination which touched in Jacob's heart the memories of the days of his own youth, when he, too, had seen wonderful visions and dreamed great dreams. So, with a dangerous partiality, he made no secret of his feeling for this particular son. He gave Joseph a coat such as princely persons wore. He loved him more than he loved the others, and the others knew it.

As a result, they hated Joseph with all the fierce heartiness of a jealous resentment. They could not understand him, and the very things which made his father love him were to them a constant offense. They were of the practical sort that takes life as one finds it, lives as others live, and is impatient of what one considers fantastic theories. They expected to spend their days in the sort of occupations and surroundings in which they found themselves, and to take advantage of the fierce, and sometimes very grossly passionate pleasures, which they thought young men had a right to. This lad, of a different temper, self-restrained, imaginative, full of great ideas as to what he was going to do and be, irritated them by his provoking difference. They constantly felt in him the undefined constraint of a nature which by its very presence rebuked the things they were satisfied with. And as is ordinarily the case with men in such circumstances, they struck at the thing which they did not like. They put their own elements of superiority forward in their minds to ward off the uncomfortable sense of the points in which he was superior to them. Strong men they were, capable and efficient, and with a kind of fierce independence in their own heedless ways; and here was this young stripling, with his large ideas and theories, treated by their father as though he and not they were the real power in the family. "This dreamer" they called him with derisive scorn, as men who have made terms with their world generally call the man who has the idea that he can change it.

But the spark which was in the heart of this lad made his life worth more than that of all his brethren. Just because he was a dreamer—because he could believe in things bigger than what he saw—he takes his place in the fellowship of the men who glorified the history of Israel. There was Abraham, first of all. What but this same quality made him great. He might have lived in Ur of the Chaldees all his life and died in obscurity there; but his dream, his intuition, his voice from God—let us call it that— told him of a larger destiny which it was worth-while to go on a long and very daring migration to seek. "By faith," says the writer of that magnificent letter to the Hebrews, "Abraham, when he was called, obeyed to go out into a place which he was to receive for an inheritance; and he went out not knowing whither he went . . . for he looked for a city which hath foundations, whose builder and maker is God." A dreamer here—and one superbly venturesome in the strength of those inspired dreams of life; a man who thought that there is something finer which a human soul has got to seek and enter into in this world than the structures which a practical worldliness can create. Joseph was of his family—not by blood and physical descent alone, but by the spirit.

Then there was Joseph's father, one of the most singular and most baffling characters in the Old Testament: a personality of deep and stormy contrasts, who at one moment impresses you with the consciousness that here is the very elemental material of human nature, with all its crudity and vastness, and at another moment makes the spirit thrill with a sense of the nobility into which that material can be transformed by the touch of God. We are not to attempt now to assess this character of Jacob, but the point about it which concerns us is abundantly clear—namely, that all the goodness which was ultimately in him came from that quality which his son also had—the power when he himself was still ignoble at least to dream nobly and dare to follow his dreams. We think of the beginning of his manhood as marked by an act of treachery against his own brother, and that is true; but we must remember that hidden by the mean expedient he used there was a purpose that had greatness in it. He was not content, as Esau was, to hunt and feed. He had another appetite than that for savory messes of pottage. He wanted spiritual privilege, the birthright of his family, the chance to achieve and to lead. He thought greatly of life and its unseen possibilities, and that is why his life was eminent at the last.

So it was in the later days with Moses. So it was with Amos, the shepherd of Tekoa, who left that desolate region where he had lived as an unknown and obscure power, and dared to go stand before kings because he believed in the tremendous reality of that larger work to which he had been called as the prophet of God. So it was with Isaiah—to name no more of the prophets—

who saw his mighty vision of the glory of God and heard the voice of God calling for a messenger and answered, "Here am I, Lord. Send me." All these men, in the noblest sense of the word, were dreamers. They were men who saw the possibility of large life and service for themselves, and dared to follow the leadings which commonplace people mocked at first as foolish.

Or, to turn from the prophets to the kings, there was that most winsome figure in all the years of Israel's history—David. There are many things about him and about his career which remind us of Joseph. He had the same sensitiveness, the same quick imagination, the same readiness to believe in the possibilities which lie beyond common perception. There were in him, as Browning says—those fancies

Which had come long ago in the pasture, when round me the sheep
Fed in silence—above, the one eagle wheeled slow as in sleep:
And I lay in my hollow and mused on the world that might lie
'Neath his ken, though I saw but the strip 'twixt the hill and the sky.

In the quiet and the solitude, he dreamed his splendid dreams. He had faith in things at which his brothers scoffed. There is no finer descriptive chapter in the Old Testament than the account of that day when the young David came down to the camp of Saul's armies where they lay facing the Philistines, and Goliath of Gath came out with his insulting challenge. To the brothers, the idea that David should fight the Philistine seemed a piece of absolute effrontery. But the lad with his impossible confidence was the hero who put his practical brethren to shame that day.

Always, indeed, the men who have achieved the splendid triumphs for themselves and for their world have been those of whom it could be said when they came upon the stage of their time's affairs, as it was said of Joseph, "Behold, the dreamer cometh." The new world waited for thousands of years to be discovered, lying embosomed in the mighty mystery of the uncharted seas; waited till there rose a man great enough in imagination to conceive the truth of an earth that was round, and until another man rose who dreamed of what that truth could mean for explorers, and fared forth from the ports of Spain to sail round the earth and find the secret of the other side. In the great monument to Columbus on the plaza outside the Union Station in the city of Washington, it is the musing of those deep eyes that makes the figure most impressive. And in the Tate Gallery in London there is a painting called *The Boyhood of Sir Walter Raleigh*, which, like the statue of Columbus, is full of the beauty of the truth that it is the vision which lies at the heart of action. At one side of the painting is a sailor, his dress and his bronzed face full of the suggestion of wide seas and distant places. One bared arm is pointing beyond the edge of the pier on which he crouches, over the water to the far horizon; and opposite him, knees clasped by his hands and the dark eyes wide and thoughtful, sits the lad who should grow to be Sir Walter Raleigh, drinking in the great suggestions of the life which one day he should claim.

Yes, it is the dreamer who fares farthest and does most in this brave earth of ours—provided always that he adds to his dreams the faith of a courageous will.

So the lad Joseph of whom we think especially today, belonged —if his brothers had only known it—through the very quality they hated to the company of the potentially great. Yet, as we try to understand him fairly and completely, we must recognize here an aspect of Joseph's character which belongs on the other side of the balance.

He had a great and bold imagination. So far, so good. But here is the counter-weight. His dreaming was essentially selfish; and this fact—though it does not account for all the jealousy of his brothers, since it was the fact of his superiority which angered them, whether that superiority was selfish or not—does give to their hostility a certain justification. Look at the two dreams which Joseph told to his brothers, and to his father also. In the first, he said that he saw the whole group of them binding sheaves in the field, and all the sheaves of his brethren bowed down to his sheaf which stood upright. The second dream was more audacious still. He said he saw the sun and moon and the eleven stars, which represented his father and mother and his eleven brothers, make obeisance unto him.

Now, these were dreams we say, those strange and unaccountable fantasies which are painted on the screen of sleep. But the fact is that dreams, even in this specific meaning of the visions which one sees when he is asleep, are not altogether unaccountable. Very frequently they are the reflections of those waking thoughts which have sunk only for the time below the horizon of the conscious. And it was in this connection that the dreams of Joseph were significant. What he saw in the night were of the same fabric as his more deliberate day-dreams. He was aspiring after his own eminence, and therefore his unconscious imaginings were of that.

So what we see is high possibilities as yet not directed to the highest end. The spirit of achievement is in him, but not the clear realization of the true goal which he must achieve. He needed the kind of spiritual education which often comes through sore hardship and discipline. It was thus that in his case it came.

II

We turn, therefore, to the second chapter in his life—the chapter of darkness.

The dramatic narrative of its outward events is familiar to us all. The very words which are our text are the prelude to it. The older brothers had gone to feed the flocks in Dothan, a considerable distance from the father's home; and when they descry Joseph coming toward them, a sudden fierce sense of power freed from the usual restraint of Jacob's nearness stirred them to take advantage of their deadly opportunity. This dreamer who imagined himself so important, this dreamer whom his father makes so much of, may save himself now if he can! They watch him as he comes near. "Let us slay him," they say, "and cast him into some pit, and we will say, some evil beast hath devoured him; and we shall see what will become of his dreams." Joseph's career, according to the story, might have ended then and there if it had not been that two of the brothers were less bloody-minded than the rest. Reuben first and then Judah protested against the extreme of actual murder. One of them suggested that he be thrown into some pit alive; the other that he be sold as a slave to one of the caravans of Midianitish merchants who went down that way to Egypt. This was the course that prevailed; and Joseph, in the possession of the caravan, was carried down into the land which was henceforth to be the scene of his strange fortunes.

It would be too long to tell the whole story of what happened in Egypt. The long chapters of the book of Genesis are filled with it. This is the bare outline. When the Midianites came into Egypt, they sold Joseph to Potiphar, the captain of the guard in the palace of Pharaoh. Very soon the young Hebrew rose to a position of trust in his master's eyes, and Potiphar put him in charge of the affairs of his house. The wife of Potiphar fell in love with Joseph, and tempted him with every seduction in her power; and when he refused to betray his master's trust she turned against him in a furious resentment and accused him to Potiphar of insult toward her. Joseph, though innocent, was thrown into prison—there to remain, as it turned out, more than two years. Here he gained the jailer's favor as he had originally gained Potiphar's, and he was made a sort of deputy of the prison. He had a chance to befriend one of the servants of Pharaoh who had been banished there, and it was through this man that Joseph was brought to Pharaoh's attention when Pharaoh was exceedingly troubled by a dream which he had had, and the interpretation of which he could not understand. It was a dream of seven lean cattle which ate up seven fat cattle, and seven lean ears of corn which ate up seven fat ones—and Joseph saw in this the prophecy of a famine seven years long which should follow seven years of abundant harvest. Pharaoh was so impressed with his sagacity that he made him the viceroy of the kingdom, and Joseph set himself with great ability and success to gather up such stores of food as should supply the needs of the people in the time of scarcity which lay ahead. And it was through this fact that the brethren of Joseph, coming down presently into Egypt to buy food, were brought face to face with the man who was their brother.

Such, in briefest fashion, is the outline of Joseph's life through the period of what we have called the chapter of darkness, and into the climax of his success which followed. But what we are supremely interested in is not the framework of events but the character of the man that meanwhile was being fashioned.

We mark first: the way in which Joseph kept his moral integrity in the midst of the apparent wreck of his life's hopes.

As a lad in his father's home, he had fed his spirit, as we have seen, with splendid imaginings of a great destiny to which somehow he should rise. His father had believed in it. His brothers, though they hated him for his ambitions of greatness, yet also took them seriously. With a confidence which was buoyant and splendid, even though it may have been chargeable with a boy's impatient pride, he felt himself standing before wide-open doors of golden years.

And now instead of entering in through these gates, he entered into slavery and exile; into a life fettered in opportunity and associations. He faced a test of the sort to which many have succumbed—and do succumb. There are circumstances in which men may say to themselves that they have nothing worth-while to live for, and throw away all patient incentives to living well. Men lose, for example—as Joseph did—the advantages upon which they built their great expectations. Some calamity takes away their fortune, blocks long-regarded avenues to advancement, changes them of a sudden from being objects of the world's envy to being objects of a sort of pity—or worse still, gets them in positions where they feel the intolerable sense of obscurity and the absolute indifference of the world as to whether they exist or not. Then many become spiritually demoralized. They lose their confidence; and either in passion fling away, or in a slow dejection suffer to drift away, their sense of self-respect. They begin to drink or indulge in worse and grosser sins. They say they want to forget their misfortunes. And particularly if it should happen that some moral compromise appears which seems to point to a way of escape out of the pit they are in does their conscience disintegrate before the profitable-seeming temptation. They have lost their money in the old business, but some shrewd and questionable scheme gives hope that they may regain it. They have lost the office they won by honorable means, but a temporary alliance with corrupt political influences may get it back again. They have been betrayed by some friend they thought was honorable; well, then, away with honor and all sorts of hypocritical theories and get ahead by any paths that offer.

That is the kind of temptation to which men may be subjected. It is the temptation to which Joseph was subjected. That peril which came to him in Potiphar's house was a terribly close one. In addition to the appeal to passion, there was the appeal to self-interest as well. The favor of this woman of prominence and position might help him far. Sore, wounded, humiliated, discouraged, broken-spirited—all these he might have been after his brothers' treatment of him. But these he was not. He kept his self-respect in spite of his outward abasement. He kept his moral nature clean and free, even though he did wear the slave's garb. He maintained his manhood under pressure.

Through the stern events which gave him a chance to do this, and to overcome the temptation to do otherwise, came the first lesson which the spirit of God had for this young dreamer whose visions and ideals had come too easily and airily before.

There was a second element in the development of Joseph through this period of darkness. It was the training of his sympathies.

We have seen that he seemed to be deficient in this respect before. He was eager and imaginative—but eager for himself. It did not seem to occur to him that his brothers' feelings ought to be considered when he was recounting his own self-exalting dreams.

In Egypt he is a different man in this respect. The fine and generous regard for others which was latent in his disposition before, but in the impetuous heyday of his own untempered enthusiasm had never been roused to expression, was of a sudden developed. He refuses to do to Potiphar the shameful wrong which the wife of Potiphar suggested, and the reason which he gives has to do not only with his own personal moral integrity but with his consideration for the man who had given him his trust. In the prison he learned that he was not the only person whose emotions and fortunes had a right to be regarded. He entered into the hopes and fears of Pharaoh's servants shut up there. As under moral pressure he had won a strength which he otherwise might never have had, so through his suffering he won the human sympathy which was not his before, and but for these sorrows might never have been his at all.

Surely there is a great message here for many lives which seem grievously beset by pain and sorrow. It may be—and this is hardest of all—that these have been brought on not by one's own fault but through the fault of others. A friend has played us false. One's own flesh and blood has been untrue. Ingratitude or injustice has balked just desires, and left the aggrieved life wounded and handicapped, it may seem beyond redemption. Then the weak spirit is embittered. It can see no other satisfaction than to carry out its rancor in a vengeance that shall strike, if possible, the persons who are responsible for its own pain; but if these are out of its reach, then humanity in general must pay the penalty. There are tragic examples of this not only in literature but in life—examples of men and women who having themselves been wronged deliberately set out to pay back to society the evil which has been visited upon them.

But there is a higher and better road to release from the burden of pain. It is the road that leads not to vengeance but to sympathy. It is the road that Joseph took. God was teaching him a lesson, which he must learn and did learn. Through his own suffering his heart was being made tender to the sufferings of others.

George Matheson, the blind Scotch preacher, has written a meditation on Joseph. The deepest and most searching part is that in which he speaks of the opportunity of the life which has itself been hurt to heal the hurts of others. It is very movingly significant because what he has written about Joseph was written out of the experience of his own heavy fate. You know the story, perhaps, of that beautiful, patient life. He became blind when he was studying for the ministry; and it seemed at first as though his aims in life were shattered, and as though his work must end. Also, he was engaged to be married, and when the girl whom he was to marry learned of his blindness she forsook him. It seemed to him, as it seemed to Joseph, that the golden dreams were shut within the hopeless darkness of his prison walls.

This is what he, George Matheson, who learned tenderness

and patience and faith from his own deep disappointments, wrote when he thought of Joseph.

How shall I pass from the life of the egotist to the life of the humanitarian? Only through my own strait gate. The wing by which I fly to your trouble is the wing which is wounded; the hand by which I help you is the hand which is maimed. In vain shall I enter your desert till I have tasted the waters of Marah. Not by fearless running I shall overtake and lift your burden, but by halting on my own thigh. The education in sympathy is the presence of personal bruises; of every true comforter we can say, "By his stripes we are healed."

Think deeper then, oh you who because your lives are hurt by misfortune think that all your great visions are at an end, you who are almost tempted to remember with a bitter scorn the fact that once you had your buoyant dreams. Look for God's great lesson and learn it while you may. He is not destroying your dreams. He is only trying to refine you with a larger tenderness and more inclusive understanding of the needs of others, that you may be fit to fulfil those dreams when the day of your final opportunity arrives.

We go forward to the third element in the development of Joseph in the days of darkness. It was this. The field for the exercise of his ambitions was changing. He was ceasing to be a self-centered individual. He was coming to find his aims wrapped up with the aims of a people.

Remember that when he was a lad in Canaan, the thing he was interested in was in interpreting his own dreams. He was bent on figuring out what sort of happy results were coming to him. In Egypt the dreams he interprets are no longer his own. He is interpreting those of Pharaoh's servants in the prison, trying to read for them the scroll of *their* joys and pains. He is interpreting the dream of Pharaoh himself, the right reading of which—and the right action in the light of which—concerned the very life of the whole nation in the face of the famine which Joseph foresaw and which Joseph took means to provide against.

Now it is true enough that certain of the details of this story are remote from us today. We are not accustomed to finding truth by the dreams which people have in their sleep. But for our present purposes this is unimportant. The essential thing is the spiritual suggestion which shines through Joseph's new relationships. His sagacity, his prudence, and the actual work of his life are given henceforth not to considering his own fortune but to working out the fortunes of the people.

Do you not see the living meaning of this thought for us? Here are men and women with their own dreams, their own ambitious imaginings of advancement and greatness. They may follow those dreams selfishly, as Joseph was in the mood originally to do. They may think that the only way to win satisfaction and success is to get those personal dreams realized: to make money, to achieve a selfish prominence, to build up their own material security no matter what may happen to the community out of which they make their profits. But the noble life is the one that comes to concern itself, as Joseph did, with those dreams which concern one's fellows as well as oneself. Out of the heart of the people today, out of that great yearning of men's minds and souls for truth and justice, there are dreams of a sweeter and better world which need some great spirit to interpret them and to tell what action ought to be taken to make them true. Here is the field for those today who like Joseph of old would be genuinely great. Every community cries out for the dreamer and the interpreter of dreams—for the man or the woman who can see the real things which a church or a city or a state ought to strive for, or can recognize and make clear the meaning in the struggling visions of others' souls.

III

So, finally, and swiftly, we touch the third chapter of Joseph's life. By inference we have necessarily suggested it already—the chapter of the final success.

That chapter emphasizes one of the most vivid and dramatic scenes anywhere in literature. Turn again to the end of the book of Genesis and see the figures moving on that Egyptian stage. Down from Canaan come the brothers of Joseph, sent by their father to try to buy food in the famine. All of them together they come—all but one, Benjamin the youngest and the one most beloved by Jacob, his old father, and by Joseph himself. These brothers do not even know that Joseph is alive. He has passed out of their ken ever since that day when they sold him to the Midianitish caravan. As far as they are concerned, he has been for these many years as good as dead. Certainly the last thing they dreamed was that he should be in any position of power with which they would have to reckon.

But when they come down into Egypt and beg at Pharaoh's court to be allowed to buy food, it is into the presence of Joseph that they are ushered. They do not know him. How should they know this figure seated in his near-royal eminence? But he knows them. He asks them of their father, and one can feel the catch at Joseph's heart as he frames his words, "Is he still alive?" He asks them of Benjamin. When he hears that these are both alive and well, he directs that they shall return home and come down again, bringing Benjamin. The brothers are staggered at this demand; but they dare not resist it. Back to Canaan again they go, and with difficulty persuade the old Jacob to let Benjamin make the journey down to Egypt in their company. In ways which we do not need to stop to recapitulate, but of which the narrative in the book of Genesis tells, Joseph lifts the situation now to an agony of tension, as he makes his brothers think that he will keep Benjamin as a hostage in Egypt while he sends them back to Canaan with the terrible prospect of telling their father that this other son also now is lost. And then, when the brothers who had sold him into slavery stand almost speechless with despair, Joseph reveals himself. His emotions sweep upon him in a flood of tears as he says to them, "I am Joseph." And then with the magnanimity of the great soul whose own victory over circumstances leaves no room in it for vengeance, he cries, "Come near to me, I pray you . . . I am Joseph your brother, whom ye sold into Egypt. Now therefore be not grieved nor angry with yourselves, that ye sold me hither: for God did send me before you to preserve life. . . . It was not you who sent me hither. It was God."

How true that is as a parable of the life which by its own heroic faithfulness turns evil into good! "It is God." Let a man be true to his great beliefs. Let him not be faithless, even though disasters seem to blot these out. Let him give himself with patient open-mindedness to God's ways—such strange ways sometimes! —that compel him to broader sympathies and more generous concerns, and his dreams for his own great service will come true at last. God will not betray the spirit of eagerness for large living which He Himself puts into any heart. Through His leading, though men may say at first in mockery, as Joseph's brethren said, "Behold, this dreamer cometh," they may say at last in amazement and in reverence "Behold, the dreamer on his throne!"

VI

THE MAN WHO COULD FORGET HIMSELF

*Choosing rather to suffer affliction with the people
of God, than to enjoy the pleasures of sin for a season.*
HEBREWS XI:25

"*CHOOSING* affliction." Mark that unusual first word. Many men may *suffer* affliction. The iron necessities of life may force them to do so. Some suffer it with an angry protest. Others crouch beneath it with a drab self-pity. The nobler type will accept it gallantly, making the best of the inevitable. But all these alike have received suffering because they could not help it. Here, on the other hand, is a man who could have helped it, but took suffering nevertheless. He did not stand still and endure it. He went out to meet it. He was not passively afflicted. He welcomed affliction by his own deliberate choice.

This man was Moses. His name is written with those of the other heroes of religious history in the magnificent eleventh chapter of the Epistle to the Hebrews—this chapter which has well been called the Westminster Abbey of the Bible—beginning with the beginning of the world and reciting the starred names of those who through the Old Testament times had glorified the spiritual record of the nation.

All these great figures belong to religion, but they do not belong to religion in any aloof or specialized sense. Many of them are men whose lives were conspicuously identified with practical affairs. So it was with Moses. He had moments of intimate communion with God. He was a man who knew the stillness of worship, a man who prayed, and listened for the divine answer in his praying. He stands also in tradition as perhaps the most important figure associated with the Jewish Church. But he was no pale mystic nor religious recluse, and certainly he was no ecclesiastic bound in small details of any church's business. He was a leader of men who took command in a social crisis and turned history in a new direction. In our own day of social restlessness and impending change, his spirit may well go before us like the pillar of cloud and fire which went before him.

Let us review, then, the stages of Moses' career and consider what these revealed concerning him.

I

The years of his first decision

According to the story in the book of Exodus, Moses was born in a dangerous time. The Pharaoh of Egypt had grown to dislike and in some measure to fear the Israelitish people, who since the days of Joseph had been living and multiplying within his borders. He had done whatever he could think of to cramp and suppress this people. Now he proceeded to a final ruthlessness. Every male child of the Hebrews should be killed. This was the order that went through Egypt, and there was terror in the homes of the Hebrew people.

A baby was born to a certain man and woman. His mother hid him as best she could; but a baby is not an easy thing to hide. Despairing of concealing him very long and fearful of the Egyptian police who might at any moment find him, she wove a little basket out of reeds, made it water-tight with pitch, put the baby in it and set it afloat on the Nile near the steps that led from Pharaoh's palace. Down the river then came Pharaoh's daughter with her maids to bathe. She saw the odd thing floating among the rushes at the river's edge and sent one of her maids to fetch it. When she opened it, there within was a baby, and the baby cried. That baby's cry went straight home to her woman's heart. She determined she would take him home, and so she did. In Pharaoh's house, therefore, this child, who was called Moses, was sheltered and grew up. The opportunities of the court were his. A strange turn of fortune had taken him out of the lot of the oppressed people of Israel and given him honor and unbounded opportunity. It appeared that all he had to look forward to was increasing enjoyment of a very happy lot.

But there came the time when Moses was not at ease in Pharaoh's house. He could not forget that he belonged to the Hebrews. Whenever he walked about, he saw how they were oppressed. Pharaoh had put them at forced labor under cruel overseers. They were driven to their work with whips. One day, in a remote place, Moses watched one of these Egyptian overseers lash a Hebrew laborer, and his anger flared. He struck the Egyptian, struck him perhaps harder than he meant to do, and the man fell down dead.

Thus, more suddenly and terribly than he had consciously intended, but nevertheless with the decision of his whole nature from which he could not have long held back, Moses cut his connection with all his life of privilege, and in that instant allied himself with the hard and perilous lot of his own people. Look again at the way in which the Epistle to the Hebrews expresses this decision. "Choosing rather to suffer affliction with the people of God, than to enjoy the pleasures of sin for a season." "The people of God"—"the pleasures of sin!" That is a strong antithesis. But was there really any such obvious distinction as this? Who are these who are called "the people of God"? A crowd of the socially and economically submerged; a poor, ignorant, unprivileged laboring class; men and women who were despised by the Egyptian overlords who held inherited power. And, on the other hand, where was anything in Moses' previous life that could fairly be called "the pleasures of sin"? What sin had Moses committed? Apparently none at all. He had been adopted by Pharaoh's daughter. He had grown up in Pharaoh's court. There is no indication whatever that in that court he had done anything of which he needed to be ashamed. For aught we know to the contrary, he was living the clean, straightforward life of a young man who was making good use of the rare privileges which had come in his way. What can it mean, then, to say that when this fine figure from the royal household stepped down to throw in his lot with that of a group of undistinguished and unprepossessing people, he was forsaking "the pleasures of sin" in order that he might ally himself with something that was divine?

The answer is, of course, that in these people of Israel there was something greater than appeared. By that vast destiny which moves through human life, this unregarded group had been chosen to be exalted. They were poor; they were unprivileged; they were in many respects unlovely and crude: yet there was something in their spirit which foretokened greatness. This people should establish a new nation, with a new sense of justice for the common man, and a new dignity for all life as held accountable to God. Moses felt this. Something deep within him understood that Egypt was not the last word in civilization. Out of these men at the bottom must come a new achievement. It was because he sensed this that he knew his place was with them. Their destiny and his destiny were both part of a divine compulsion. And this was the reason why the privileges of Egypt, no matter how fine and desirable intrinsically they may have been, were for him "the pleasures of sin." If he had clung to the prerogatives of Pharaoh's court, it would have been the sin of the lower choice. It would have been the sin of refusal to follow the highest—and the hardest—that he knew. It would have been the sin of the betrayal of his best.

So Moses *chose* affliction. When he turned his back on Pharaoh's house, he knew that he went out to a life stripped of its emoluments, full of new hardships leading on to sacrifices even greater than anything he could foresee. He who was not obliged to come to this decision made it by the free action of his own soul. He who was not afflicted rose to the heroic choice of enrolling himself among the men who knew affliction.

Thus Moses became the forerunner of those who in their successive generations have stepped down from the ranks of privilege to serve the multitude. Paul the Apostle did that when he left the company of scholars and distinguished leaders of the Jewish Church to go out and share the fellowship of despised groups of slaves and lowly people to whom he had carried the message of the cross. Francis of Assisi did it when he left his father's house to live among the poor. John Wesley did it when he forsook the congenial affiliations of his cultured Oxford to carry the gospel of a new life to the common folk of England. Samuel C. Armstrong did it when he gave his life to build at Hampton a great school for the negroes who, set free from slavery, stood groping on the borders of a new existence. Jane Addams did it when at Hull House she carried the ministry of her own life and of the lives of those who joined her down among the neediest immigrants in the Chicago slums. It is not a numerous company, this succession of the men and women who have disassociated themselves from the easier and more spacious life they might have lived and have gone to give their leadership to those who need it most. Their sort of imagination and their sort of devotion is rare. Their heroism is perhaps the highest heroism to which this human nature of ours attains.

But for courage such as this and consecration such as this there is crying need in our world today. Out of our ranks of privilege this spirit of self-denying leadership must somehow come forth if the critical issues of our civilization are to be greatly met.

That these issues are critical few will doubt. Our civilization in the America of this twentieth century is astir with forces similar to those which moved in the civilization of Egypt more than three thousand years ago. There is a restlessness among the multitudes at the bottom of the social pyramid. Outward conditions are different; but there is a revolt of the spirit not so different from what it was in those days when Moses allied himself with the Hebrew toilers. Men labored then under the whip-lash. Today they feel upon their backs the equally terrible scourge of unemployment, insecurity, and fear. We today in the West have built a social order marked by many iniquities of conscious and unconscious cruelty. We have produced our Pharaohs of privilege, demanding much and giving little; and have produced at the other end child-labor, the drear poverty and the soul-destroying ugliness of coal-mining towns, the drab monotony of factories and mills where men and women labor unceasingly and never inherit the beauty or spaciousness of life. Some years ago Reinhold Niebuhr wrote a book which has commanded nation-wide attention because of the power with which he told the truth that most of us who belong to the comfortable classes do not want to face. He called it *Moral Man and Immoral Society*; and his thesis is that there is an inherent selfishness in social groups which makes it almost impossible for any privileged class to realize the injustices by which it thrives. He believes that some sort of social revolution will be necessary if the cruel inequalities of our present system are to be set right.

If such a revolution comes, how will it come? Will it come with bitterness and bloodshed, as in Russia? Will it come with an overturning so violent and savage that many of the fair and beautiful things which have blossomed out of our admittedly imperfect civilization will be destroyed in a blind convulsion? It may so come. Who can look at the volcanic forces trembling beneath the crust of our present life and dare say that any ominous possibility is unthinkable? But if we want to avoid in America a cataclysm such as Russia has already known, and such as that which Central Europe may be facing, what is the thing we most surely need? We need a blossoming of the human spirit which can produce as leaders of the social changes (which unquestionably will come) men such as Moses was in the crisis of his place and time. If our civilization is permanently divided into two hostile and suspicious groups, on the one hand those who have and who intend to keep, and on the other hand those who have not and who intend to seize—then the resulting collision some day will be terrible. As human history moves on, the power passes to the multitude; and if the multitude is led only by its own embittered leaders, their impact on the old order will be ruthless. A better way of change can come only if leaders issue out of the ranks of the privileged to become the champions of the unprivileged, carrying to the men at the bottom the wider perspective and more sensitive imagination of the man who is not blindly struggling after the best, but who already in his own experience knows what the best can be.

To some degree, this leadership is being already furnished. There are ministers who, in spite of every temptation to voice the instinctive prejudices of well-to-do congregations, are the fearless and sometimes lonely champions of the poor and the disadvantaged; there are young men in college or just out of it who cannot rest in the complacent ideas of their families or their social group, but wrestle in mind and spirit with the insistent question of how to take their place in the world's everyday affairs and still be just and fair and generous; there are women who in settlements or in organizations like the Consumers' League have daily contact with the problems of the poor, and have transferred their passionate loyalties from the class into whose exemptions they were born to the class with which vicariously they have become identified. I believe that an increasing number of people are in some measure doing this. There are some of you who know that you cannot now be content, as perhaps you once were content, to consider wealth or comfortable conditions as your natural prerogative, and to feel no responsibility for such radical alteration of social conditions as shall leave you less and give the poor more. We look out upon a world which is shaken with the tremors of industrial and economic protest. We remember the near-insurrection of farmers in the west in the early 1930's against the load of debt and the foreclosures on their farms. We see the growing swing to radical measures among the organized and unorganized groups of labor. What attitude will you take toward these? Will you react toward them with that protective selfishness which Reinhold Niebuhr so unsparingly delineates in the book to which I referred just now? Will you echo all sorts of convenient arguments by which you rationalize your own advantage and try to make your own profit appear as though it were a matter of high-sounding principle? Or will you instead do this: —If not in the kind of active leadership which Moses gave, and the kind of leadership which many of the finer men and women in our present generation are prepared now at great cost again to give, then at least in your willingness to think justly and to create a public opinion which makes for justice, will you encourage in our time the spirit which breaks down the barriers between the class at the top and the class at the bottom, and meets with a generous and understanding sympathy all those movements which are trying to set men free? The creation of this sort of sympathy, and the furnishing of leaders of this type, is today the most crucial test which the Christian Church must face. God, who weighs men and institutions in the balance of His moral accounting, is forcing us to reveal whether we of the Church will hide ourselves in Pharaoh's house, or whether we dare to go

out and identify our strength with all the distressed among whom
God's purposes are moving.

> The Lord said "Say We:"
> But I shook my head
> Clasped my hands behind my back and said
> "No Lord. 'I' "
>
> The Lord said "Say We":
> But I looked at all those other people grimy and all awry,
> Myself in those twisted, dirty shapes, "Never:"
> I turned away—"No Lord, 'They.' "
>
> The Lord said "Say We": and I at last
> Richer by a hoard of years and tears
> Looked in their eyes. And then like a shamed schoolboy
> I bent my neck and bowed my head and said "Yes Lord, 'We.' "

II

The period of postponement

We pass now to the second stage in Moses' life, which was
of a sort that can be treated briefly.

When Moses had killed the Egyptian, he fled from Egypt. There
was nothing else for him to do. He escaped into the Arabian desert to the north, and there he lived as a shepherd and nomad.
He is a long way off now from Egypt and the immediate problem of his people. There in Egypt he had seemed to hear God's
call in his own heart to do something to help his people's
affliction; but the impulsive thing which he had done had led
to no result. Was the idea, after all, a mere vagary? When he
cut himself off from Pharaoh's court, perhaps he had made only
a reckless and useless sacrifice.

There in the desert Moses had to face that possible reaction
of his spirit. The first hours of impulse and enthusiasm were
gone. He had waked now to what seemed a long, drab, morn-
ing-after. He was facing the test which repeatedly faces the
souls who have had in them the possibility of becoming great

in devotion and in leadership. It is the test of the inevitable depression which sets in after exaltation; but it is the test which the Spirit of God for its own purposes seems deliberately to impose. Jesus himself was driven by the Spirit into the wilderness for forty days after the high experience of his baptism. Paul the Apostle, after his conversion, went for three years of silence and solitude into the same Arabian desert where Moses himself had gone. It was as though God's Spirit said, "Stop, and be sure. Ask whether you will be ready to pay the long cost of consecration. Determine now the issue with your own soul, and see whether you can not only take up a great task, but whether also you can carry it through."

In the desert Moses found what he needed to find, namely, that his urge to go to the aid of his people was no shallow flare. It was a fire that burned in his soul and could not be quenched by distance or by time. One day he had a vision. In the shimmering heat of the desert, beneath the blaze of that eastern sun, he saw a bush that seemed on fire, and the bush was not consumed. What that vision meant, we can, of course, never positively know. We can only infer its meaning; and *this* inference, perhaps, is as near the full truth as any other we could arrive at. The burning bush which was not consumed was like the undying conviction by which Moses had been possessed. It would not burn itself away. He could not get rid of that fire. As long as his life lasted, that fire would be there, burning, burning, refusing to turn to ashes, no matter how the years went by.

That was an understanding about his own soul. There in the desert also there came to Moses a new and deeper understanding about God. When the urge to go back to Egypt and take up the burden of his people had become irresistible, Moses prayed more earnestly. He asked God to tell him His name; and *this,* in the mystic experience of his praying, came back to him as the answer: I AM THAT I AM, or, as the revised version has it, I WILL BE THAT I WILL BE. A baffling answer, we think. How strange and impossible a group of words to constitute a name!— "I am that I am." "I will be that I will be." But an immensity of suggestion is in them, like the depths beneath the rolling surface of the sea. God is not to be limited by any description. He is not to be confined within any partial record, even in the way in which He is revealed. He is the whole profound meaning of life that is and that is to be, as this meaning gradually and continuously is set forth. All great memories of the past, all remorse for failure or gratitude for faithfulness, all deeds of today or hopes for tomorrow—these are part of the continuous impact of God on human life. It was as though the divine voice had said to Moses: "You cannot know me by anything that I shall tell you now. You cannot recognize me, as you imagine, by any fleeting signs that I might give. You will know me only as day is added to day; and from every day lived in loyalty to the highest that you then know, you gather your increasing understanding of what life and God mean."

III

The days of endurance

Back from the desert then Moses went to Egypt, and in the book of Exodus there follows the stirring narrative of his conflict with Pharaoh, his mobilizing of the oppressed people, his leading them across the arm of the Red Sea, and the long and weary marching until they came to the borders of the promised land, where Moses himself should die.

Moses has been made fully ready now for his task. The iron in him has been fashioned into steel. As he stands before Pharaoh and demands that Pharaoh let the Hebrews go, there is a majesty of moral courage in him which is stronger than the power of the king. He is unmoved by Pharaoh's anger, unterrified by his threats. At length, overborne by a series of calamities which had fallen on Egypt and which he had attributed to Moses, Pharaoh yields. He will let the people of Israel go. In that moment, it seemed to him that he would do anything to get rid of this intolerable man. If Moses was not afraid of Pharaoh, it is certain that Pharaoh had moments when he was afraid of Moses. His resistance had been beaten down by Moses' indomitable will. His confidence in himself was undermined by superstitious apprehension of what Moses would accomplish next. The plagues which fell upon Egypt seemed to him to come from Moses' hand; and Moses himself appeared to him to be the worst and most detestable plague of all.

But then a curious thing happens. This man Moses, who could be so terrible to Pharaoh, leads the Israelites out of Egypt into the wilderness. At first the deliverance seems to be vivid and wonderful; but very soon the people begin to realize that they are face to face with a long and weary experience. The desert seems full of terrors, and certainly it is full of hardships. They march across its blistering sands; they get lost in wastes where there is no water; their food gives out, and they are hungry. Then they begin bitterly to complain. As compared with this desert, even Egypt seems to be desirable. "Were there no graves in Egypt," they cry, "that thou hast brought us forth to die in this wilderness?" And then their minds go back to all the advantages of the Egyptian civilization, which they think if they could get again would make them gladly reconciled to slavery. "Would to God we had died by the hand of the Lord in the land of Egypt, when we sat by the flesh pots, and when we did eat bread to the full."

Then what did Moses do? Did he fall into a rage with the people? Did he abandon the effort of his leadership in disgust, or did he set himself with some sort of cruel dictation to break down any opposition, and to stifle all complaint? Did he exhibit himself as the kind of man Pharaoh thought he was, proud, over-bearing, and implacable? He did not. On the contrary, he showed a patience beyond measure. Even when his own sister Miriam and Aaron his brother stirred disaffection against him, he was steadfast, kind, and forgiving.

There is a strange contrast here between the man who stood before Pharaoh and the man who led the people in the desert. As Dean Hodges has put it in his inimitable way: "Do you suppose that if Pharaoh had been catechized according to the New England Primer, and somebody had said, 'Pharaoh, who is the meekest man in your dominion'—do you suppose that he would have answered Moses? He would have replied, 'I don't know who is the meekest man. But I will tell you who is the

most imprudent man, I will tell you who is the most mischie-
vous man, I will tell you the only man of whom I am afraid—
his name is Moses.' "

And yet this contrast, remarkable as it appears, really is not
strange. It is always the great man who can be most meek. It
is always the man capable of terrific power who has the strength
so to subject himself that he can be patient with ignorance and
folly. The secret of Moses' bearing in both instances went back
to the most central fact about his soul. He was not thinking
about Moses. He was thinking about God and God's commis-
sion. He could seem terrible before Pharaoh because his heart
was filled with compassion for this people whom God had
appointed him to lead.

Are not both of these qualities needed in our own day? If out
of the Egypt of our social confusion there is to be some great
exodus of human forces which leads on toward a new land of
promise of the purposes of God, we need first an unflinching
courage, a courage that confronts old iniquities and vested
wrongs, a moral courage like that of Moses which will be terrible to all those whose interests and whose prejudices block
the human emancipation which God would work out in this
present time. We need the voices of the prophets both in the
pulpits and in the fields of politics; we need those who will
speak the ringing word, no matter if it sounds like bells of
judgment and disaster to some of the comfortable things that
we have known. But no less, and perhaps even more, we need
that other spirit which Moses represented, the spirit of meek-
ness which can make eager and idealistic people patient during
a long and often disillusioning process through which their
ideals alone can arrive at the destined goal. The children of Israel
were often a very cantankerous lot. They were called "the children of God"; but frequently they acted like limbs of Satan.
They were stubborn, stupid, rebellious, fickle. They would praise
Moses, and they would glorify God when everything went well;
but there was nothing too bitter to say about Moses, and nothing too doubtful to think about God, when, as frequently happened in their estimation, things went ill. A little man would
very soon have grown tired of that. He would have abandoned

the whole disagreeable business, and done it in the name of his ideal. He would have said that this people did not even know enough to recognize a great purpose, but insulted it and made it useless. Let them take care of themselves, and he would go back to his own concerns. How easy that would have been, and how natural! How hard it was, so hard that every day had to be newly heroic, to go on with a patient effort long after the first exultant glow had passed! On that day when he broke the resistance of Pharaoh, Moses knew what it was to "mount up with wings as eagles." Now he had to learn the infinitely more difficult achievement of the man who can "run and not be weary," who can "walk, and not faint."

Do you not see the relationship of this to our own life today? Many young idealists go out into social work or into the settlements or into the labor movement or into politics with a true desire, like Moses', to take their privileges and put them at the service of the common man. They glorify the great democracy. They believe in the virtues of those whom they somewhat romantically think of as "the poor." Then they begin to find that the poor and the depressed groups generally are by no means altogether virtuous or altogether agreeable. They have limitations which have been bred in them by their narrow lot, together with the other defects of the human nature we all share. They are not easily led in the right way, even by generous leaders. They often will be selfish and suspicious. They cannot always look forward to long goals, but are impatient for short cuts and quick results. They may listen to the demagogue and turn a deaf ear to the statesman. And then what? What will happen with the leaders then? It will depend upon the sort of soul which these would-be leaders possess. If they are only common clay, they will desert, as Moses might have done but did not do. They will become disillusioned, and adopt a sour cynicism in place of the ideals which they once believed in, and which they say now that human facts have made impossible. Or they may keep on like Moses because, as in the great words once written of him, they are "seeing the invisible." They do not see human nature merely as it is. They see it with a divine compassion and a divine expectation which they have learned from God. They see God through man, God's infinitely compassionate and loving purposes trying so patiently to win their way through men's slow understanding and acceptance. And because they thus see the invisible, they will not be dismayed by the obvious and the temporary. They will be meek to endure, as Moses did, much complaining and resistance, because their souls are mighty with a faith that will not be conquered by petty things. They will keep on desiring, believing, trusting, leading in the right way, and knowing that some day, whether in their time or afterward, the multitude will follow.

So at the end I go back and strike again the note of the text which has been echoing through our thought since its beginning. In the great social relationships of our world today, it may be possible that those who have been born to privilege at least temporarily avoid affliction. We may hide ourselves in the Pharaoh's courts of our own comfortable privileges of condition and of class. We may do nothing either to understand or to help forward the great movements which are pointing in the direction of a freer and more spacious life for the masses. But somewhere out of the Christian Church there must come the leaders, and everywhere from the Christian Church, if that Church is not to fail, there must come the increasing sympathy which deliberately brings the power of those who have had much to the side of those who have had least. For those who have once caught that vision, the sojourning in Pharaoh's house is sin. No longer can we desire to avoid affliction. Rather we must go out to choose it, as Moses did—and as Christ did—in order to take our part in serving God's purpose for His people.

VII

THE FRIEND IN THE BACKGROUND

*The soul of Jonathan was knit with the soul of
David, and Jonathan loved him as his own soul.*
I SAMUEL XVIII:1

HOW wonderful the Bible is in its vitality. The more we
know it, the more we understand how inexhaustible are
its meaning and its interest. We may think that we are familiar
with the great personalities that move through its pages, and
then some day we see one of them from the fresh angles of our
own experience, and in countenance and in character he is new.
Or out of the multitude of the well-known personalities suddenly some other one emerges from the crowd, and we see his
figure alive and vibrant. All the years and centuries have not
made them stale. They live today, these figures of the Bible,
whenever knowledge and imagination turn again to look at them;
and intimately they move into the circle of our own consciousness of what life means and ought to mean.

It might be imagined that for any one who has to read the
Bible a great deal, as a preacher, for instance, does, the Bible
would have no more surprises; but this is never so. It is forever
disclosing faces that one had not before been sharply aware of.
For twenty-seven years I have been preaching from the Bible, and
recently I asked myself, as every preacher in the moments of the
emptiness of his own thought must ask, "What is there left to
say? Where shall a new sermon come from? What figure in
the Old or New Testament, which have been reviewed so many
times, can stand forth in any fresh significance?" And then to
my amazement there moved out of the background of the Bible
a face into which I had never directly looked before. I had heard
of him, of course, and thought of him indirectly, but always in
secondary fashion. Now the man himself stood there, not sub-
ordinate to any one else, but distinct and separate, and I realized
that here, in this man of whom I had never specifically preached

in twenty-seven years, stood one of the great souls of all human history. It was exactly as though he looked at me with clear, level eyes, not troubled as to whether any one paid him tribute or not, but having in that look an inner greatness independent of all accident of recognition or non-recognition.

"What is his name?" you ask.

I

It is Jonathan. You have heard of him, of course; but you have heard of him in all likelihood as a sort of echo to the name of David. David and Jonathan: they are the symbols of an immortal friendship. But it is David who generally stands in the foreground and Jonathan who is in the shadow. It is David who went on to a career of many exploits, ending in the kingship, while Jonathan's career was short. The result is that, though we hear a great deal about David, we tend to forget about Jonathan. Yet the fact is that his appears to have been the nobler spirit. He is one of those very rare characters in the Bible on whose record, as we find it written there, there is not one single blemish. Nearly all the other figures, even some of the very great ones, have very obvious shortcomings and very ugly scars. Abraham was an exalted spirit, but he had his hours of weakness and discredit. So did Isaac. So did Jacob. So did even Moses. So conspicuously did David. But so far at least as all we know about him goes, not Jonathan. From beginning to end of his history, he never did a mean thing nor ever failed to do what was magnanimous. He became the great example of the generosity of a human friendship which went beyond all selfish bounds.

Consider now his story, and let us see whether this high-hearted and gallant figure of a far-off day will not come to be as real to all of us as out of the pages of the record he suddenly made himself to me.

When we first see Jonathan he is the young warrior son of Saul, the king. Those, of course, were the distant days when civilization and the social conscience had not even come in sight of that point in human evolution when war itself would be arraigned as evil. In their perilous and uncertain world, warfare for the tribes of Israel was a constant and inevitable fact, and Jonathan lived and moved within the framework of that time, a spontaneous soldier without fear and without reproach.

The earliest incident in which he figures showed him immediately for what he was, a man who cared for accomplishment and not for credit. He had led the fighting men of Israel against the Philistines. Saul, his father, had kept under his own command the greater part of the fighting forces; but it was Jonathan and the men he led who drove ahead to victory. Then the chronicle goes on with this curiously revealing statement: "And Saul blew the trumpet throughout all the land, saying, 'Let the Hebrews hear.' And all Israel heard say that Saul had smitten a garrison of the Philistines." It was the king's name, not Jonathan's, that thus was proclaimed abroad in connection with the victory; but there is no hint that Jonathan was offended. The success was won. That was all he cared for. What did it matter whose name was sounded with it?

The next scene is again a scene of battle. Once more the Israelites were at war with the Philistines, and the Philistines were entrenched among the hills. Jonathan with his armor-bearer conceived a dare-devil exploit which to the ordinary man would have appeared as scarcely less than madness. He climbed up a cleft in the rocks and fell upon the Philistines' camp, believing that the Philistines would consider that nobody would have risked this unless great numbers of others were following at his back. Exactly this happened. The Philistines fell into a panic and began to retreat, and the rest of the fighting forces of Israel, seeing this, fell upon them from the flanks, so that the rout of the Philistines became complete.

But the history of the day was not ended, and it threatened to end in a strangely different way from that in which it had begun. All day long the intermittent fighting of the pursuit continued. The men of Israel were hungry and faint because Saul had issued a grim command that no man should have anything to eat that day. Jonathan had not heard of this, and, passing by a tree where bees had made their honey-comb, he took the honey and ate it as he went forward. One of the fighting men near Jonathan, awe-struck, told him of the curse which Saul had laid upon any man in the army who dared to eat that day. Jonathan was indignant not for himself primarily, but for his men. It was wrong, he said, that the king should have laid this hardship upon those who were already growing faint. But at the end of the day, when Saul halted the pursuit, he consulted the omens as to what he should do next, and could not get an answer. His superstitious dread was aroused. Somebody, he thought, had offended the heavenly powers. He had lots drawn to see who it might be, and the lot fell upon Jonathan. Then he discovered that Jonathan had disobeyed the curse which he, Saul, had laid upon the army against taking anything to eat that day. In his fierce resolution, he swore that Jonathan should be put to death for this offence. But the army was in tumult. Jonathan, they shouted, had been the hero of that day. Not even Saul himself should touch him.

A great Scotch preacher and interpreter of the Old Testament has made a revealing comment upon this story and upon Jonathan as he moves through it. He points out what of course was the fact, that in those days the wars of Israel were recorded by the Israelites themselves as an act of God against the powers of the world. He points out also that Saul had the idea, which many men in his age and since have had, that the way to please God is by inflicting pain upon oneself. "It is strange," he writes, "how persistently the idea has survived that the value of divine worship lies in its difficulty." We can see that in a certain grim note which runs through many religious influences all down the centuries. We see it, for example, in the Jewish law concerning the sabbath-day, which limited by the strictest prohibition every sort of normal activity till that day was past. We have seen that same idea persist in what used to be the Puritan Sunday, in the bleakness of the Puritan houses of worship, and in those extreme sects of Christians which think that even ornaments in dress are sinful in the eyes of the Lord.

Saul thought that day that if he made his army endure enough in obedience to a vow, God's authority would be pleased by that obedience. Thus in the name of religion he could be ruthless to his men. But Jonathan had a warmer and more human sympathy. He rejected the king's harshness not only for his own sake, but for the sake of all the ordinary people. He had a truer instinct that made him know that there was something wrong about a religious idea which laid on men burdens that were unreasonable and then supposed that these were flattering to God. It is as though there had dawned in Jonathan's awareness in that far-off century something which only later ages of religious development were to make men understand more deeply, namely, that the meaning of God may best be found not apart from but within the throbbing facts of everyday existence. In him, perhaps, was a foregleam of the truth which Christ himself long afterwards summed up when he put the supreme spiritual duty in these words: "Thou shalt love the Lord thy God with all thy heart, and with all thy soul, and with all thy mind, *and* thou shalt love thy neighbor as thyself." Doubtless Jonathan did not think out his conclusions in words as explicit as these, but in his heart he *felt* that the worship of God is not something which is opposed to consideration for human life, that we do not please God more when we regard and protect men less, but that, on the contrary, religion ought to go hand in hand with kindness. Jonathan loved the common man, and in that he was to some degree at least a prophet of the greatest One, who should come to show in Galilee and on Calvary that love is the fulfilling of the law.

And now the story of Jonathan moves from scenes of battle to scenes which, if sometimes not less dangerous, were yet more beautiful. A new figure comes upon the stage. It is David, a young shepherd, son of Jesse; David, the intrepid stripling who, coming down to the camp of Israel on the day when Goliath of Gath challenged the armies of Saul, went out alone to fight Goliath, and overcame him with his shepherd's sling. Many emotions must have been in the army that day. Saul the king— for he too in his best hours could be magnanimous—was filled with admiration. Some of the men doubtless were in another mood. David's own brothers had been churlish and distrustful. Others may have envied him that day. But the emotions which Jonathan poured out toward him were like the rush of a mountain brook. "The soul of Jonathan was knit with the soul of David," says the chronicle, "and Jonathan loved him as his own soul."

It was not long before Saul's feeling toward David turned abruptly. It happened thus. Shortly after the victory over Goliath, when the armies of Israel came back from the pursuit of the Philistine foes, the women came singing out of the cities, and they chanted this: "Saul hath slain his thousands, and David his ten thousands." Instantly Saul recognized the implication of that. Here was this newcomer who was eclipsing him, the king. Here was this unknown boy, this upstart as he saw him now, who was being lifted up by the crowd's enthusiasm as a hero. There was danger in that to Saul, danger to his dynasty.

From that time on, with brief impulsive reactions to the nobler generosity which he could never quite destroy in his own soul, Saul began to hate David, to project his own resentments upon him, to try repeatedly to kill him.

And now Jonathan moves into the light in the full revelation of the manner of man he was. He must have perceived the reason for Saul's hostility to David. He must have seen that on the stark basis of obvious advantage Saul was right. It was not madness, but a cold correctness of calculation that made Saul perceive that his interests and those of David must be in deadly opposition. If David increased, Saul would decrease, and Jonathan would decrease with him. That is why, when David was playing the harp before him, Saul's brooding resentment flamed into uncontrollable hatred and he hurled the javelin which, if his aim had been better, would have pinned David to the wall. That is the reason why he hunted him afterwards through the wilderness of En-gedi while David hid in the clefts of the hills. But meanwhile to Jonathan it was as though these reasons for fear of David had no existence whatever. It was possible that David might some day become king instead of himself. But if he ever thought of that, it poisoned his spirit not at all. He loved David. David was the one thing he cared for most. Here was a man to whom his whole soul went out in unreckoning friendship. Their friendship was a bigger thing than any preferment that might or might not come to him. One day in a rush of his affection he "stripped himself of the robe that was upon him, and gave it to David, and his garments, even to his sword, and to his bow, and to his girdle." Repeatedly he stood between David and the danger which Saul's hate always held. He warned David when his father's mood was ominous. He confronted Saul with frank and fearless defense of David when Saul's anger blazed. Once the king was so beside himself that he actually threw his javelin at Jonathan because Jonathan had said to his father of David, "Why should he be slain? What has he done?" After he had seen his father thus turn in deadly fashion against himself, Jonathan, as the chronicle tells, "arose from the table in fierce anger." But in anger for what? The next sentence goes on with its astonishing revelation of this man's superiority to any self-concern. It was that "he was grieved for David, because his father had done him shame."

He went out into the fields after that to meet David, when it was no longer safe for David to come back to the court of Saul. He protected his friend with a devotion that took no reckoning of the danger to what might have been his own personal interest, and at the risk even of his life.

Yet all the while the extraordinary thing is that Jonathan was no indifferent son to Saul. He could disapprove the things his father did and withstand him to his face; but never for a moment was he at heart disloyal. Neither was he any easy-going, flabby person who surrendered advantage and shrugged away the duties of his position because he was too weak or too indifferent to defend them. On the contrary, he was a patriot after the fashion which in that day was the highest that men knew. He was a soldier of unswerving courage and inflexible determination. He stood at his father's side in every crisis which he could meet with a clear conscience. He could see the kingship pass away from him without a shadow of resentment because of his great love for David, but not for an instant would he flinch in defence of the kingdom through any indifference or cowardice. In his short life he had won brilliant victories; but he was no less great in the hour of defeat. When Saul his father went out to the last great battle with the Philistines at Mount Gilboa, Jonathan was there; and when the battle turned into disaster Jonathan fell beside his father, high-hearted and valiant to the end. No wonder that David sang of him:

> *"The beauty of Israel is slain upon thy high places:*
> *how are the mighty fallen!"*

II

Such, then, is the story of Jonathan. It is an astonishing thing that three thousand years ago there lived a spirit so clean and high and gallant, and that there could have been found a chronicler to put his story into a record so transparent for the spiritual beauty which it contains.

When we deal with a personality such as that of Jonathan, it would be foolish to try to dissect it and turn it into moral lessons applicable in this or that precise advice to us. One cannot deal with a living soul that way. There he stands in his far-off time. Yes, if we are sensitive, here he stands vibrant and inspiring in the midst of our awareness now, the whole man with the whole impression of him. It would cheapen our theme for us to say in moralizing fashion, "Thus and thus he showed what it is to be a friend. Thus and so, therefore, let us go out and practise being friendly." No, the matter of friendship is not a matter of maxims. It is the contagion of a great suggestion. Here was a man who stands among the winsome figures of all time because he showed how great the soul of a man can be when it loves enough to forget its own selfish interest.

It is this supreme suggestion, therefore, that we would remember and make sure, if we can, of its relationship to those issues of life which were real a thousand years before the cross, are real now, and will be real forever.

First, there is the fact that back of numberless lives which we rate as the outstanding successes of our world there may be another power less conspicuous, but not less great, which friendship has put there. We cannot always trace this quiet other presence. We cannot always see the self-effacing friend. But it is safe to believe that almost always behind the man who registers the conspicuous achievement the friend is there. Sometimes it is a comrade. Sometimes it is a man's mother. Sometimes it is his wife. Sometimes it is the associate in business or in work, or the teacher, or some sympathetic spirit in the ways of life to whom a man or woman instinctively goes when problems are difficult. But in all these embodiments the essential friendship may be the same. Here, that is to say, is the power of a sympathy and an understanding that is not seeking anything of its own but is giving all it has to the one whom it is befriending. Without some such background as this, it would be found, I think, that few lives either of the past or of the present could have advanced as bravely on the ways of life as the best of them have done.

Certainly this was so of David. We think of him now as unquestionably great. He has become one of the dominant figures in the religious history of mankind. But who can say what David would have been without Jonathan? It was not only that Jonathan's friendship protected him against physical danger and was his shield more than once against actual destruction. The gift of Jonathan was greater than this. Natively David had great courage and daring; but he had also elements in his nature which, unrestrained, could be very cruel. The dark chapter of his treatment of Uriah the Hittite showed that. Who knows how much of the magnanimity which also came to mark him was due to Jonathan? Who can tell whether the fact that he could be thought of as a man after God's own heart was not due to all the purifying and ennobling influence which had come to him from Jonathan's heart? Years afterward there was a depth of devotion in his own soul which could cry concerning Absalom, "O my son Absalom, my son, my son Absalom! would God I had died for thee, O Absalom, my son, my son!" The love of which he was then capable may be traced back in large part to the love he had learned from Jonathan who had been willing to die to open the road of life for him.

Or take some of the other great figures of the Bible and of later life. Moses became the hero of the deliverance of the nation. But how would the story of Moses have ever begun save that in the background there was the gentle figure of Pharaoh's daughter who lifted him as a baby from the rushes of the Nile, nurtured and befriended him, and gave him all the first opportunities from which later he was to go forward on his own adventurous way? Or, passing to the New Testament, look at the figure of the man who stands second only to the Master himself, Paul the Apostle. How would his new life as a Christian ambassador have begun if it had not been for Barnabas? Barnabas the quiet and the generous, Barnabas the man who took Paul when all others distrusted him, welcomed him and sponsored him, Barnabas, to whom attached the name that every one who aspires to be a friend might well covet—"Son of encouragement." And if we want to leave the distant past, even though it have to do with the pages of the Bible, and come down to our time, there is such a friendship as that of Frederick Maurice and Charles Kingsley; there is that lovely enrichment of two lives which has been brought so vividly to our thinking through *The Barretts of Wimpole Street,* the friendship of Robert Browning and Elizabeth Barrett, which grew into a great love, but a love in which that deep understanding of spirit which friendship ought to mean was never lost in mere emotion. Or to come still closer to our own present, one may read such a life story as that of Jane Addams, a woman whose spirit and accomplishment made her known across the world. Yet one will find that in the beginnings of Hull House, it was not only Jane Addams but her friend, whose very name most people are unaware of, who helped to make possible the work which both of them did but for which one only of the two was increasingly remembered.

But it is possible, I know, that some one at this point might say: "Yes, but these are a very few selected instances. Against the recognizable examples of persons who owed their great achievements in some large measure to a friend who stood behind them in the shadow, there are innumerable other instances of the great ones of this earth who seem to have wrought their achievements out of their own lonely courage. What friend did Elijah the prophet have? What friend did Savonarola have? What friend did innumerable others who have stood in great posts of public service have? Often we do not know."

Ah, yes, exactly so; but that leads us to the second and further point which we ought to emphasize. The friends who matter most may sometimes not even have left their names behind. They may be so wrought into another's life that they are not remembered in the public records as having been at all. But when we look deep within the heart of our own experience and our sense of the daily values of life, do we not know that it is scarcely possible for any of us to go forward far on the way of brave and steady living if we are wholly separate and alone? Somewhere, somehow the friend is present. It may be, as I have said already, a mother, or a wife. It may be the comrade and counsellor whose name never gets into any public print. It may be indeed some very humble person whose role is known only to those who daily are served and helped, sometimes not quite consciously acknowledged by even them: yes, known perfectly only to the eyes of God. There is in another city a woman who has been conspicuously able and generous in various wide ways of service in her community. Some of those who knew her were marvelling at the range of what she did. "How is it possible," they said, "that with limited resources of strength and of possessions, and with her family responsibilities, she has been able to do so much?" Most of them did not know the real answer, did not know, for how should they know, of the Irish maid who for more than a score of years had been the background for the daily routine of that family life, nurse and friend of the children, confidant in troubles, responsible for everything in which her cheerful sagacity could help. But one of them knew, knew why the woman whose public service was notable could do what actually she did. "The reason," she said, "is Jane." And then she smiled and said thoughtfully: "I expect every life which is amounting to much has somewhere its Jane."

And so it is. Let us not make the mistake of estimating the value of friendship in this world through the conspicuous examples to which we can attach a name. Along innumerable ways through the whole field of human life the beauty of friendship flows, flows so quietly and in such familiar fashion that we scarcely stop to notice it. Its reality has no need of noise or of display. It comes to make the whole earth beautiful like the quiet flowing of a brook by fields where flowers grow and little children play. It shines like sunlight through which alone the beauty of the spring awakens and the seeds of all planted things are stirred to life, and the harvest is ripened and fulfilled.

So the theme which we have been following brings its suggestion which no argument should be needed to enforce. If we have seen again the figure who moves in his brave and magnanimous manhood through the Old Testament story, we shall have seen that which we can never quite escape thereafter as an ideal toward which the best in us is drawn. It may not be given to us to be among the Davids of this world. That is to say, we may not attain conspicuous achievement. We may not win that seeming royalty of privilege which comes only to the few; but something surer and nobler too can be within our grasp. We can understand and reflect the soul of Jonathan. We can remember how beautiful a thing is friendship, mark every aspect of it which has blessed our lives, be grateful for it, and know that there is nothing else which counts so much. And we can, each one of us, try to be a friend and *such* a friend as was the man whose face is beautiful and living still across three thousand years. We can try to let our souls be warmed by that same glow which was in the soul of Jonathan. And if we do that, we shall not be far from the spirit of one who was greater than Jonathan—even Jesus.

VIII

A FATHER AND A SON

*And the king was much moved, and went up to the
chamber over the gate, and wept: and as he went,
thus he said, O my son Absalom! my son, my son
Absalom! would God I had died for thee, O Absalom, my son, my son!*

II SAMUEL XVIII:33

WE ARE to think of the story of a son who failed his father
and of a father who lost his son.

It is written for us in the book of the Old Testament
called the Second Book of Samuel. In the First Book of Samuel
there comes upon the stage of Israel's history that most winsome figure among all the characters in the long Old Testament pageant, David the son of Jesse. We see him first as a
lad, fresh and guileless, the youngest of eight brothers, anointed
by the prophet Samuel to be the future king of Israel. From
the mountain pastures where he kept his father's sheep, he
comes down presently, clean of limb and clean of heart, to
the valley of Elah, where the army of Saul is confronting the
army of the Philistines; and there David takes up the challenge of the huge Goliath, and with his shepherd's sling and
a small stone taken from the bed of the brook, he slays the
Philistine champion. Then follows the story of one of the love-
liest friendships recorded in all literature, the bond of unselfish
brotherhood between David and Jonathan the son of Saul. Because of Jonathan's friendship and because of the whispered
rumor that the old Samuel has prophesied that David will ultimately be king, Saul in his morose jealousy hunts David to kill
him. Twice David, pursued by Saul in the wilderness, has his own
opportunity to kill the king, and twice he refuses. During that
pursuit by Saul occurs an incident which reveals like a flash of
sudden sunlight the character of David and the quality of devotion which his leadership aroused. Standing opposite Bethlehem

one day, David looks toward the village of his youth and sighs for a draught of water from the familiar wells of Bethlehem. Two soldiers standing by him hear his wish. Out through the line of the soldiers of Saul they go that night to bring back to David a cup of water from the dear familiar wells which he desired. There was something in his spirit which made men willing to die to protect him—yes, made them willing to hazard their lives to satisfy what might have seemed his unimportant wish and to win the gladness of his smile.

The years go by. Saul and Jonathan have passed to their death in the fateful battle of Mount Gilboa, and David is king. Now, in the Second Book of Samuel, the story finds him a mature man with grown sons. The old sweetness and gallantry of spirit which marked his youth are in him still; but the scars of life are on him. That nature of his, so passionate in affection, has had its moments of passionate evil also. And now, out of life's strange retributions, tragedy has come to him from the quarter where he might have least expected it.

I

Among his sons there was one whom David apparently loved best of all. His name was Absalom. Perhaps one reason why David loved him was that he must have aroused continually the wistful memories of his own brighter youth. For Absalom in seeming at least had many of the qualities which made the young David the hero of the multitude. He was handsome to look upon. "In all Israel," says the Book of Samuel, "there was none to be so much praised as Absalom for his beauty: from the sole of his foot even to the crown of his head there was no blemish in him." He had a lavish and generous way. He could meet men with an outgoing interest and exercise over them that same fascination of confident leadership which his father had always had. But the magnanimity of the soul of David was not in Absalom. Instead of the chivalry which twice made David refuse to take the life and seize the crown of Saul his pursuer, Absalom had a consuming ambition which made him conspire even against his father's throne. Adroitly he won the favor of many men in Israel. At last he lifted his deliberate banners of revolt and marched upon Jerusalem. David and those who remained faithful to him were obliged to abandon the city and Absalom pursued him. Presently the battle was joined between the forces of David and the forces of Absalom; the fighting surged into the forest of Ephraim, and there, as he rode under the trees, the glorious long hair of Absalom became entangled in the branches. In that moment he was helpless, and as he hung entangled there, Joab, the friend of David, came upon him with javelins in his hand.

Meanwhile in the nearby city of Mahanaim David waited for news of the battle. He had said to the leaders of his army as they went out, "Deal gently for my sake with the young man, even with Absalom." With what conflicting emotions now did he wait the tidings of the struggle! Would this thing that seemed an evil dream pass by? Would Absalom come out of the battle changed in heart? Would his rebellious spirit turn back again to his father? So wondering, David waited—waited by the gate of the town. And now the watchman upon the wall perceives a runner far off across the plain. He cries to the king that a messenger is coming. And the king answers, "If he be alone, there is tidings in his mouth." Then the swift narrative continues. The watchman sees another man running, "and the watchman called unto the porter and said, behold another man running alone. And the king said, he also bringeth tidings. And the watchman said, Me thinketh the running of the foremost is like the running of Ahimaaz the son of Zadok. And the king said, He is a good man and cometh with good tidings."

Then comes Ahimaaz near, this panting messenger from the victorious army of David with his exultant news that Absalom, the king's son, is dead. He begins to pour out his eager news. "Blessed be the Lord thy God, who hath delivered up the men who lifted up their hand against my lord the king." Then he looks upon the king's face, and his message goes dumb upon his lips. David is not thinking of victory. One great emotion of anxiety struggles in his heart. "Is it well," he says, "with the young man Absalom?" And Ahimaaz, who had come to bring his message of victory, falters, and in sudden pity he stammers out a lie. He saw a great turmoil in the battle, but he knew not what it was. He cannot tell the outcome. "And the king said unto him, Turn aside and stand here. And he turned aside, and stood still."

Then as the first messenger stood by David, there came the second. His was a cruder spirit than the spirit of Ahimaaz. He takes no note of anything in David's face that might warn him back from the hot news he has come to tell. "Tidings, my lord the king," he cries, "for the Lord hath avenged thee this day of all them that rose up against thee." "Is the young man Absalom safe?" David asks. And at that the messenger bursts into the fierce climax of his tidings. "The enemies of my lord the king, and all that rise up against thee to do thee hurt, be as that young man is." Absalom is dead. Joab, the captain of the king's army, had thrust three darts through his heart.

That was all. In the silence even the second messenger could understand the ghastly wound with which these words of his had pierced the heart of David. There at the gate the two messengers stood looking at one another in hushed dismay while the slow figure of David passed from them to the room above the wall, and they heard him cry: "O my son Absalom, my son, my son Absalom! would God I had died for thee, O Absalom, my son, my son!"

II

Such then is the story of David and Absalom. Let us think now of the two men themselves.

Absalom went to his death in an evil adventure. But he was not all evil. On the contrary, there were mingled in his nature elements exceedingly winsome and promising, together with those elements that led him to his destruction. In him, as in so many of us, our human nature revealed those struggling forces of glory and of shame, the conflict between which makes the eternal significance of life.

To begin with, Absalom had a sense of honour which, in certain relationships at least, could be passionate in its attachment. In the years before his rebellion against his father, there came into his life one incident sufficiently calculated to arouse his whole

nature into fierce action. His half-brother committed against his
own sister a deed of infamy, and from that time on Absalom
never forgot that his sister's cause was his. He did not rest until
his half-brother was in his power, and then he killed him at a
feast to which he had lured him in his own house. After that he
fled, and for a period of years remained in banishment. That
was the beginning of his estrangement from his father. The way
in which he slew his half-brother was cruel and treacherous. Of
that we shall speak later. But in order to understand the whole
character of Absalom, it is right at first to give full recognition
to all those partial elements in him which were honourable. He
had a wholesome capacity for indignation against an abominable
wrong. Even though he followed it down blind and terrible ways,
he was at least following something chivalrous when he felt that
he must go to whatever ends seemed necessary to express his
loyalty to the sister who had been infamously wronged.

There is much that is attractive, too, in a certain dashing and
debonair wholeheartedness with which Absalom went out to
meet his world. He was young, handsome, and attractive, and
he knew it. His enemies might have called him vain. But people
at large would have described him more warmly. Vanity is a
word that suggests a kind of soft and affected satisfaction, a
preening of oneself before the mirror of self-conscious regard;
and it was not this sort of vanity that men felt in Absalom.
Rather they felt in him a frank and unembarrassed consciousness
of his own gifts, a quick exercise of the leadership which he
knew his brilliant personality won, and a lavish way of expecting
much from life because life already flowed at high tide in his
own nature. He lived magnificently; but the crowd had a sense
that he was not separated from them, but that somehow they
were taken up into his magnificence. He rode in a chariot with
fifty men to run before him. He was the aristocrat, but he was
not aloof. He was the prince, but he was the prince who came
heartily out among the people. He was no idler either. He would
rise early in the morning and come out to the gates of Jerusalem
when the common people were first astir with the day's business.
He would talk with the porters of the gates, with men and women

coming in with their market produce, with citizens generally who had their ideas of how affairs in Jerusalem ought to be managed and who were flattered at the idea of standing face to face with the son of a king. Especially if men had grievances, he was sympathetic. He made them think how much better things would be if Absalom were in power.

Who shall say that there may not have been some measure of sincerity in Absalom's reaching out for the affection of the people? He had the genius of the human touch. Also he had the ambitions of youth. Doubtless he could look at David's kingdom and see much that was not as it ought to be. It was not hard to convince himself that his father was at fault and that a more impulsive energy could sweep away old evils, and a fresher leadership make all the land more prosperous and happy. With untempered confidence in his own abilities, Absalom began first to question and then to resent the existence of an authority which stood in the way of his own leadership. So in the name of youth as against experience, of tomorrow as against today, he persuaded himself of his right to revolt against his father. It was the age-long story of the new generation lifting its challenge against the generation into whose world it had been born.

Where now is the line of difference between the adventure which is the fine liberty of the new life and a reckless assault and unfruitful rebellion such as Absalom's turned out to be? That is a question which has reference not alone to our interpretation of a far-off tale. It has reference to our own world and our own age. Absalom interests us, not only for what he was as an intensely vivid human individual of the past, but also for what he is as a type of human tendencies today and tomorrow. When we ask why was it, and in what respect was it that Absalom failed, we are asking also why it is and how it is that the spirit of youth today, fascinating and inspiring though its possibilities are, may also run the chance of failure.

The answer reaches to one deep yet simple lack in Absalom's whole spirit. He thought that he was sufficient unto himself. He had no fixed loyalties to which he was deliberately and devotedly true. Like a meteor, he shot with a kind of wild and blazing beauty through the firmament of his world, and like a meteor, because he was not held by the great attraction of some mightier central sun, he collided with the fixed stars of moral principles that were steadier than himself; and the brightness of his possibilities were swallowed, like the dust of a dead comet, in the emptiness of space.

There was no religion in Absalom. I use that word now in the sense of that beautiful throbbing reality which it ought to mean. In the stories of the Old Testament, one encounters, of course, men who had much so-called religion, which, however, was of a kind that meant very little to them and would have meant very little to Absalom. There was a religion which had to do with perfunctory worship at shrines, with superstitions and half-believed formalities, with prayers forgotten in ordinary moments and resorted to only in some time when danger and perplexity seemed to offer no other resource. But the great figures of the Old Testament had a religion which was something different from this. They believed that the secret of this world is not contained in the things which are seen. They believed in the mightier spirit of a living God, with whom the highest instinct of our human souls bids us be in touch. They heard the accents of the still small voice which speaks to the conscience within, and in comparison with which the tumults and the shouting of our outward world are trivial. They knew that their lives could not move forward with certainty and power until they were linked in deliberate awareness with those purposes which are eternal. The religion of Moses was such as that. More real to him than the voice of Pharoah was the voice of God. More shining than the splendors of Egypt was the fire that flamed in the burning bush. Out from his own ease and advantage, out to the long adventure of his costly leadership, out to the great cause wherein he merged his own life in the larger destiny of his people, it was religion that led him, as the central sun of some great universe leads its obedient star. Such a religion Elijah had, as he dared to set the moral certainties of his own soul against all the corrupt authority of Ahab. Such a religion Isaiah had, as he, in the midst of the shifting politics of an unprincipled time taught men how

they could establish, if they would, the city which hath foundations, whose builder and maker is God. And such a religion in
its deep essentials David, Absalom's own father, had. He was no
unmarred saint. On the contrary, he was scarred by deep marks
of evil which branded him with the everlasting witness of his
human weaknesses. But through his whole life of mingled victory and defeat he was reaching out toward something higher
and steadier than himself. "Create in me a clean heart, O God."
"Out of the deeps have I cried unto thee." "I will lift up my eyes
unto the hills, from whence cometh my help." "My help cometh
from the Lord." "Like as the hart desireth the water-brooks, so
longeth my soul after thee, O God." "My soul followeth hard after
thee: thy right hand hath upholden me." These are the echoes
from the Psalms, traditionally linked with the name of David; and
whether or not they are his words, they do express what was the
aspiration of his soul. He had the sense of a higher truth to
which he must be true, of a higher law to which he must be
loyal, a higher life in the spaciousness of which alone he could
truly live. And Absalom had none of this. That was the secret of
his small life and his unworthy failure. He had no vision that
lifted him above himself, and therefore his ends were circum-
scribed and mean.

When a man possesses thus no mindfulness of God, and therefore no steady sense of spiritual duty, he makes the instincts of
his selfishness the pivot round which his thoughts and actions
turn. What he plans and what he does have no bigness of conception. Take, for example, in the case of Absalom, the killing of
his half-brother. That he should have felt that this man, because
of the brutal wrong he had done to a woman, ought to be
punished, was natural. In that undeveloped civilization where
justice was capricious, it was also not strange that Absalom should
think that he himself had to be the instrument through which
punishment must come. But he pursued his purpose in a way
which no man would have taken who held himself to be accountable to a holy and eternal justice which is above the mere impulse
of human revenge. He killed his brother at a feast in his own
house, killed him in the presence of his family, and thus made
the punishment into another crime. He had nothing higher than

his own proud wilfulness to refine his motives and to shape his ends. So, therefore, when it came to the question of his ambition to be king, he had again no consciousness of God to act as corrective to his own impulse. The thing he wanted to do was the thing he would do. The thing that for the moment seemed advantageous was the thing that he persuaded himself to be his rightful destiny. Upon the unbridled exercise of his own self-expression he thought he could ride to the goals of life.

That is the peril of youth always when it does not lift its eyes above itself. We are told that youth is in revolt now in our own day. That revolt may be a noble thing. It is noble if the spirit of youth can be clear-eyed to see and clean-hearted to choose the truth which is a higher and a holier thing than some of the inherited ideas of the older generation, but also is a higher and a holier thing than its own unfettered and undisciplined instincts. Let youth try to discover what is the kingdom of the spirit which God intends it to inherit. Let youth, considering history and weighing the actual facts of life, learn what are the things which always have been and by their quality always must be true and honorable and of good report. Then the spirit of the rising generation will not fling itself into a mere selfish and reckless collision with the old. It will ask how it can take its place in that long progress of human life in which no new day can afford to throw away the gains of yesterday. It will revalue the ideas of its fathers, but it will also purify its own by those principles which the long religious experience of the best among our human race has proven to be the power by which men are lifted to the kind of living which befits the sons of God. If any new generation has no better ambition than that of Absalom, and sets out merely to destroy whatever authority stands in the way of its own recklessness, then it is likely to find that the patient realities of life league against it and destroy its revolt as Absalom's was destroyed. It is not by Absalom against David, but by the nobler Absalom bringing his strength to the side of David that the better kingdom of the purposes of God will be established. It is not by the spirit of youth self-centered and self-sufficient, but by a spirit of youth that reaches up to God for light and leading that the new possibilities of our time and of every time must be fulfilled.

We have thought of Absalom. We turn now to consider the figure of David.

What did he think there in the room above the city-gate? Over what long road of bitter memory did his thoughts go back, as he sat there wrapped in the black realization that Absalom was dead? He had just received the tidings of a great victory. Did he think of victory? He knew now that his throne was safe. Did he contemplate his throne? What were victory and dominion to him now but dust and ashes? What would these things mean to any man when suddenly he realizes that all the sweetness of his human hopes, in relationship to which alone his power, his wealth, his practical successes have had any value, now are gone? What does all the rest of the world matter when Absalom is dead?

Perhaps there came and confronted him first of all the awful knowledge that out of his own weaknesses some of Absalom's weaknesses had been inherited. Through his own flesh and blood led perhaps the entail of his own passions and sins. What should he say now to the recollection of that one chapter of his deepest guilt when he had compassed the death of another man in order that he should have Bathsheba as his wife? How should he forget now the words of Nathan the prophet, "The sword shall not depart from thine house for ever." Here was the sword now, striking not at his own life, where he would willingly have endured it, but at the life of Absalom. Let the hearts of fathers in all the years since David's time down to ours answer whether there is any more dreadful realization than that. Your son has sinned. He has gone down some dark road of wild rebellion from which you cannot call him back. All the respectability of the world condemns him. The judgment of the world pursues him. They do not blame you, but they blame him. And then as you look into your own past, from whose secret rivers the nature of this your son, in some way that the world knows not, may have been tainted, you know that the thing men hate and punish in him may be the thing that you have put there. He is faulted for what may first have been your fault. He goes out perhaps, as Absalom did, from his father and his friends. He takes his own wild way among the strangers who alternately exploit or despise him. He is looked at by the self-righteous as an alien rebel who ought to be condemned. But you, in the moment of your soul's loneliness for the son whom you cannot call back to your side, see in him only the face of the little boy upon whose spirit are the stripes that might better have come to you.

Or even if David had had no such bitterness of reaction such as this, even if for him, or for any other father, there is that measure of thankfulness which comes in knowing that he has tried to give to his son an inheritance that is at least preponderantly good, still there may be the consciousness of the failure to give to that son the comradeship which might have kept him true. There are many men who give to their children everything except the one thing which matters most, the comradeship of an affection which understands the child and which the child can understand. There is no doubt that David loved his sons; but there is not much evidence that he took time to love them with a wise imagination. He was too busy building kingdoms to enter much into the kingdom of the heart of a child. He dealt with Absalom spasmodically, with bursts of affection and with periods of abstracted inattention. And Absalom had grown away from his father's fellowship. Great as David was, therein he had failed. And many a man in our own day is drifting down that same stream of failure toward the wistful awakening that may come too late. In an essay printed not long ago, there was the account of a certain business man, who had attained great success in his material affairs, but from whom the sweeter possibilities of his life were slipping unobserved away. One day his daughter came and sat down a little timidly on the arm of his chair, and, with her arm around his shoulder, said, "Daddy, I could love you so much if only I had a chance to know you." But the years go fast, and the chance may pass before we turn with frightened hearts to seek it. The little boy Absalom grows up and is gone, and there may come the time when his father's voice, no matter how it call, cannot bring him back from the woods of Ephraim.

"O my son Absalom, my son, my son Absalom! would I had

died for thee, O Absalom, my son, my son!" That cry was the depth of David's tragedy. It was the height of his soul's divineness too. It was the voice of the love that had been implicit in him from the beginning, the love that swept all thought of Absalom's unfaithfulness before it like a flood, the love that would have given its life to redeem its son. That is the cry of the father-heart always, when God has touched it with His own glory, and the great need of our life's ordering is that the expression of that love should not come too late.

But I would not close this chapter, which has to do with the drama of two human figures, without remembering the mightier figure who stood behind them both. In the story, David and Absalom seem to stand alone. But they are not alone. Through the heart of David enters—God.

As long as David lived, his love would follow Absalom. Down the tracks where the dead walk, still his love would follow, and who knows but that, sometime there beyond the mystery, he would overtake and find his son?

So certainly it is with the love of God. That great cry of David in the room above the gate is the lifting of the curtain for the entrance of the love that is perfect in its purity, unflagging in its purpose, invincible in its appeal. If that day Absalom could have heard his father's voice, he might have turned home again. And today, if we will hear it, to our errant and rebellious souls the voice of God is calling: "My son, my son! Not only I would die for thee, but I *have* died for thee." In Jesus Christ the very love of God came down to tread the long road of man's denial, to die as the seal of its last persuasion, as the triumph of its willingness to redeem. Is there not need today that the Absalom spirit in our own hearts should hear and answer that voice of God that cries, "My son, my son!"?

IX

THE MAN WHO OVERCAME DEPRESSION

And, behold, the Lord passed by, and a great and strong wind rent the mountains, and brake in pieces the rocks before the Lord; but the Lord was not in the wind: and after the wind an earthquake; but the Lord was not in the earthquake; and after the earthquake a fire; but the Lord was not in the fire: and after the fire a still small voice.

FIRST KINGS XIX:11-12

WE ARE to consider one of the great examples in the Bible of a man who was doubtful and discouraged, and who had his doubts and discouragements taken away by what the spirit of God taught him to do. That man is Elijah, the vivid story of whose life we may read beginning with the seventeenth chapter in the First Book of the Kings.

Recall briefly what we know of him. It was in the ninth century B.C. that he lived, in the reign of Ahab, King of Israel. In the long line of Israel's kings, Ahab was one of the worst. He had a moral indifference which made him inclined in any case to drift toward evil; but in addition he was pushed that way by the powerful influence of the queen. He had married Jezebel, a princess of Tyre, and Jezebel was one of the most forceful personalities of whom the pages of the Old Testament have any record. Unfortunately all her force seems to have been turned in the wrong direction. She had brought with her to Israel the worship of the Baal gods, and priests of the pagan rites of Baal swarmed in the capital. Her imperious will made her determine that the life of her husband's kingdom should be ordered in the way that suited her and in the way that she thought suited him. And she brooked no interference by any spokesman of a religion built upon the Ten Commandments, or any other inconvenient moral law.

In a society dominated by such an influence, Elijah appeared.

The words in the Book of the Kings which describe his entrance on the scene are laconic: "Elijah the Tishbite, who was of the inhabitants of Gilead, said unto Ahab, As the Lord God of Israel liveth, before whom I stand, there shall not be dew nor rain these years, but according to my word." Exactly where Elijah came from we cannot tell. What he had been doing before, we do not know. Neither do we know anything about the inward circumstances of the call which made him become a prophet. Simply this man appears out of an empty background, a solitary figure heroic in the power of his moral conviction, to confront a king and to tell him that there will be a drought and famine in his land which will not come to an end until he, Elijah, in the name of God has said so. No wonder that Ahab was startled and outraged. No wonder that presently he began to hunt everywhere for this ominous prophet, who meanwhile had disappeared. When after a time Elijah came again out of the wilderness as suddenly as he had come before, and stood again face to face with Ahab, Ahab looked at him and said, "Art thou he that troubleth Israel?" And Elijah answered, "I have not troubled Israel; but you and your father's house, in that you have forsaken the commandments of the Lord, and you have followed Baalim."

Then there comes into the story a description of the conflict between Elijah and the priests of Baal. Here, as occasionally elsewhere in the Old Testament narrative, there is a dazzling fringe of miracle around the central figure, like the corona which in the moment of an eclipse one may see shooting from the edges of the sun. It is not strange that in the atmosphere of tradition and legend which gather round heroic figures there should be this reflected light. But the central matter is independent of these miraculous occurrences. The central matter is the flaming personality of the man himself, which in sheer moral grandeur shines through and above all accidents of the telling. Elijah meets the prophets of Baal and wins a victory over them which enlists the wild enthusiasm of the people on his side. The crowd falls upon these Baal priests and nearly exterminates them.

Ahab is frightened and appalled. But this is not his last encounter with Elijah. Later on he becomes involved with one of his subjects named Naboth concerning a vineyard, next to the royal palace, which Naboth owned. Ahab wanted this ground. He tried to get it from Naboth; but Naboth, loving it as an inheritance from his fathers, would not let it go. Then Jezebel enters the picture. She brushes aside disdainfully Ahab's hesitation. Is he not the king? Why should he bargain and palter with this Naboth? Why not take the thing he wants? She will get for Ahab what he is not forthright enough to get for himself. So she contrives to have Naboth falsely accused of blasphemy and treason. He is condemned and put to death, and then she goes to Ahab and says, "There is your vineyard." Ahab goes down to take possession of it; and at the gate of the vineyard, whom should he meet but the awesome figure of Elijah. "Have you found me, O mine enemy?" he cries. And Elijah answers: "Yes, I have found you, because you have sold yourself to work evil in the sight of the Lord." And then he pronounces against Ahab and Jezebel the judgment of the terrible doom which before long was fulfilled upon them both. A man clothed with nothing but his moral authority had proved himself more irresistible than the royal might. Not Ahab, and not Jezebel, but Elijah, was the ruling influence of his time.

But it is not with any climactic moment of triumph that the particular words of our text have to do. They show us Elijah at one of those crises in his career when he seemed to be defeated. It is the time immediately after his encounter with the priests of Baal. It looked at first as though he had won a staggering success. But suddenly in that unguarded hour which may often accompany the reaction that follows a terrific over-expenditure of all a man's energy, Elijah was struck by a blow which almost overthrew him. A message came from Jezebel, a message hot with all the hatred of her implacable revenge. "God strike me dead," she said, "if by tomorrow I have not done to you all that you have done to my priests of Baal and more too." Before that message Elijah recoiled. Doubtless he was emotionally exhausted, and suddenly the victory which he thought he had won as the crowd turned against the Baal priests tumbled into fragments around his feet. It was as though his whole world went black. What was the use of these fierce struggles if at the end of them the central impersonation of evil in his world was as implacable as ever?

So Elijah turned and fled. He went as far as the limits of the land would let him, down to Beersheba on the extreme southern border of the Jewish lands. Nor did he finally stop even there. He fled down into Arabia, to the desolate and rocky mountains of Sinai, and there he flung himself down under a bush and cried out to God, desiring that he might die. "It is enough"; he said, "now, O Lord, take away my life; for I am not better than my fathers!" It seemed an almost complete collapse. Elijah was plunged into a doubt and despondency which made him in that hour not a heroic but only a bruised and pathetic figure. It seemed then as if he were, after all, no more than a very ordinary man, a creature of life's changing weather, walking with his head up when the sun was shining, but shrinking into dejection when the clouds came across the sky.

It is true that in this incident the one who was supposed to be the great man did appear as small men do. But there was a difference. The thing which had thrown Elijah into this momentary near-despair was no petty consideration. He was despondent, but he had not been made despondent through any casual whim which had happened to himself. He was thinking fundamentally not of himself but of something infinitely greater. It was true that he was in danger; but he had been in danger before. What shook him to his foundations was the sudden feeling that the whole fact of God in his world might be in danger. To fight for righteousness and to suffer in the process, that was one thing; but to fight for righteousness and to have it amount to nothing, that was something else and far more terrible. "I am not better than my fathers," he cried. No; and nobody else was either. It seemed to him that all life, instead of going forward, was drifting back. What was the use of moral effort?

I say, then, that his despondency revealed an element of weakness which showed the kinship of his nature with human nature generally; but I say that there was a difference between his despondency and that of ordinary men. The difference was in the grandeur of the plane on which this man's thoughts were moving, and in the greatness of the concerns which brought him down. The average man may be depressed by trivial things which the man like Elijah would never notice. He may go out to his day depressed and out of sorts because his coffee did not suit him at the breakfast table. He may be depressed because he has not received the word of praise he would have liked to have and the lack of which he resents. He may be depressed because some business venture on which he had pinned his hopes has not been as profitable as he had expected that it would be. Great moral causes may be abroad in this man's world; but he is not concerned with them. It is the matter of his personal fortunes which affects his spirit and determines whether he will be buoyant or glum. But the great spirit like Elijah is oblivious of trifles such as these. Nobody could ever think that Elijah was concerned for his own comfort. Nobody could think that he would be much deterred by his personal peril; but he was concerned about what was happening for the working out of God's will in this world. Men like him in our own time would be the men who take on their consciences our social problems and our social sins, men who are sensitive enough to understand and great enough to care what happens for good or evil in our industrial and economic life, in our politics, in the vast forces that affect war and peace, and in the destiny of our whole human race. The small man does not even feel these things. They are outside the range of his vital awareness. It is at least a kind of indirect tribute to a great soul that it is capable of being touched by great despondencies—by despondencies, that is, which a man will only be exposed to when his loyalties are so large that it is not with petty personal fortunes, but with the grand issues of universal right and wrong that he is grappling.

Understanding, then, the kind of depression by which Elijah had been overcome, let us go forward to think of the way God dealt with him to help him overcome it.

I

In the first place, it is as though the Lord had regarded Elijah with a kind of divinely humorous compassion. According to the narrative—round which, as I have already said, there is the framework of miraculous wonder—it is said that God sent an angel to lead Elijah to a cake baked on the coals and a cruse of water. At any rate, however it happened, Elijah found food. It is as though God were saying to him: "Elijah, the trouble with you is that you are hungry, and so you are out of sorts. What you need is something to eat, and I am going to give it to you."

How true that is to the working of God. The divine fact is never out of relation to the realities in the midst of which He has set us here. He has made us not as disembodied spirits but as souls whose growth and fulfilment must be accomplished in conjunction with these material bodies and this material world in the midst of which we dwell. Napoleon said bluntly that an army marches on its stomach, and the same thing may be said not only of an army, but of every ordinary human soul as it goes upon its progress along the ways of everyday existence. The spirit of a man and the spirit of a people cannot indefinitely advance unless their fundamental material needs are reasonably met. Jesus said, "Man doth not live by bread alone"; but he never said that man has no need of bread. He knew that men do need bread, and his whole life and ministry were full of a realistic tenderness with which he tried to meet the needs of the hungry and relieve the burdens of the poor.

Let us take care, then, that in our thought of religious loyalties we never make these so airy and remote that they become dehumanized. Our ability to serve God greatly must in the long run be founded upon a sensible regard for those things which keep men in everyday health and strength. Therefore, the kingdom of God in this world is not built only by those who work for those conspicuous expressions of spiritual thought which would rise high above the common earth. These may be the towers and turrets that climb up into the sunlight; but down underneath them are the foundations, and without those foundations they could never rise. All honest work that adds to the values of human existence is essentially religious, because it is a necessary part of that whole ordering of life which God Himself has ordained. The labor of the man who sows the seed and drives the plough to raise the wheat by which multitudes are fed, the dependableness of the locomotive driver whose freight-train carries the commerce of great cities, the daily work of men in coal mines and in mills and factories and foundries, the faithfulness of every single individual who may seem only an insignificant cog in the great industrial machine; all these must have their glory in the sight of God because all of them are necessary to make the complex fabric of our existence and the ground out of which everything that is upreaching in mind and spirit alone can grow.

Surely, then, we cannot as religious people be indifferent to the material fortunes of people anywhere. How can we expect that people will be anything else but doubtful and depressed if they are hungry? How could we be surprised if they should begin to doubt anything and everything which we should like to believe most certain, doubt the value of a civilization which we might prefer to consider so desirable, doubt the worth of this particular social order that our forefathers have set up, doubt the value of religion, doubt, as men have so devastatingly doubted, in Russia, in Mexico, and in Spain, whether the Church has any right to go on existing. When men are hungry, they may be, as Elijah was, not merely annoyed at their own personal difficulties; they may become filled with a thorough-going and terrible scepticism as to whether there are any decent forces of right and justice in the world they actually know. Suppose there are around us human forces today which cry out despairingly in the same sort of disillusionment which shook Elijah when he said: "O Lord, take away my life; for I am not better than my fathers." Suppose there should be—as in some nations there already are and in every nation there might be—multitudes who begin to say: "This life which we have is not worth enduring. Nothing is getting better, but rather worse. We are sick of the world as it is now, and we are ready for any desperate expedient to make it different." How should we meet this protest? Should we meet it by threat and punishment? Should we meet it by suppressing free speech, throwing men into jail, or intimidating them by mobs when we do not like what they try to say? If we do, we shall fail and we shall deserve to fail. The only way to cure today the doubts which are beginning to spread concerning the value of our civilization and the vitality of religion is to make these reach down vitally to touch men where they are most instinctively alive. Toward all the people who today may be hungry, hungry for actual food, and hungry for justice and hungry for larger opportunity, our first obligation is to say, as the wisdom and the love of God Himself would say: "You need food, and we propose to see that you get it. You need to have your essential desires met, and we will not be content with any social order that does not meet them."

II

So the first thing that God did for Elijah was to say to him, "Arise and eat"; but this was not all. The second thing he did was to rouse him to his need for action.

"God said, 'Go forth, and stand upon the mount before the Lord.' And behold the Lord passed by." See the picture which those words and the great words that follow go on to portray. There in the desolate gorges of the Sinaitic mountains stands the lonely and troubled figure of Elijah. The one thing he wants above all else is to regain his confidence in God. He wants to believe again that there is a right and wrong that matter, that there is a power not ourselves which makes for righteousness, that no matter how relentless and terrible evil may seem, there is a goodness which is stronger yet. And then what happens? As Elijah stands there at the mouth of a cave, with the awful solitude of the rocky canyons and crests of the mountains below him and around him and above him, there comes a mighty wind, roaring as the winds can roar nowhere more terribly than in that region where the bleak heights of the mountains draw to themselves the hot currents that rise from the surrounding desert to collide with the colder air above. "And a great and strong wind rent the mountains and brake in pieces the rocks." Elijah's soul, desperately desiring some awful revelation of the power of God to come to his aid against his enemies, would have wished that God might be as irresistible as that wind. Yet, nevertheless, as he stood there, there came to his soul no assurance. "God was not in the wind."

After that there came an earthquake. Oh, that God might be

like an earthquake to make the very ground tremble beneath the feet of those who walked on evil ways! "But God was not in the earthquake."

And after the earthquake there came a fire, a fire of lightning, splitting the darkness of the mountain storm, and Elijah must have cried instinctively, as James and John, the sons of thunder, long afterwards were to cry in the presence of Jesus when they were confronted with the insolent rebuff of the Samaritan village that would not take them in, "Oh, that God would send his lightning down to shock men like these into their senses, and that he would show the kind of anger that ought to be let loose on people who will not listen to persuasion! God like a lightning bolt. What other kind of God could Ahab and Jezebel understand?" "But God was not in the lightning."

And then, as Elijah stood still at the mouth of the cave, and as he wrapped his face in his mantle, there came to him a different revelation. It was a still small voice. It was the quiet, inescapable sound of conscience speaking in his soul. What it said to him was this: "What doest thou here, Elijah?" It turned his thought from the violence he wanted to the inward faithfulness he had forgotten. It made him ask himself what he was doing there, empty-handed, idle, and inactive. Not in the wind, and not in the earthquake, and not in the fire, but *there* in that still small voice was God.

How true to all deep human experience that immortal picture is! So often and instinctively men who, like Elijah, have given their best effort to some great enterprise and then, in a moment of emotional reaction, plunged into a terrible doubt about it all, have desired just what Elijah desired. They have wanted God to come with some sort of catastrophic violence and do the work that needs to be done in the way they think it ought to be done if it is to be done at all. They have done their best, they say. Now let God attend to the matter Himself. Let Him change conditions. Let Him make plain to the world that He cannot be contradicted with impunity.

But presently men begin to see, as Elijah saw, that this is not the answer. The inescapable quietness of God presses home to their hearts with a deeper question. The real world, the world of men's beliefs and motives and choices, that inner world out of which alone any moral order which is to last must rise, cannot be shaped by wind or earthquake or fire. It must be created by the power of human souls that will be obedient when God sends them out to manifest his spirit. "What doest thou here, Elijah?" That was the question he had to answer first.

When Elijah began to realize that in this voice and only in this, God was drawing near, he did not at once have a complete understanding of the way in which all his future life was to open out. He did receive from God the revelation of certain particular things that he was to do; but there was a great deal that as yet he did not know. He could not be sure yet how he was to meet Ahab and Jezebel when he dared go back within their reach again. He did not know what particular ways there would be in which he would have to witness to God's requirements in the face of their denial. But the one thing he did know was that he would have to go back, back to the arena of the old struggle, back to the conditions of the difficult faithfulness in which he had partly succeeded and partly failed before. The conviction which came home to him was much like that which has been expressed by John Bunyan in the immortal opening paragraphs of his *Pilgrim's Progress*. To the pilgrim, halting doubtful and bewildered, comes the figure of Evangelist.

Then said Evangelist, "Why standest thou still?"

He answered, "Because I know not whither to go."

Then said Evangelist, pointing with his finger over a very wide field, "Do you see yonder Wicket-Gate?" The man said, "No." Then said the other, "Do you see yonder Shining Light?" He said, "I think I do." Then said Evangelist, "Look always at that Light, and go up directly thereto; so shalt thou see the Gate; at which, when thou knockest, it shall be told thee what thou shalt do."

Life is often like that. We may not see clearly yet the gate through which we have to go or all the particular paths of duty which will open up beyond it. But what we do see is a shining light, the light of an intuition which tells us that in this direction rather than another is the path we have to follow; and it is when we obey the leading of that light that we come to the place where it is told us what we must do.

Let all men and women remember this in their hours of doubt and depression. "It shalt be told thee what thou shalt do." Thank God for the voice of the practical conscience within us which fulfils that promise. A great deal about the future may be still dark; but if you know of some one thing which obviously you must do, you are on the way of being saved.

The truth of that reaches down into the most ordinary and fundamental facts of life. Go and look at the crowds of people streaming every morning into the subways and out of them again as they go to their ten thousand places of work. Here are men and women who have responsibilities to meet. They do not begin the day with shilly-shally indecision as to whether they will go or not, as to whether they will do this or that, or as to whether they will stay at home and do nothing. They have particular obligations they must meet, whether they feel like meeting them or not. The result is that in this great body of the people there is a fundamental integrity and a kind of virility of native power beside which the pale irresponsibility of many more privileged people is weak and pitiable. These men and women cannot afford to be neurotic. They have no time to sit down and play with their own symptoms. Life lays compelling hands on them, and it molds in them a stuff that endures strains and meets hard demands with steadiness. People like these seldom fall into long depression. They are too busy meeting facts realistically to stand off and brood and begin to fear. They have escaped the sin which Elijah temporarily fell into, and the sin which thousands of people in our own day are likely to fall into all the time, and by which they are sent into a wilderness of feeble scepticism—namely, the sin of turning their backs upon the world of urgent duty, the sin of being slack.

And so in all other ranks of society, and most conspicuously among those who take up duties, not perhaps because material necessity compels them, but because the duty itself has won them, doctors, nurses, social workers, men who have gone with some positive ideal into politics, men in the industrial system who keep their heads above the level of merely selfish interest and see the large social objective they want to pursue—this same power of a work to do has been life-giving. If ever they flee, like Elijah, to the wilderness of some dark question as to whether their whole effort is worth while, they will not stay there long. They too will hear the still small voice of the accepted responsibility which has a divine assurance in it, and back they will go to do what needs to be done, and in the doing find the strength that is of God.

III

But there was still a third thing which God had to do for Elijah. He had sustained him with food. He had helped him overcome his slackness. And now also He helped him overcome his sense of isolation.

For one of the things which lay heaviest on Elijah's heart was the feeling that he was alone. He had fought for righteousness in Israel, and nobody else seemed to care. How could he go on battling unaided for God's cause? What could one man do against a whole hostile or indifferent people?—indifferent, it seemed to him, when the pinch came, no matter how they might shout around him in excited moments. This sense of isolation has been the sore burden which other great souls besides Elijah have borne. And if they were ever tempted to despair, it was perhaps this more than anything else that overcame them. It is a terrible thing to feel morally and spiritually solitary. The very nature of religious loyalty makes a man reach out for comradeship. It is so great a thing that a man's heart cannot contain it alone. He must have somebody else to share it with him, somebody else to validate it, somebody else to make him go on trusting through the dark moments that the ideals he has believed in are not too beautiful to be true. It is not the weak souls but the strong souls, the souls capable of great hopes and great adventures, who need this spiritual comradeship and who shrink from isolation. Martin Luther, at the very time when he was moving on to his most heroic commitments, wrote to John Staupitz, the head of the Augustinian monastic order, and the one who had been his father in God: "You forsake me too much. Last night I dreamed of you. I thought you were leaving me, and as I was weeping and lamenting most bitterly, you waved your hand and told me to be quiet for you would return." In the second letter of Paul to Timothy there are these poignant sentences: "Demas hath forsaken me, having loved this present world, and is departed unto Thessalonica. . . . At my first answer no man stood with me, but all men forsook me." Who can read those words and not feel in them still the wistfulness of a great spirit who could meet any forces of opposition, but who could not bear to think that he was separated from those who ought to have been his friends?

To Elijah in the wilderness bowed down by *his* sense of isolation, there came the voice of God saying: "Yet have I left me seven thousand in Israel, all the knees which have not bowed unto Baal, and every mouth which hath not kissed him."

Seven thousand! Where had they been, and why had Elijah not known of them? Well, they had been there in Israel all the time; but they had never taken the trouble to tell Elijah what they thought and felt. Doubtless they said to themselves, and perhaps they said here and there to one another: "Thank God for Elijah! He is the sort of man the nation needs. He is worth more than a hundred Ahabs. We believe in him. He stands for the things that all decent men ought to want. We hope he will go on speaking and acting just as he is doing now." Yes, but they never told Elijah that. They somehow assumed that he would know, and they never stopped to think how much it might matter to him if he did know.

Was that characteristic only of the men of Israel in that far-off past? Or is it not likely to be true also of the same sort of group in every generation—the seven thousand men who have not bowed the knees of their self-respect to the particular Baals of their own time, yet who have never made their better allegiance plain? Always and everywhere there are the few moral and spiritual leaders who champion the ideals which the best men want, the men who stand for refinement against vulgarity, for the spirit as against the flesh, for God as against Mammon. And always there is in the general population at least a large minority which sympathizes with the great souls but yet may fail to say so. The reason why better standards in any field of life often are beaten down or gradually abandoned is not because there are none who might support them, but because so many who do support them in their intentions never make their convictions plain. In one of the current magazines there is an article entitled, "The Art of Pleasing Everybody," and its main point is the fact that in the modern field of radio the cheap things often flourish and the best programs are often abandoned simply because those who really wish the best things do not so much as write a letter to indicate what it is they want. Now and then some man who might be a leader in cleaner politics and more generous public service fails for the same reason. If by honesty and fearlessness he offends some selfish group, he will bring down upon himself that group's quick retribution. But those who admire what he has said and done may never make him realize that they do support him. How many are there, I wonder, in every church congregation who, when their representatives in municipal, or state, or national government have stood up above the crowd of common men through their championship of some fine cause, have ever sent them a message to tell them of their admiration? If the Elijahs in the field of education, or in politics, or in the Church, are not to be driven into the wilderness, the seven thousand in Israel who have not bowed the knee to Baal had better let them know that they are there.

Yet, after all, they *are* there. That is the final fact which God made Elijah understand; and that is the conviction which the worship of the Church is meant to bring home to all those who, like Elijah, would overcome their doubt and depression by overcoming their sense of isolation. In the house of God we meet to remember that in this moral and spiritual struggle no soul is alone. There we know that we are a part of the great fellowship of those men and women who also are trying to be faithful. And there we remember not only those of the present but also all the immortal comradeship of the past: saints, confessors, heroes, martyrs, who from generation to generation have passed along the torch of the living flame of men's eternal loyalty to God. If there is any single soul today whose life is bruised; if there is a single one tempted, like Elijah, to doubt whether the moral and spiritual struggle is worth while; if there is a single one who, having fought hard for goodness, is driven almost to be despondent in the face of the evil of your world—remember that the climactic note of this message is for you. Your doubt and your depression can vanish when your sense of isolation vanishes. When you remember that great company of the witnesses of God in every age who strengthen you by their comradeship, you will know you cannot fail; for their heroic witness is enough to show you that this world holds no adverse forces which courage and consecration cannot overcome.

X

THE PROPHET IN THE MINORITY

And the king of Israel said unto Jehoshaphat, There is yet one man, Micaiah the son of Imlah, by whom we may inquire of the Lord: but I hate him.

I KINGS XXII:8

THERE is a good deal of human nature in that remark, "But I hate him." Why did he hate him? The sentence goes on to give the reason: "He does not prophesy good concerning me, but evil." In other words, here was a man who had a way of saying things which the man who heard him did not want to hear, and so it was no great wonder that he was not regarded with affection.

The text comes, as you will have noted, from the Old Testament, and the Old Testament, of course, is a very old book. But the curious thing about it is that in its significance it often seems not at all old. It is most astonishingly modern. The man who spoke the words we have just read was named Ahab, and he was king of Israel about 850 years B.C.; but so far as the up-to-dateness of his feeling was concerned, his name might be the name of one of us, and he might be a citizen of these United States in this year of grace 1937. For what Ahab said was this: that when a man said what he did not like to hear, he did not like the man; and that is exactly what every one of us is disposed frequently to say when we are as explosively honest as Ahab in that moment happened to be.

It is a curious story from which the text comes, full of interest and not without unconscious humor too. Let us refresh our minds concerning it.

Ahab, the king of Israel, and Jehoshaphat, king of Judah, had determined to join in a war against Syria. It had been three whole years since they had had any war, and that seemed too long, and life was growing dull. So they joined their forces and were about to launch what they thought would be a pleasant and profitable little piece of conquest. Ahab, however, had an uneasy conscience. His record was bad, and he knew it. He had deliberately acted on more than one occasion as though no such thing as a God of righteousness existed; but he had a secret and uncomfortable feeling that perhaps He did. He had round him a company of men who were supposed to be prophets of God, and he had an impulse, half religious and half superstitious, to get these men to give him a sort of advance blessing on what he was going to do. Jehoshaphat the king of Judah felt the same way. But apparently he was a cautious man and liked to make sure of things. So after four hundred of these hand-picked prophets had unanimously declared that God could certainly be expected to be on the side of Israel and that the war was bound to go well, Jehoshaphat asked whether this cleared the whole ground, or whether there might be any other prophet about who had not been in at the roll-call. Then Ahab made his disgusted admission. There was one man, a person named Micaiah; but no one wanted to hear him. He was the sort of prophet who always had some disagreeable contrary idea to put in the way of what a man wanted to think and wanted to do.

Jehoshaphat, however, thought that it would be better to hear what Micaiah might say, and an officer was sent off to get him. In the meanwhile, Ahab and Jehoshaphat put on their royal robes and mounted themselves on two thrones to look as impressive and formidable as possible, and all the four hundred yes-men recited their pleasant prophecies all over again. They said that if Ahab wanted to capture the city of Ramoth-gilead (which was what he did want to capture), he could go and do it, for the Lord would certainly deliver it into Ahab's hands. Meanwhile the messenger who had gone off to get Micaiah thought he would do him a service by giving him some sensible advice. So he told Micaiah that all the rest of the prophets had said what the king wanted to hear, and that Micaiah had better do the same. Micaiah told him that God had a concern in this matter, and that what God prompted was what he meant to say.

He came in then before the two kings, and Ahab began to question him. He wanted to know what Micaiah's counsel was. Should he and Jehoshaphat go up and attack Ramoth-gilead or should they not? "Certainly," said Micaiah, "go, and prosper." Didn't they know that the Lord would deliver the city into their hands?

It looked as if Ahab ought to have been satisfied with that; but the odd thing was that he could not be satisfied. Something kept him from believing the very thing he wanted to believe. He saw that Micaiah was speaking ironically. A queer compulsion of his own conscience gave an intimation of the truth which, in spite of his own desires, he somehow had to draw out into the light. So he said to Micaiah angrily, "How many times must I adjure you to tell me nothing but what is true in the name of the Lord?"

Oh, so it was the truth he wanted? Very well, then Micaiah would show it to him. So he answered like a man who stands in awe before a sudden vision. "I saw all Israel scattered upon the hills, as sheep that have not a shepherd: and the Lord said, 'These have no master: let them return every man to his house in peace.'"

"There," said Ahab, "didn't I tell you that he would prohpesy no good concerning me, but only evil?" After which Micaiah went on to make his prophecy more explicit, and he warned Ahab against the lying prophets who had told him the smooth things he wanted to hear.

Ahab's answer was to have Micaiah arrested and sent off to prison. He was to be kept there, he said, until he, Ahab, came back triumphant from the battle. But Micaiah did not stay in any prison until Ahab came back, for the very good reason that Ahab never came back at all. In the battle against which Micaiah had warned him, he was shot by an arrow, and that was the end of Ahab.

Such, then, is the story as the Book of Kings narrates it. Let us consider the facts now from the point of view of Micaiah and then from the point of view of Ahab.

I

What made Micaiah important was the fact that he spoke not as though with the authority of Micaiah but as though with the authority of God. Here was a man who dared to say, "Thus saith the Lord," and who had a right to say it. For he had evidently gone down into those deep silences of the spirit where the human soul stands face to face with eternal truth. He had thought much and prayed much. When he spoke, he was sure of himself because he was sure of something larger than himself. The power of the Highest overshadowed him and an infinite resource was at his back.

That is the way it is always with the authentic prophet. He conveys the impression of a man who has come into this world out of another one, and he brings with him something of the awe and majesty of that larger moral universe in which his soul has moved. The light of it is in his eyes. The power of it is in his bearing. The flame of it is in his speech.

Such a man does not depend upon majorities. There were plenty of persons ready to flock to Ahab's retinue who called themselves prophets. They had, perhaps, all the conventional marks of religious men. They could cast their speeches in pious terminology. But they were moved by surface impulses. They registered the opinion of the crowd. Their ideas of importance, of power, and of probability were the crowd's ideas. They made the complacent assumption that everything would happen in their world according to what their world wanted. If Ahab the king wanted God to take care of his particular affairs, God presumably would be there. It was a very pleasant sort of religion which thus lent sanction to the prevailing purposes of the time. The so-called prophet could speak very boldly when he was saying what everybody believed already. It did not take much courage for that kind of utterance. But Micaiah had the kind of courage which did not need to be fortified by a crowd. He could proclaim his truth with intrepid steadiness even when he was alone, for all the time he knew that he was not alone. Back of him was God.

It is this sort of prophethood which has made the glory of religion down the whole course of human life. God does not leave Himself without His witnesses. From among the multitude the great souls somehow are raised up, the men who in their spiritual stature tower above the ranks, men who belong not only to the earth but to the sky. Thomas Carlyle expressed the truth when he wrote

common languid times, with their unbelief, distress, perplexity, with their languid doubting characters and embarrassed circumstances, impotently crumbling down into ever worse distress toward final ruin; —all this I liken to dry dead fuel, waiting for the lightning out of heaven that shall kindle it. The great man, with his free force direct out of God's own hand, is the lightning.

Medieval Italy sinks into corruption and indifference, and there arises a Savonarola. The new machine age one hundred years ago, with its hot pursuit of the sudden chance for riches, its raw materialism and its human cruelty, is brought to a new accounting of its conscience by Lord Shaftesbury and Charles Kingsley and Frederick D. Maurice. There are men and women now living who can remember the preaching of Phillips Brooks, and the very thought of it stirs emotion in them yet. Doubtless there are some today who remember Studdert Kennedy—remember how their hearts burned within them as they looked upon that strange, homely little figure, and saw him as he spoke become transfigured by the divine passion that clothed him like a flame. Men like these bring God into the ordinary place and the ordinary hour. They throw a shaft of splendid light to mark the straight path through what otherwise might have been our crooked sophistries. They reveal the truth which, once seen, we cannot forget or willingly forsake. They speak the brave word which stirs the laggard moral strength of multitudes who otherwise might have been content in a mean compromise. In the midst of unbelief and indecision, they lift up great loyalties which command the whole allegiance of our souls.

I think that all of us would say, when we stop and face reality, that it is prophethood such as this that we want associated with the pulpits of the Christian Church. We do not want men who ladle out some milk and water pabulum that happens to suit the taste of the idle crowd. We want men instead who come with challenge and with provocation. Otherwise the pulpit would become mere clanging brass and tinkling cymbals. Surely nothing is more pitiful than when the pulpit does thus become a tame accompaniment to an opinion which it flatters and does not rouse. Who really wants a preacher who comes to people with a saccharine and fawning message and says to them in effect: "My dear friends, we ought all to be so proud that we are as good as we are. Our church and our religion and our ideas of life are already a great credit to Almighty God"? Who really wants a preacher who turns our popular and profitable ideas into an idol and pretends that all we need to have a better world is that everybody should be as sensible and wise and well-disposed as we are? Who would choose a preacher who would say, as the four hundred well-drilled prophets said to Ahab, that whatever we want very much will surely come to pass because it would be very rude of God to introduce any disturbance into our nice affairs? No. We want an utterance different from this. We want a message that has in it the ruggedness of uncalculating truth. We want men who will carry into their pulpits the look of those to whom God has given something authentic to proclaim.

Let us not forget that it is the congregation which helps to make the preacher. There can be no great preaching without a great soul in those who listen. The kind of message which will be preached in the pulpit now, the kind of men who will come into the ministry in the next generation, and the kind of men whom the ministry will hold, will all depend upon the sort of desire and expectation which are in the pews. If the men and women who come to church are satisfied with nothing more than the recitation of pious axioms, they will destroy the spirit of prophecy. If the word of God is to be truly spoken, it can be spoken only to those who are willing to think and willing to be disturbed. For the word of God, as Jesus said, must always come "like fire cast upon the earth." It must come like flame, beautiful, but terrible too; terrible, that is, to our little earthbound selves, that our larger selves may be set free. The preachers of the present generation do not matter so crucially for the destinies of the Church. Our work and worth are already revealed for much or little, as the case may be; but the great and decisive question is as to the quality of the men whom the Church will call from the ranks of the oncoming generation and ordain to be its spokesmen. God give us a spirit in the congregations which will make the best men know there is work for them to do and a word for them to speak. Only tame men will come into the Church if all that the Church wants is tame preaching. But deep will answer to deep. Men who have something great to say will come when it is clear that it is the great things that the churches want to hear.

I am not unmindful of a danger which must be avoided here. No preacher, old or young, may dare to assume that he is wholly the teacher of the congregation and that the people are only learners. Individually and collectively they have much to teach him. He had better measure his thoughts with their thoughts, his intuitions and his ideas with their experience of living in the world which they confront. He had better be sure that he never dogmatizes and that he always keeps the spirit of one who knows that the truth he sees is only part of the larger truth. But when all this is remembered, the great, central fact still rises clear. The preacher ought to set forth a message that has in it the note of a divine authority. He ought to seem unmistakably to be a man who does not echo the crowd opinion, but who thinks and speaks for himself; no, rather who dares let God speak through him. If he does this, he will be trying to turn the light of a divine interpretation upon those real issues which are both crucial and contemporary. He ought to be, like Micaiah, one who, having seen what he believes to be the way God is moving in the world, turns the eyes of other men to see it also, no matter what the results to them may be.

II

We pass now to the other side of our subject. Let us look at it from the standpoint of Ahab.

Ahab had set his heart on something which he wished to do. His ambition was involved with it. His prestige seemed to be involved with it too. He wanted to show that he could carry through successfully the plan which he had launched and to which he seemed to be committed in the eyes of his friend the king of Judah, and in the eyes of all his own nation. He was going out to capture the city of Ramoth-gilead. If he did capture it, then obviously he would be ranked as a figure of greater consequence in the line of Israel's kings. He would expand his own personality by the measure of that success.

That was what he had thought, and there seemed to be no reason why he should not go ahead. The great majority of those who called themselves prophets encouraged him. Then this one inconvenient and annoying figure of Micaiah appeared. Micaiah said he could not do the thing which everybody else expected that he would do. Micaiah said that the current of reality did not run that way.

Of course Ahab was irritated and angered. Most of us in his circumstances would have felt exactly as Ahab did. He felt that he had collided with an arbitrary force which threatened all his impulses with frustration. He had an uneasy feeling that Micaiah might be right. But he did not want to acknowledge that he was right. He hated the stubborn contrary probabilities which Micaiah was pointing out; and because it was Micaiah who had forced these into his notice, he hated him.

The trouble with Ahab was that emotionally he had not grown up. He could not look at his world objectively. He could not detach himself from his own impetuous wishes and look facts squarely and courageously in the face. He preferred to believe that the inconvenient facts were not real and that the man who pointed them out did so only because he was unfriendly. He knew in spite of himself that he ought to stop and make a reappraisal of the situation; but his pride and petulance were stung by the idea of being balked. He wanted to capture Ramoth-gilead, and he thought that this would show him to be a great man. He might better have remembered the wise old words of the proverb: "He that is slow to anger is better than the mighty, and he that ruleth his spirit than he that taketh a city."

One of the difficult but vitally important lessons of life for us in every age is to learn to avoid the blunder of Ahab. His blunder has its roots in every man's instinctive human nature. All of us are born and grow up first as children, and the danger is that we may never quite cross over the hard bridge from emotional childishness into the self-mastered recognition of the real world which is essential to the man who would be strong. The child is a creature of impulse and has at first very little reflective self-control. Every one of us has seen children who, when they were turned aside from something they had set their hearts on, knew of nothing better to do than to fall into a fit of crying, and to wail, "But I want to! I want to!" They transferred to their nurses or to anyone else who happened to be in control all their angry disappointment. They could not see that their own purposes needed to be changed, but felt instead that the person standing in their way must somehow be battered out of it. "I hate you! I hate you!" they cry.

When the years carry us along so that we are adults according to the calendar, we nevertheless may have failed to become adults at heart. In our reactions to reality we may be children still. Yet the slow adjustment to inescapable facts, the readiness to see things as they are, and to fit our response to their necessity, is the essence of education. Walter Lippman has expressed it unforgettably in the brilliant pages of his *A Preface to Morals*:

For unless a man has acquired the character of an adult, he is a lost soul no matter how good his technical equipment. The world unhappily contains many such lost souls. . . . It is full of semi-adult persons who secretly nurse the idea that they are, or that by rights they ought to be, Don Juan, Croesus, Napoleon, or the Messiah. . . . Their purposes are merely the relics of an infancy when their wishes were law and they knew neither necessity nor change. When a childish disposition is carried over into an adult environment, the result is a radically false valuation of that environment. . . . The childish pattern appears also as a deep sense that life owes him something, that somehow it is the duty of the universe to look after him and to listen sharply when he speaks to it. . . . The childish pattern appears also as a disposition to believe that he may reach out for anything in sight and take it, and that having gotten it nobody must ever under any circumstances take it away.

Who has not seen this spirit, for example, in young men and women about to enter upon what ought to be their adult life? A boy or girl may fall in love. It may be to any calm judgment a foolish and shallow infatuation. The older friend or the father and mother will try to point this out. If the young persons are capable of maturity, they will at least listen. They will recognize at least the possibility that they may be seeing things through the fog of their adolescent storminess, and they may look again to see whether the real facts are what their first impulses made them think. But if they are incorrigibly childish, they will merely suppose that the one who stands in their way does so because he is hard and alien and lacking in sympathetic understanding; and, like Ahab, they will go their own way to disaster.

We may see the same thing happen with older men and women. They come to some crisis in their affairs, and they want to embark on an adventure that seems to them to promise sensational reward. The ordinary voices of their world would tell them to go ahead. "Of course it is what everybody wants," they say, "and you can get it. You can have the new adventure in the field of sex. You can move out of the ordered and disciplined life you have led and seize the exciting opportunity of the moment. In practical affairs you can turn your back on the old virtues of hard work, with its moderate rewards won by clear integrity of service, and you can transfer your interest to some plausible speculation that will make you rich." The unstable adolescent in us answers to ideas such as these. Yet our better judgment and our clearer conscience, embodied, perhaps, in some one else who is brave enough to tell us the truth, stands across the glittering pathway and says, "This is not the road for you." Impulsively we may be tempted to cry like Ahab, "I hate him, for he does not prophesy good to me but evil!" But if we are mature, we shall thank God, as Ahab might well have thanked Him, for the voice that comes and speaks to us reality.

It is important for us, however, that we should not let our thought come to its climax in a way that would seem to identify the voice of God with a negative implication. In the story of Ahab, the prophet who represented the truth of life did stand across the king's pathway as a barrier; but the reason was that Ahab was the kind of a person whose active choices were not good but evil. All the record of his previous life as one reads it in the Book of Kings had shown that. It was not for beneficial purpose that he was out to capture Ramoth-gilead. The need was that he should stay in his own kingdom and promote there the justice which he had ignored, rather than launch some merciless venture for his own prestige. Therefore, in his case, although the whole company of the false prophets said "Yes" the true prophet must say "No." But often the conditions may be reversed. If a man is set to follow the best he sees, if the affirmative choice of his mind and will move in the direction of the values of God and not against them, then it may be true that for him it will be the false prophets who say "No" and the single lonely voice which will say "Yes" when he stands at the brink of some great decision. Said Emerson, "Our friends are those who make us be what we can." For the evil man that would be a terrible kind of friendship, but for the good man that is the kind of friendship which is the gift of God. When a man wants the best, then the danger of childishness in him will be exactly the reverse from what it was in the case of Ahab. *His* danger of remaining the emotional adolescent will be in listening to the chorus of those who discourage him from any great spiritual effort, who mock at his ideals, who think that nothing in life matters enough to take much trouble about, and who would have him settle down to a soft convenience. *His* danger is lest he become impatient not with the voice which tells him what he cannot do, but with the voice that tells him what he *can* do, if he tries with all his heart.

But whether the way of decision lead this way or that, the great fact always to be remembered is that the counsel of God is most likely to come not out of the easy majority but out of the minority. Ahab knew in his own soul that the voice of truth spoke not from the four hundred prophets but from the one; and what Ahab ought to have admitted for his warning, other and happier souls may well recognize for their encouragement and their inspiration. If your life is lifted up to God, and if you have made up your mind that as truly as you can you want to serve Him, then you can turn your back on all the crowd of cynical and disbelieving prophets and listen to the clear brave voice, even if it comes to you from the lips of only one person in this world, that tells you to go forward in God's name!

XI

THE MAN WHO WAS NOT, *BUT* ——

*Then answered Amos, and said to Amaziah, I was
no prophet, neither was I a prophet's son; but I
was a herdsman, and a gatherer of sycamore fruit:
And the Lord took me as I followed the flock, and
the Lord said unto me, Go, prophesy unto my
people Israel. Now therefore hear thou the word
of the Lord.*

AMOS VII:14-16

ONE of the characteristics of real religion always is that it
helps men to become what they have not been before.
Without the power which religion gives, a man's life may move
on the dead level of the uninspiring commonplace. With the
power of religion, he goes up over the hills of difficulty and scales
the heights of great achievement. He looks back on the period
before his life had been lifted up by God, and he remembers what
he was not. Then he says to himself, "I was not purposeful, clear-
sighted. I was not strong. I was not, *but*. But now the facts are
different. By the grace of God, I am no longer what I used to be.
By the grace of God, I am what I am."

It is with the record of such a man that we are now to deal. He
is an individual; but he is also a type. He revealed in his vivid
history the sort of experience which can be renewed in every time
—the experience of life lifted into unshakable significance through
religion.

It was a long time ago that this particular man lived; but that
is no matter. The realities of the spirit are alike in every generation, and the figures who speak to us from the Bible are so
obviously comrades in spirit with us that they speak with as clear
a voice as though they were standing at our side. This man's name
was Amos, and we call him one of the prophets; but he might
have any name, and he does not need a title for him to speak to
us with the accents which fit the understanding of great manhood
in any time.

Here are the circumstances of what he was and of what he did.

The period was the eighth century before Christ, and the scene was Palestine in that period when the kingdom of David and Solomon had been divided into two kingdoms, a northern and a southern one, which together made up the people of Israel. Over the northern kingdom reigned perhaps the most powerful of all its line of rulers, Jeroboam the Second, and the capital which he had built at Bethel was for the standards of that time a flourishing and an opulent place. The state religion also was centered there with its temple to which the worshipers brought their rich offerings. Amos lived in the southern kingdom in the land of Judea. When he went into the north, therefore, though he was of the same blood which all the tribes of Israel shared, he was also in one sense an alien. He had no privileged standing as a citizen in Bethel. Moreover, he was not a man of any wealth or rank. He herded sheep in that half barren country which drops down from the plateau of Judea to the desert gorge of the Dead Sea. He went to Bethel not by invitation but simply in the course of marketing his sheep. Nevertheless, this man, with nothing to fortify him save the fire in his own soul which God had lighted, looked at the life of Bethel with fearless eyes and dared to speak unflinching truth about it. He was one of the first figures in human history who proclaimed what we in our own time have not even yet fully accepted, namely, a gospel that had to do not merely with small matters of personal conduct but with the formidable demands of social righteousness. He said that as he looked at the life of Israel he had seen a vision of it as a wall which God was measuring with a plumb-line, and that, like a wall built crookedly and on false foundations, it should fall. He condemned in explicit language the commercial greed of the civilization round him. He pointed out the bitter contrast between the luxury of the rich and the misery of the poor. He showed the way in which the prominent man could get justice while the little man was denied it. He said that religion had become a gilded show, and that the pious maintenance of churches went hand in hand with business rapacity. When God looked, he said, at the kind of worship which was going on, the worship of sleek men who laid unction to their own souls while they did nothing to make religion real in the life outside the sanctuary, God's awful voice would say of this very religion which was offered in His name: "I despise your feast days. . . . Though ye offer me burnt offerings and your meat offerings, I will not accept them: neither will I regard the peace offerings of your fat beasts. . . . But let judgment run down as waters, and righteousness as a mighty stream."

It is no wonder that the city buzzed with furious excitement. Here was this man Amos who had insulted, so they said, everything great and honorable in Bethel. He had denounced the priests. He had challenged the rich and powerful. He had defied the king. And who was he anyhow? A nobody from Judea, an upstart who ought to go back where he came from out among the scrub bush of his own Judean desert tending sheep. The priest Amaziah took it upon himself to attend to Amos. He would get rid of this intruder. So up to him he went, and he said with angry contempt: "You seer, you, go back from here to the land of Judah, and eat your bread and do your prophesying there. But let us have no more prophesying from you at Bethel. This is the king's sanctuary, and it is the king's court."

And what of Amos then? Did he stand cowed in silence? Did he turn and go obediently away? He did not. This is what he said with quiet dignity which yet had in it a flame of challenge that was devastating: "I was no prophet, neither was I a prophet's son; but I was a herdsman, and a gatherer of sycamore fruit. And the Lord took me as I followed the flock, and the Lord said unto me, Go, prophesy unto My people Israel. Now therefore hear thou the word of the Lord!" And Amaziah heard, heard because he could not help it, the indignant moral condemnation which Amos went on to pronounce against all who had degraded and denatured religion as Amaziah had.

Let us consider, then, the suggestions in the process by which Amos, who seemed originally a nobody, became a man with whom a whole civilization had to reckon.

I

The first suggestion is contained in his own words, "The Lord took me."

What does it mean when the Lord takes a man? That is to

say, how shall we know when the spirit of God commissions some soul for an outstanding opportunity? Our first instinct is to believe that it must come by some manner of miraculous sign. If God has a peculiar destiny for a man, surely He will indicate it, we think, in a way which nobody could mistake. A man will have a vision or hear a voice from heaven. He will be lifted up on wings of some tremendous mystical experience. Thinking thus, we separate the prophet from our own ordinary sphere. If God wants any man to be His spokesman, He will single that man out in a way altogether different from his fellows; and if a man is not thus singled out in unmistakable fashion, then we think we may rest on the assumption that no particular spiritual responsibility belongs to him.

But the truth of it as exemplified in the person of Amos may be very different. There is no record that Amos was marked out by any miracle. His conviction that God had a work for him to do grew out of exactly that sort of reaction between a man and his environment which any one of us ought to be able to understand. Amos lived in a world that had need of the cleansing and redeeming word of God. Anybody could see that who had clear eyes and a sensitive conscience, and the man whose courage was great enough could feel the implications of that for him. Here was a civilization marked by the growth of material values and the neglect of human values. Here was a civilization—and if you read the prophecy of Amos you can see it drawn as sharply as though with the strokes of an etcher's steel—in which rich men were growing increasingly callous to the social consequences of their getting rich and in which the poor were wretched and rebellious. Here was a civilization in which religion was becoming the paid apologist for vested privilege—just as in our own day it became in czarist Russia and in Mexico, and can be in peril of becoming in any land. Amos perceived these things as doubtless other men of his time may have perceived them; but the difference between him and other men was this: that whereas their perceptions were theoretical, his were vital. He responded with the whole of his nature to the things he saw. If his world was full of need, then that need had a consequence for him. There were many men in Israel who knew the need, but did not care.

There were probably those who were vaguely stirred in conscience and may have said like ineffectual Hamlets:

> The time is out of joint: O cursed spite
> That ever I was born to set it right!

But not so Amos. If things were crooked, then there was something in him that made him want to set them straight. If things were wrong, then he was there to bear his witness for the right. Face to face with evil, his soul could cry, as Isaiah was presently to do, "Here am I, Lord, send me." Confronted with a moral emergency, he could offer to God at least the courage of one man whom God might use.

Thus when Amos said, "The Lord took me," he was expressing that sense of compulsion which is registered in a man's own soul when the facts without and the moral sensitiveness within leap together like the currents of two electric poles into the flash of sure conviction. God took him not by outward sign, but by that inner signal, the signal which can always flame in any man if the moral energies in him are equal to the urgency of the needs that gather in his world. Then indeed the Lord takes him as truly as though a hand were laid upon his shoulder and he were bidden go.

Not long ago there came to America one of the great spirits of our contemporary world, Kagawa of Japan. When history is written five hundred years from now, he may be reckoned as one of the supreme souls in all the Christian centuries, a man perhaps as near to Christ in spirit as any who has lived on this earth since Francis of Assisi. Since he became a Christian he has been the leader of a redeeming work in the slums of Tokyo and among the poor of Japan. He is perhaps the greatest voice in that country for freedom of the spirit as against the tyranny of the state, for the values of man as against the hard values of money, for human brotherhood as against nationalism running riot, for the difficult ideals of peace as against hatred and violence and war. And what called him? Again no miracle that belonged to him rather than to others, but a recognition of a crying need and a courage in his soul to meet it. Once in New York at the time of an earlier visit to this country, he said very simply, but with those strange eyes of his shining, "Somebody may have to die for the sake of the kingdom of God. Why not I?" He too like Amos could say, "The Lord took me." And that compulsion of the love of God that did thus take him called him not as a grudging servant but called him as one is called to knighthood, with a spiritual accolade that sent him out clad in heavenly armor like a flame.

But it is not alone a conception of the evil in the world that wakes a man's conscience and makes him feel that he has had a call from God. It is rather that evil shot through with the higher gleam of the good that ought to be. Suppose, for example, you stand in the window in some high building which commands a vista of a modern city and look out over its streets and houses and let your thought and feeling dwell upon the strange vast thing that lies beneath you. You can consider, if you wish, the elements which are sordid and sad. You hear the shrill voice of the newsboy crying the extra edition that tells you the details of a murder. You hear the clang of a bell, and the patrol wagon goes by with the thief huddled in its shadows. You see under the bridge, where the moving tide of life flows back and forth, the roof of the jail, like an ugly cesspool, into which the dregs of the city's squalor and shame and wretchedness have gathered. You watch the aimless tramp going from door to door with his shifty plea for money. You look down upon the places where other men are plotting and scheming so narrowly to make fortunes for themselves that they have lost the largeness from their living, and you say to yourself, Such is the city.

Such, it is true are some of the facts in its great complex. But the impression of those thoughts on you will depend upon whether or not there is in your heart a hunger after something larger—after a light that is to illumine the shadows, after a goodness that is destined at length to transform the things which are gross. Disillusioned we may be with many of the elements of our human struggle. Disillusioned we well may be at the perishableness of much of the fruit of our human ambitions, at the waste and wreckage of what with thoughtless hands we build. But if there is in us the desire that makes us sensitive to another truth, we shall behold it. We shall look upon the city, and there within those walls we shall see the mother bending over the cradle of her little child. We shall watch the nurse going her way down the ugly streets to minister to the sick among the poor. We shall see the man in his office making the gallant decision which has cost him money and favor because he would not compromise with the doubtful things that could have made him great. We see that other man, rising up and leaving his own affairs that he may go out and give his thought and energy to some unselfish public-spirited citizenship. We see the churches where men and women, conscious of their weakness and their sins, go week by week to try to consecrate themselves afresh to God's purpose for their lives. Remembering those things, we see the vision of the holy truth; we hear, as it were, the voices of the seraphim who cry that the whole earth is full of the glory of God. We ourselves have seen it but imperfectly, but it is much to have caught even the glimpse of it, and to know that in goodness, wherever it is manifested, there is a reality and permanence beside which everything else passes away, and into which there enters a glory that ultimately will be all there is.

And God needs today the prophets who will look out not only upon the life of one community, but upon the life of the whole world that more and more is being inextricably bound into one destiny, and will try to trace the eternal purpose which is moving there. We watch the tumultuous forces surging upward from the masses of the people in other nations—dark hands lifted to lay hold on the stuff of life and mold it into new patterns. Some call it chaos. Some think of the challenging new forces of the time as so much defiance to their own settled interests, and are prepared to fight against them to the death. Some see only a sordid struggle of class against class and nation against nation, in the midst of which the only wisdom is to be strong, and the only policy is for each man and each group to seize as much as it can and as quickly as it can for itself. But the time will not be redeemed unless there are souls capable of seeing another thing—seeing the vision of the plan of God which men may ignore or defy at their peril but which, when they link their own purpose with it, will lift all their lives into a new nobility. And that purpose is the reshaping of all the relationships between men and nations so that human souls among every people may have a better chance than they have had before to dwell in peace, in justice, and in largeness of life.

II

We pass on now to another consideration concerning Amos. We have thought of how God took him. We shall think now in the second place of what God said through him.

The message of Amos is written in the book of his prophecy. It is significant, to begin with, because of its definiteness. It would have been easy to bring to Bethel a smooth religious message by which everybody might have been pleased. The people of Bethel had planned a religion of a certain kind. They were ready to be told that they must honor God provided they honored Him in their accustomed fashion. They would have been willing to be told how pious their forefathers were and that everybody must observe the old ordinances of worship as a genteel tradition. What they did not want to be told was the relation of religion to the kind of activities they were pursuing in business and financial circles. Neither did they want their dealings with other races and with other nations commented on by moralists. They would practice religion within the borders of the temple; but like other men before and since, they wanted to be what they called practical in the things of this world. Priests like Amaziah could help them draw this convenient distinction. They knew how to make men feel in good standing ecclesiastically without having altered their standards outside the church. But Amos spoke with a disquieting plainness. He talked about the sort of luxury rich people lived in while the poor went hungry. He talked about people who got drunk. He pointed out the sharp practices and the hard bargains by which some men took advantage of their neighbors. In other words, he made it uncomfortably plain that the kind of religion he was concerned with had to mean something drastic in men's everyday self-discipline. It took courage to preach a message such as that, and it took more honest humility of heart than the people of Bethel possessed to listen to it.

Moreover, the moral judgment which Amos proclaimed was

one which knew no favorites. The people of Israel were accustomed to think that, whatever happened, they were ultimately secure in the favor of God. They were confident that they were God's peculiar people. Their patriotism and their religion were linked in the sense that they made it a point of religion to believe that whatever their patriotic desires wanted God was somehow pledged to give. They had the same sort of arrant nationalism which crops up like a disease from age to age, and which one may see today exemplified in Italy and in Hitler's Germany. God and the nation are identified, and to do homage to the nation is to exalt God. But Amos had a different message. "You only have I known of all the nations of the earth," he said of Israel. They were willing enough to hear him that far. That was exactly what they liked to listen to and believe. Theirs was the one nation which God had singled out for His regard. But they were not prepared for Amos's conclusions. "You only have I known of all the families of the earth: therefore will I visit upon you all your iniquities."

It was an unpopular doctrine that Amos was preaching. The real message of religion often has to be that, and we may as well admit it first as last. Men inveterately want to have smooth things said to them, and if these smooth things are said in the name of God, so much the better. But the real man of God cannot always, or even mostly, say smooth things. He must speak as Amos did, with a terrible and unsparing sternness. Let us remember this always when we appraise the worth of preaching. If it is always popular, it may win plenty of human applause; but it may lie under God's condemnation of unfaithfulness. The religious message which proceeds from reality and dares to speak real truth with honest words may have its surest sign of loyalty to God in the opposition which it stirs among men. It is important that we American Christians should ponder this. The day may come when it will be desperately important for our spiritual salvation that the Church should defend the freedom of those, both in its pulpits and in its pews, who hold to difficult truth. The world today is full of ominous examples of the way in which some obsession may grow so great within a nation that the effort is made to silence the voice of those who speak the eternal correctives of God as against the passions of the time. Unless the sure standards of God's truth are seen and maintained by a minority that refuses to be stampeded with the crowd, it is possible for a whole people to be given moral poison in the name of patriotism. Black can be turned into white and evil into pretended good. The holiest words can be so perverted that they become the cloak for shameless wrong. Before the lessons of recent history fade, remember how in despatches from Japan the Japanese invasion of a helplessly subjected nation was announced as a campaign "to free" north China. Mark how the war of Italy against Ethiopia was paraded in Italy as an "extension of civilization." Mark how in Germany the campaign to stifle all brave utterance in the Church is carried forward "in the name of the German soul." It is a perilous thing in those nations now for any prophet of God to speak. Conditions might so develop that it would be equally perilous here in America, perilous for the men who should speak against a growing fascism, or against race hatred, or against war. Already in some quarters there is an effort to muzzle the Church when self-appointed guardians of protected interests imagine that the Church might be dangerous to them. A bishop of the Protestant Episcopal Church was recently stopped by a group of vigilantes in an industrial conflict when he went to a confirmation at a church in the Imperial Valley of California, and this group of self-appointed protectors of the vested interests of that region demanded to know in advance what he proposed in this church service to say. Most free citizens in America, and most members of the Church would today be indignant at such insolence as that; but it is always possible for public fears to spread, and for the mob mind so to be inflamed that even good men gradually are caught up into a kind of intolerance that would make them sacrifice our great heritage of freedom. Our need is that we should be on our guard in time. Our need is to discipline ourselves to listen to every honest word that may have in it the counsel of God, even though it be unpopular; and to defend, as we would defend the dearest treasure of our souls, the right of the truth to be spoken and to be heard.

III

We go on then to the third consideration concerning Amos. We have seen how God took him and what God said through him. Let us note now what God did in him. It is obvious that the power of God made Amos into another man. He had been a nobody before; but he was lifted into a spiritual nobility now that made him invincible. "I was no prophet, nor a prophet's son"; he said, "*but*." But now God's strength was wrought into the fiber of his being. God's fire burned in him, and shone through him. God's voice spoke through his voice. Now, therefore, he could say, "Hear thou the voice of the Lord."

As we have said already, Amos was not an individual only, but a type. Always it has been true that when men have given themselves into the hand of God to be fashioned and to be used, they have been lifted to a whole new plane of power. They have become like the psalmist who could sing, "The Lord is my light and my salvation; whom then shall I fear? The Lord is the strength of my life; of whom then shall I be afraid?" They have become like Paul the Apostle, saying as his life moved on to its dangerous climax, and his friends anxiously besought him to take heed of the gathering peril: "But none of these things move me, neither count I my life dear unto myself, so that I might finish my course with joy . . . to testify the gospel of the grace of God."

This kind of strength which comes to the man who is God-possessed can lift him up above the scepticism of associates, the luke-warmness of the timid, and the solemn advice of those who like to think that they are prudent and cautious, but really are cowardly at heart. A century and a half ago in England there lived a man concerning whom every indication was that he would move through an insignificant existence and die unknown. He had no formal education, no rank or position, no powerful friends. He was a cobbler of shoes. But this man had a vision of God's work not for one country only, but for the world. He dreamed what has come to be the great adventure of the modern missions of the Christian Church. When men with whom he talked tried to dissuade him, he answered: "You are wiser than I, especially in foreseeing difficulties. Therefore I like to counsel with you but to execute without you." And when at a ministers' meeting he outlined his purpose of going to India and carrying the Christian gospel there, he divided what he said into two great affirmations: "Expect great things from God. Attempt great things for God." And in that spirit, William Carey went out to do more perhaps than any other single individual from the West had ever done to carry to a great continent the best which our civilization knew.

And now at the end let us not imagine that because some of the illustrations we have used are of those who became great in history therefore these have no immediate relevance for us. On the contrary, they speak straight home to us even though spiritually we may seem to belong to the undistinguished crowd, as Amos at first might have seemed to belong. God's strength comes to any man whenever that man makes a brave and true decision. It has been grandly said: "God makes His presence known with irresistible conviction in the act of will by which a man surrenders without reserve to the highest he knows." The real possibilities of our souls are achieved not by anything which we work out alone. They are achieved when we listen to the voice which somehow and at some time every man hears speaking in his heart, when he follows the higher leading that marks out a shining path amid what otherwise would be common things. We may not have the name of prophets, and we may not be ordained to any special office; but that does not touch the heart of the reality. Any single human soul, whoever and wherever it may be, can become one of the spokesmen for the divine truth and the divine goodness, if day by day that soul is trying to be sensitive to the will of God. There are many people in this world who have brilliant abilities; but in the last analysis, all that they will ever say is only so much thin and idle chatter which never wakes an echo in the deeper levels of our human life. But there are other men and women, some of them apparently without shining gifts, some of them in humble places, whose everyday words have a genuineness and force that make all who hear them stop and listen. These are the people who have learned what Amos learned, and what all of us who want to can learn again, namely, that when a life has let itself be God-possessed, then uniquely it possesses power. We are not made great by any instruments, not by wealth, not by possessions, not by formal honors. What we want to be able to say is not, "I take this or that"; but rather, at some great instant of spiritual commitment, "God took me." When a man can say that, then he can go to bear his witness among the men about him in no deprecating way. When such a man's consecration gives him words, then he will be saying not "Hear me," but "Hear thou the word of the Lord!"

XII

MEN WHO WOULD NOT FAIL

But if not.—DANIEL III:18

THESE words come from the midst of one of the most stirring hero stories of the Old Testament. Turn back to the third chapter of the book of Daniel and read it there. Nebuchadnezzar, king of Babylon, has set up in the plain of Dura a great image adorned with gold which represents the god of his empire's proud success. He commands that all people shall come and bow down before the image, and there is a vast ceremony with music and the assembling of dignitaries and the pouring together of the crowds. But three young Hebrews, captives in Babylon, refuse to worship this pagan god of Nebuchadnezzar. The king is furious. He threatens that they shall be thrown alive into the furnace which was kept for cremating dead bodies. Still they will not flinch from their refusal to bow down to his image. Into the fire they go. And then the old story tells the tradition of their miraculous deliverance.

So much for the account of these men who in the end were saved from what seemed certain death. But in the course of the story there is a disclosure about these men which is more important than the story itself. In the climax they were delivered, but they had faced the possibility that they might not be delivered. They believed that in their danger God would intervene. But suppose that belief were disappointed; suppose there should be nothing ahead but defeat and death. Then what?

To answer that question took a kind of faith that was not built on easy calculation. Being confident of God's help, they would be faithful; but that was not all. They would be faithful anyway. Whether God saved them or let them suffer, they would be true to their convictions. "Our God whom we serve is able to deliver us from the burning fiery furnace, and he will deliver us out of thine hand, O king. *But if not.*" If not, then admit that you have leaned on false reliance, and surrender to the thoughts that cowardice would whisper. But these men said no such thing. Whatever the conditions were, they had a duty notwithstanding. Come life or death, they would not falter. Even if no help from God appeared, even if there were no vindication and no evident fulfilment of their faith, even if the fire were all that faced them, nevertheless they would carry on. That—we instinctively acknowledge—was magnificent. It is an inspiring fact from the past to read of. But is it something to live by today? This is the question which directly matters, and which we need to consider as clearly as we can.

Our thought falls naturally into two divisions. First, we shall recognize the facts in our own experience which are like the facts the three men in this story faced; and then we shall ask how we may become able to meet the issue as they did.

I

It is a natural thing for men, if they want religion at all, to want a religion which seems to work. If we worship God, then God will take care of His worshipers. "Doth Job fear God for naught?" asked Satan in the prologue of the Old Testament drama, which bears Job's name. As a matter of fact, Job did serve God without conditions. "Though he slay me, yet will I trust him," he cried. But it is not only Satan, but our average human nature which instinctively assumes that religion ought to bring obvious benefits in its train. If a man follows after goodness, then the result ought to be demonstrably good. If he is righteous, then the plain issues of his life ought to turn out right. If we trust in God, does this not mean that we can be confident that in hours of necessity God's deliverance will be at hand?

To think in these terms, may, of course, make religion a poor thing of selfish bargaining. But that is not necessarily true. The craving for a God whose truth can be seen in practical results is not always ignoble. It is linked with the instinctive desire of every human heart to feel that it is not living in an empty universe, but that there is an unseen Friend on whom it can depend. Men want to be sure that God is not an illusion, that His help is real, and that not only in the light but in the darkness He is there.

Yet the times come when this desire is contradicted. If God's presence could be felt, then the soul could be courageous. But He is hidden. Faith may try to believe in His sufficiency, but faith seems to be left groping in a void. One side of us goes on saying, "God can deliver us, He can deliver us, and He will"; and the other side of us is answering uneasily, "Perhaps it is so. We hope for the hand of God. But we cannot see it, and, if not, what then?"

Take, to begin with, our personal relationships, especially those which involve our deeper affections. As long as men have faith that some benevolent purpose is watching over these, they can stand a great deal of suffering. If they see some reason in it, even though it be a far good that is working out through pain, they can march straight into the furnace of affliction and not be dismayed. But the more terrible ordeal lies in those things which seem irreconcilable with any thought of God which they can frame. How often does one hear men and women say after some shattering crisis in their affections, "I used to think I had faith, and now I do not know whether I have faith in anything." As long as they could believe that God at least was in the not too distant background, ready to appear before any great disaster happened, they could hold steady. But the realization may be forced upon them that disaster is closing in inexorably, and that no help from God will intervene. A man's own health is shattered. He sees his powers of service broken and defeated, or, worse still, he sees sickness fall upon someone whom he loves better than himself. Death lays its hand upon that other life, his friend, his wife, his child, and he is powerless. As long as he could hope that worse would not come to the worst, as long as there was still a chance for some divine deliverance before it should be too late, he could stick to his affirmation of religious faith. *But if not.* If the last light on his horizon seems to go down into darkness, if he cries for understanding and yet cannot understand, what shall he do then? *But if not!*

Or take the field of practical affairs. Watch men in their business. It may be that they have gone into it with high ideals. Boys grow up in Christian homes, are taught in Christian Sunday-schools, imbibe the suggestion of Christian worship, and then with fine sensitive instincts go out presently into the competitive struggle of store or factory or broker's office. They realize that in this new world of theirs there is another god beside the God they were earlier taught to worship. It is the gilded god which the Nebuchadnezzars of our modern Babylons have set up, the god of so-called practical ambition, of riches and success. "Bow down to this god," men say, "and you shall have the world's reward; and, when you do bow down, you only follow sensibly where everyone else is pointing the way. The dignitaries will be there just as they were in Nebuchadnezzar's time. The crowd will be there. The brass bands of popular opinion will be drowning out any small uneasy voice of conscience." Faced with that situation, the young idealist will remember God, the God of the spiritual values as against the material, the God who is known through service and not through selfishness, the God who puts into men's hearts the motive of the golden rule. "I ought to be able to carry my best religion into all these business relationships," the young man says. "I ought to be able to believe that God will stand beside me and vindicate my trust in Him by making me a success on these highest terms." That is what he wants to think, but the day may come when he is disillusioned. He comes to the conclusion that, no matter how agreeably religion may sound on Sundays, it does not work on week-days. He has had to face the question, not only of what he would do if God made his conscientious inclinations easy, but what he will do if God seems to do no such thing. God ought to be able to deliver him from the practical necessity of worshiping the golden idol. God ought to make it so that he can accumulate as much money and get ahead as rapidly while he keeps his religious idealism as if he let it go. But when he finds himself facing a conflict with his spiritual faith on the one side and his material fortune apparently on the other, what shall he do then? If God would only show that religion is more profitable than irreligion, that would be ideal. *But if not.* If not, what is left to a man except to be a realist and to take the world as he finds it, golden image and all?

Or, again, people may be confronted with the problem of the hiddenness of God, not in matters which primarily concern them personally, but in those great movements of the world in which all life's values are at stake. Such is the case, for example, with Christian men and women in Russia today. Maurice Hindus in his book *Red Bread* draws a pathetic picture of a Russian priest caught in the terrible confusion of trying to sustain his belief in God in the midst of conditions where there seemed to be no sign that God was there. "Don't you suppose," he said, "if He made himself known people would flock back to Him? Of course they would. They would bow in repentance and promise to believe and obey and worship. Yet here are we His servants, waiting, waiting, and nothing happens. Sometimes I say to myself, 'If He does not care, why should we?' Or is He merely trying us out to see how much we can endure? Perhaps. Who knows? But it is so hard, so very hard on us, His servants." In America and in most other countries of our Western world, we have no such conditions as those which prevail in Russia. Nevertheless it is possible that, though in different ways, yet in no less acuteness, the Christian religion and those who think that they believe in it will be put to mortal testing. It is entirely possible that religion, which heretofore has been treated with a tolerant respect even by those who had no active interest in it, may be despised and assailed. It is relatively easy now to be at least nominally religious. Church going and church membership are still intellectually and socially respectable. Great endowments and generous gifts from an older generation have often established the Church in affluence. But these things may change. Another generation is growing up which may have another attitude. The time may conceivably come in America, and come sooner than we think, when belief in God and loyalty to religion will not be easy things to profess. The idol of some hard paganism may be set up to challenge it under the name of science or enlightened psychology or social efficiency, or any other similar name. It may be held, just as it is now held in Russia, that religion is bound up with reaction, and that all its mysticism must be got rid of, in order that men may grapple relentlessly with the real world. In that time men may say, "If only I were quite sure that the faith I once was taught is true. If I could be certain that God would make plain to everybody that we, the religious people, are right, then of course I would stand my ground. But what if this does not happen? *But if not*—what can I do then but surrender?"

Those, then, are some of the actual possibilities in our present life which run parallel to the situation in which the three young men found themselves in the old story of the Book of Daniel. Now, as then, men will have to meet the issue involved in that "But if not." We have got to determine whether we shall trust God only when we can see, or whether there is a religious heroism which can trust Him beyond our immediate seeing.

II

We pass on, then, to the other and more creative aspect of our thought. How can we learn to meet victoriously those crises when the divine help we need does not appear?

We take up in the same order those types of crises which we have already recognized, and first come to those which have to do with our personal lives and our personal affections.

Few men or women go through this world without having some drastic experience which challenges their religious faith almost to the point of obliteration. They have always assumed that God exists, and that God is good. They want to believe that still, but in the stark facts which confront them they cannot honestly say that they see any signs of goodness. It is as though God Himself had been overthrown by evil, or as though, if God still exists, He is so remote and unintelligible in His ways with men that life is no better off than if it were alone. That is what a man or woman, stricken by grief and bereavement, is tempted to feel. God's deliverance does not come. And since it does not, what can they do, and what can they cling to now?

Well, the magnificent fact is that human souls in exactly these circumstances have again and again clung to that faith in the unseen, gone straight ahead through the darkness, and on the other side of it touched the invincible assurance which they knew to be the hand of God. That is exactly what Jesus did. His "nevertheless" in Gethsemane was like the "But if not" of the three young men in the story of Daniel. Every outward circumstance of that hour seemed to deny the reality of his Father's help. He was facing mortal suffering, and facing it in loneliness with the load of seeming defeat resting heavy on his shoulders. Up to the last hour he seems to have hoped that there might be some conceivable other way of faithfulness for him to take rather than that way which led to Calvary. "But if not," he would walk unflinchingly upon that road. He dared to believe, in spite of crucifixion, that in the end his Father's redeeming purpose would be fulfilled.

That same test of the cross comes back again and again to human lives. Religion is not an easy thing. It has never guaranteed that it would or could make every hour smoothly happy. What it does promise is that it can make life heroic, and that the heroism will be worth its cost. There are hours when men and women have to hold hard to the best they have believed in, even if every circumstance seems to challenge that belief. Life is often full of mystery which we cannot by any hasty verbalisms dispose of or explain away. But again and again men have felt that in the mystery something great was moving which in the longer perspective of tomorrow they would better understand. Viewing life as a whole, we begin to perceive that out of no less difficult a process could God have produced the values which are highest and most to be desired. In a universe where there were no pain or bewildering bereavement, there could be smooth and comfortable existence. But in such a universe how would it be possible to create souls capable of sacrifice, or to reveal a Christ capable of a cross? Helped by this realization, from the midst of every deepest shadow those who trust to their best belief in God will be led on to fulfilments which will make them glad they did keep faith with their highest, and will vindicate at length the goodness in which they dared to trust.

It is exactly in the face of such necessities as this that we understand best how nobly human nature can measure up to great requirements. Others can learn to say what Studdert Kennedy, that gallant interpreter of the meaning of God to every life, could say when from the trenches of the World War he wrote:

The first prayer I want my son to learn to say for me is not, "God keep daddy safe," but "God make daddy brave, and if he has hard things to do make him strong to do them." Life and death don't matter, Pat, my son; right and wrong do. Daddy dead is daddy still, but daddy dishonoured before God is something awful, too bad for words. I suppose you'd like to put in a bit about safety too, old chap, and mother would. Well, put it in, but afterwards, always afterwards, because it really does not matter near so much. Every man, woman, and child should be taught to put first things first in prayer, both in peace and war, and that I believe is where we have failed.

Other lesser men and women have likewise learned how to put first things first, and in so doing have found the meaning of their life. What they have learned is not a peculiar accomplishment. It is a revelation of what is possible for us all. Dr. Maltbie D. Babcock wrote to a friend of his in great distress: "You cannot understand, or explain, but you know as well as I, that back of everything is God, and God is light,—we shall see. And God is love—we shall be satisfied. It may be a long while, but it will be worth waiting for. Trust Him all you can—you will be glad you did." And to another friend he wrote: "Trust God now in the dark, when it means something. It will be so easy to see it all, and to be thankful, when the perfect day dawns." And may it not be that, in the great day of our final accounting, we shall be ashamed if we had been able to trust God only in the light?—ashamed if, unlike those men in the old story, we had failed in the difficult hour and, desiring to receive religious consolation, had been unwilling to say that, if it did not come, we would still be faithful?

Take then, in the second place, the question of our need for God out in the world of business and of material affairs. It is quite true that real religion there seems often set at nought. Practical affairs may not be ordered with reference to religious ideas. Many men and women also in the industrial world are caught in that perplexity. Their ideals make them want to live one way. Necessity seems to force them to live another. They want to be unselfish, and they seem caught in a process which is fundamentally selfish. They want to believe in God, but apparently they have to bow down to Mammon.

Now in these circumstances there are two things to be said. If a person seems forced to compromise with situations where there seems no ideal way out, and where any choice is less than the best he really wants, then at least let him keep his sensitiveness of soul which feels the wound to conscience, and which will make him do his best to alter circumstances so that those wounds will not recur. There is a figure in the Old Testament whose experience was like that of some of us, and the prayer he made can be as genuine and fresh today as it was when he first voiced it. Naaman the Syrian had come into Israel seeking the prophet of God for his own healing. He had been healed, and he was deeply grateful and spiritually deeply stirred. He wanted to worship the God of Elisha the prophet, but he knew that when he went back into Syria he would have to enter, as a servant of his master the king, into the temple of Rimmon. His heart would not be there, but his feet would have to go there. He did not have the courage yet to say he would not go, but he did feel and acknowledge an unrest in going. "When my master goeth into the house of Rimmon to worship there, and he leaneth on my hand, and I bow myself in the house of Rimmon: when I bow down myself in the house of Rimmon, the Lord pardon thy servant in this thing." Let men and women today who feel that they are carried by their relationships with others into the house of Rimmon listen to the cry in their own souls that makes them rebel at anything that compromises their loyalty to God. Let them not stifle that cry beneath a hardening cynicism. *That* is the greatest peril which faces young lives caught in conditions which they know to be materialistic and unspiritual. They are tempted to shrug their shoulders at last at the possibility that religion can have any place in their practical world, to abandon their ideals altogether, and to play the harsh game of selfish realities without compunction. But God forbid that that should happen. It is better to be confused than to be cowardly, better to hold on to such fragments of ideals that we can still defend than surrender, better to be uncomfortable in inconsistency than to quench all the light of God within us which gives us our unrest. Even if God does not seem to work out our problems, even if He does seem to leave us in conditions where we want to serve Him and cannot fully do it, still we want to go on believing in the best and trying in spite of every defeat to measure up to it as fully as we can.

And the second thing is this. We cannot expect religious victory which has in it no element of the cross. There are times in a man's life when he has got deliberately to face sacrifice. He must lose money, lose possessions, lose the friendship of powerful and successful interests if need be, rather than sell his soul. He must be willing, as those men in Babylon were, to go straight into the furnace of affliction rather than submit to the idol which will crush out the dignity of his life.

When that point of devotion is reached, then men have risen superior to consequences. They can move on with shining eyes to meet whatever may await them. They may not come out of the fire unscarred, as the men in the Book of Daniel were said to do, but they will come through it. Whatever may be their material loss, they will emerge spiritually triumphant. They have laid hold on eternal convictions which nothing can shake, and in those they are satisfied. They will understand what that great spirit, Frederick W. Robertson, meant when he wrote:

Thrice blessed is he who—when all is drear and cheerless within and without, when his teachers terrify him, and his friends shrink from him—has obstinately clung to moral good. Thrice blessed, because *his* night shall pass into clear, bright day.

I appeal to the recollection of any man who has passed through that hour of agony, and stood upon the rock at last, the surges stilled below him, and the last cloud drifted from the sky above, with a faith, and hope, and trust no longer traditional, but of his own—a trust which neither earth nor hell shall shake thenceforth forever.

Finally, there is that larger circle of the world which has no particular relation to our personal interest, but represents that great drift of moral forces common to us all. That drift, as I said before, may be in the next generation toward irreligion. More particularly, the institutions of religion may be attacked, and those who choose to stand for the ideals of Jesus as these are or ought to be embodied in the Church, may find themselves more solitary than they are now. Already in many quarters there is a sort of airy condescension toward those who are interested in public expression of loyalty to God. "Do you really go to Church?" said one woman to another. "I did not suppose that anybody like you could be so old-fashioned." Religious loyalty may increasingly be faced with those subtle weapons of derision before which so many men and women gradually surrender without clearly knowing that they have done so. Their shrinking from seeming to be peculiar, the uncomfortableness of being the only one in the household or in a group of acquaintances who takes the trouble to go to Church, the difficulty of seeming to push a personal opinion against a majority indifference, can make people little by little abandon that which used to represent religion and stop defending something which they think is no longer defending them. It is possible also that the assault upon religion may become more direct and definite. In some respects that is already true. Idols are set up upon the plains of our public life which a man cannot worship without abandoning his loyalty to the God revealed in Jesus. There are forces in our modern capitalism obsessed with money-making, blind to human welfare, exalting the so-called sanctity of property above the sanctity of life, which Christians individually, and which the Christian Church, must resist to the utmost on peril of their souls. There is the idol of an exaggerated nationalism as in Nazi Germany, which is becoming increasingly arrogant in its demands. Even through the Supreme Court of these United States that nationalism has made its voice heard through the court's pronouncement that no one shall become a citizen of this country who in time of war will not scrap his conscience and follow the majority vote, whatever it may command. Against these forces of industrial ruthlessness and of nascent militarism, those convictions which come from God through Jesus Christ may seem impractical and powerless. They may require of a man a prophetic denunciation of existing evils and a prophetic willingness, if need be, to suffer for the truth he sees which will lead him to the doors of a modern fiery furnace. In such an hour he may feel terribly lonely. In his weaker moments he may think that his religion is requiring of him an awful cost. But in that same moment he may take upon his lips those words which stout-hearted Martin Luther spoke that day when, in the loneliness of his own conviction, he went up to the Diet of Worms to face the Emperor Charles V and all the other great ones of his time.

My cause shall be commended to the Lord, for he lives and reigns who preserved the three children in the furnace of the Babylonian king. If he is unwilling to preserve me, my life is a small thing compared with Christ's, who was wickedly slain to the disgrace of all and the harm of many. Expect anything of me except flight or recantation. I will not flee, much less recant. So may the Lord Jesus strengthen me.

"So may the Lord Jesus strengthen me!" What a magnificent climax for him and for us. Not "May Jesus relieve me of my difficulties." Not "May religion be my safe and smooth reliance." *But* "May religion give me strength to face what conscience tells me must be done and go forward to do it, believing that, if not today, then tomorrow God's vindication will appear." Blessed are the moments when we are able to say: "Our God whom we serve is able to deliver us in our need." But better and braver still are the times when we look for God's immediate revelation, and, even if it does not come, resolve that nevertheless we will not fail!

XIII

WHAT THE HERODS DO NOT KNOW

*Now when Jesus was born in Bethlehem of Judaea
in the days of Herod the king, behold, there came
wise men from the east to Jerusalem,
Saying, Where is he that is born King of the Jews?
for we have seen his star in the east, and are come to
worship him.*

MATTHEW II:I, 2

VISUALIZE the scene which those words suggest. Its background is the royal court of Herod at Jerusalem. For a long time he had been entrenched there in the power which he had gained under the aegis of the world-wide Roman Empire. Subject only to this great over-lordship, he dominated Palestine. He was an old man now, proud, watchful, and implacable. He had matched his wits and strength against the realities of his world, and apparently he had won. He was king, and lesser men cowered before his kingship.

If Herod, then, is the first figure in the scene which rises thus before us, the second group of figures is made up of men who have come from far beyond Herod's horizon. They are called in the beautiful story of St. Matthew's Gospel "wise men from the east." The tradition is that their home was in that far country beyond the Tigris and the Euphrates from which the most ancient races of mankind have come. They were perhaps worshipers of Zoroaster, men who found a clue to this universe in the eternal struggle of light and darkness and saw in the stars the heavenly lights in which they read the thoughts of God. These men of uplifted faces, these men of mighty dreams, came now at the end of a long caravan journey to Herod's court to tell him that they had seen a new star in the east, and that they had followed its light until now it had led them to Jerusalem. They said that the star was a sign that somewhere one should be born who was to be King of the Jews, and in that kingship was to bring a new redemption to the world. They wanted to ask at Herod's court where that king might be.

As a matter of fact, he had been born, though Herod did not know it. In Bethlehem in the arms of a maid from Nazareth a baby lay. Nobody but the little handful of folk who gathered round the stable of the inn knew that this child was born, or cared. Nevertheless, in him there had entered into the world a power beside which the power of Herod should be revealed as only tawdriness. In him had come the fulfilment of the vision of the Magi and of all other men of many centuries who had been looking to the heavens for a sign.

As a sheer piece of human drama that scene in Herod's court is breath-taking. Imagine what Herod felt and what went on within that dark and crafty mind of his. Here was he the king, a king who thought himself secure, and here were these strange unheralded men from a distant country with this unearthly look upon their faces, coming to ask him about another king who was supposed to have been born. Another king! The blood of Herod's courtiers must have run cold when they heard these strangers breathe such words as those. To even whisper them was treason. When they looked at Herod's face, they remembered what he had done already to more than one supposed rival of his kingship. They knew what perhaps the Magi did not know, that he had slain his own wife in a fit of jealousy, that he had had three of his sons executed for challenging his power, that he had had another rival strangled in a public bath. And here were these three dreamers from the east asking so naïvely about another king! Would they ever go out alive through Herod's doors?

But Herod as we see him there in that tense moment was crafty as well as cruel. His mind, even in the moment of amazement, was master of itself. He knew how to disguise his emotions for his own ends. His thought pierced at once to the center of the whole concern. His interest was not to let his anger flame against the visionary followers of a star. His concern was to strike swiftly at this king they talked about. So he found out by careful questioning where and what this child might be, and he sent the Magi with all seeming benevolence upon their way. Let them go and see exactly where the child was, and let them come back again and bring him word, so that he might also pay his homage. So he told them, while the controlled mask of his face hid the passion that was behind it. But what he did was to send soldiers after the Magi as they went to Bethlehem, with orders to kill every young child in the town. Thus he thought to settle once for all this threat of a rival to his power; and according to the gospel story he was frustrated only because Joseph, being warned in a dream, fled from Bethlehem in time with Mary and with Jesus.

A great dramatist could make an immortal drama for the stage out of that figure of Herod and of the other figures of his story. But there is another drama in it which is greater than that of any one historic personage: it is the drama of all life symbolized there. For in Herod and the wise men and the Child Jesus are typified three elements that enter life always, and we may well consider their relationship.

I

The first is worldly wisdom.

Herod represented that. He was the type, that is, of the man who deliberately sets out to make terms with the world as it is, to accept the rules of the prevailing game, and to play it so ably that he wins the prizes which it has to offer. "Be practical," the world may seem to say to the ambitious spirit, "be realistic. It does not matter what you might dream that life ought to be. Look to see what life actually is. Adjust yourself to facts, and then you can begin successfully to adjust facts to you. The impractical man collides with hard reality, and all he can do is to take the consequences. But those who are shrewd enough can *make* the consequences to suit themselves."

Many men in many ages have followed that sort of interpretation of the meaning of their world. Herod followed it conspicuously. He was the son of Antipater, an Idumean who had had the shrewdness to ally himself with the Roman power as Rome extended her sway along the eastern Mediterranean. Herod the son was even abler than his father. He was a military leader of courage and resourcefulness, and he never flung the hazard of his fortune blindly. He lived in a time when the Roman Empire

was shaken by great conflicting powers, and when it took almost
uncanny foresight to guess from one day to another which way
the tides of success would run. But Herod had the adroitness to
make himself valuable to each one of the Roman masters whose
authority reached Palestine. The first of these was Julius Caesar,
then Cassius, then Mark Antony, and then Augustus. These men
might be enemies of one another; but Herod managed to make
himself the ally successively of them all. At last he became the
undisputed legate of the Roman rule. Although in his own
blood he was only remotely allied to the Jewish people, he married
the heiress of the Asmonæan line, who represented all the glorious
Jewish memories of the heroic period of the Maccabees; and
when he rebuilt the temple in unprecedented splendor, he won
for himself the favor of many who thought that thus the people
of God were honored. It appeared, therefore, that his life in all
great ways had triumphed. He had won every prize which his
proud ambition coveted.

But at the end what happened to him? A lonely and horrible
death through a wasting disease. There were many who obeyed
him, even more who feared him, but none at the end who loved
him. He was an old man with haunting and embittered memories, an old man with the blood of his own wife and of his sons
upon his hands. When he died, the whole realm began to breathe
again as though the shadow of a long fear were lifted. But his
name went down into a deeper shadow; and when today men
think of Herod, they think not of a man whose reign was
splendid, but of a grim and evil figure who stands as a foil to
the thought of Jesus.

And yet one wonders what Herod was in the beginning and
what a different man he might have been. There were great
qualities in him. He had intrepid courage, both physical and
moral. He had the instinctive power of leadership which ordinary men could acknowledge and obey. Like Saul, the far-off first
king of Israel, whose kingship like Herod's was in the end a
tragedy, Herod had the dominance of personality which seemed
to stamp him as by nature royal. Like Saul there were aspects in
which he rose above the crowd, "from his shoulders and upward
higher than any of the people." He could command homage, and

there was a time at least when there was something winsome in him which could reach home to human hearts. Once he had deep emotions too. His love for Mariamne his wife was passionate, and might have been ennobling. Stephen Phillips in his poem *Herod* dramatized the beauty and tragedy of that love. But at last there was nothing left of it except the terrible scorched emptiness where the old fires once had burned. For there had been something else in Herod which was stronger than love and stronger than loyalty. That other overmastering thing was his ambition. He wanted power, power unquestioned and unchallenged; and when there crept into his mind the slightest thought that any one near him put opposition in his way, immediately he flamed with resentment, jealousy, and distrust. And so at the end, although he seemed to have gained his world, that world was only a hollow shell, and his soul was dead within him. Being the sort of man he was, of course Herod could respond with nothing but hatred when he heard from the Magi of the child who was born in Bethlehem. At first he knew only that the child was said to be a rival to his kingship. If Herod could have known more about him, he would have hated him all the more, for the spirit of Jesus should symbolize in the world all those things which Herod had repudiated and which, therefore, he feared and wanted to destroy. Jesus represented the power of the spirit; but Herod wanted no inconvenient talk of spiritual ideals to disturb his entrenched advantage. Jesus represented the power of purity, and Herod, stained with many sins, could not allow his conscience to admit that purity had any place in this world's hard realities. Jesus represented the power of love, and Herod had built all his power on the conviction that only force and cunning can carry a man ahead. Herod could not exist in a world in which the spirit of Jesus should prevail.

Herod as a figure in history lived and died a long time ago, and human life never exactly repeats itself. There have been no other figures who at all precise points are parallel to Herod. Nevertheless, the type of man which Herod represented is repeated in many generations. We may see those who are contemporary Herods, some on the grand, and some on the petty scale, some of them like the tiger and some like the jackal, but all of them akin to Herod in the fact that they imagine that life can be successful by selling itself to the shrewd and crafty methods of a conscienceless ambition.

A generation ago there was a young man who started out through doors of generous opportunity in these United States. He had been born into a family which had been not devoid of public service. He inherited great wealth and the impulse toward broad culture. He received the best education America could give. Then he started out upon a career which offered great influence and which could have enabled him to make an almost measureless contribution to the public good. But it grew increasingly evident that this man cared for power. There seemed no device which he would not use to make his papers sell. His papers catered to the lower elements in the public taste. Nothing seemed sacred to them, neither the sensibilities of individuals nor the honor and integrity of great public causes. His influence has been a corruption and a poison to his time. His name was not Herod; but his name was William Randolph Hearst. And of him another newspaper in Seattle not long ago, putting into words in a front page editorial what numberless other newspapers had doubtless long been thinking, wrote:

In his campaign of frightfulness which he has undertaken to browbeat and stifle all Americans who won't accept his brand of politics, this mad hatter of yellow journalism has at last gone too far. It is high time for the pendulum of public opinion to swing back the other way and to bump this bullying dictator off his paper throne. What America most needs right now is not protection from communists but protection from William Randolph Hearst.

About the same time another man began his career in the life of America. He too had every opportunity. He too, like the man whom we have just mentioned, had the privilege of education and of many inspiring contacts. He started out as a young man of alert ideals, dedicated, so at least he thought, to the career of a reformer in politics, but he changed his mind before long, and deliberately allied himself with the most corrupt and sinister influences in his state. He became a great power in party politics, but one whose power was exerted usually in hidden ways. He became as much as any other man in his time the type of those who used public office for the interests of secret, favored groups. His name was Boies Penrose. In the December, 1936, number of the *Columbia University Quarterly*, President Nicholas Murray Butler has left of him a curious record. Senator Penrose had opposed for reasons of his own the adoption of the constitutional amendment providing for the election of senators no longer by the state legislatures but directly by the people. But after that change had been made Penrose met President Butler in Washington, and he said: "Butler, give up fighting the direct primary and the direct election of senators. I thought they were going to be bad, but they are wonderful! In Pennsylvania a grateful people has just sent me back to the Senate by a majority of 250,000 at a time when no Republican legislature would have dared to re-elect me." "Nothing," said President Butler, "could more fully record Penrose's scatching cynicism in all that had to do with politics." And the blight that will always rest upon this man's name is the fact that, like another Herod, not only was he himself cynical but that he made many of his contemporaries cynical of all those beliefs in this world which are not based on crafty calculation.

But whether or not they seem to win their fleeting successes, the Herods of the world suffer ill at the hands of history. The mistake which men often make lies in forgetting that life has its long perspectives. The man who follows the way of Herod may seem for a moment to rise above the crowd into the sunshine of success; but in truth his feet are set upon a descending way which takes him, and all memory of him, down into the valleys of ultimate darkness and dishonor.

II

We pass then from Herod to those other and brighter figures represented in the scene with which we began. Confronting Herod were the Magi. Against the self-deceived and self-destructive spirit which calls itself "worldly wisdom," there stands the different spirit which sees great lights and follows them upon a shining way.

The quality which the wise men represented, and which their

successors represent in every age, is imagination. Here were men who were not shut within the boundaries of the obvious. They could believe in that which had not yet been proved. They could see significance in signs which pointed to fulfilments that could be reached only at the end of a long, courageous road.

It is this quality of imagination which makes this story of the wise men so everlastingly beautiful. They might have gone about their own concerns in their own country as multitudes of others did. There was no reason why they more than others should have dreamed that the world and the future held something greater than any one had yet seen, held the promise of a divine deliverance, and a new redeeming spirit that was somehow to come down from heaven upon our earth. There was no essential reason why they more than others should have been concerned to search the skies. The gift of imagination, and especially of spiritual imagination, is a strange and wonderful thing. Judged by results, it would seem that few are endowed with that great gift, and yet perhaps more have it than the final reckoning would seem to show. For imagination does not come at first in its full flower. It comes in little gleams, hints, intuitions, the sparks of a divine unrest, and many there are who quench these first beginnings of imagination, and so deny to themselves the growing gift which might have been theirs. But it is plain to any one who reads with thoughtfulness the long record of human history that it is only through imagination that the race goes forward. We might all have been cave-men, cowering in the cold and in the darkness, if somebody ages ago had not had the bold imagination to dare the use of fire. We should all have gone with eyes in the dust if the first seers and prophets of the soul of man had not dared to believe the voice within them and to lift their faces up to God. Every subsequent advance—both in the material basis of life and in all its spiritual unfoldings, in its security, its plenty, and its peace, in its music, its poetry, and all its winged ecstasies—has been due to the men who had imagination. In every age, above the common earth where the common crowd goes up and down, there dawns in the sky of the human possibility some new and shining star. There will be those who see it because they want to see. There will be those who behold the light because they have desired the light; and if their imagination is brave as well as clear, they will see, as the Magi did in their star of new suggestion, a reality greater than all the rest of the world they had known before. They will be willing to follow it on long and difficult ways. They will believe, in spite of immediate appearances, that God has a great meaning for life to be found by those who are determined to discover it. They will be of those who make the world better, and who make it new, because they dare to trust that God intends that the morrow should have in it something better than the best we have known today.

The trouble with most lives which fail and come short of their great possibilities is not in any wickedness or evil will. It is simply in the lack of imagination. It is in the fact that day by day we may grow so bound by customary things, so matter of fact and unillumined, at last indeed so stodgy and so dull, that we are not looking for anything thrilling and creative. We may get into a round of life when it seems to us that the only realities are figures on a ledger, the routine of business and commercial practice, and all the kinds of commonplace assurances which so-called practical men want to cling to. We are fenced in by precedents and afraid of anything whose end is unpredictable. We fear to launch new ventures in social justice, in international cooperation, in the larger daring of a Christianity bent upon reunion, because we do not really believe in the shining of the star. We are not like the Magi, but like the Magi's neighbors. We want to stay in the conditions to which we are accustomed, and we do not trust that some great new gift for human life could really come down into our midst if we set out to find it.

I beg you to stop and think of this now. Remember how fatally easy it may be for us to lose—and lose without knowing of our loss—the spontaneity of our minds and spirits. It is a tragic thing to see any man or woman begin to lose imagination, to become day by day a little less sensitive to new ideas, a little less ready to kindle to lovely possibilities, a little more resistant to hope and faith. In an unforgettable essay by A. Edward Newton in the January, 1937, *Atlantic Monthly,* he says with gentle wit: "But for the unimpeachable integrity of Charles Lamb, we might well doubt his observation that 'lawyers were children once.'" The legalistic mind is not necessarily confined to those who are professional lawyers; and what Charles Lamb has said is worth pondering by us all. Any intricate civilization such as ours is not only based upon the law, but may become mired in the law. That is to say, it may be so identified with the type of mind which believes only in what has been, and is not awake to the signs of what might be, that we fail both as individuals and as members of a community to seize great chances that might be creative. Yet "lawyers *were* children once"; and all men and women whose minds have grown legalistic and dusty and unfruitful once were children also. We dare not forget those tremendous words of Jesus: "Whosoever shall not receive the kingdom of God as a little child, he shall not enter therein." Only at our peril should we fail to carry into our maturity something of the everlasting meaning of the child's expectancy and the child's desire. We must try to keep the lifted eye and the eager heart. We must pray God to continue in us the capacity for imagination. God pity us if ever we should become unable to see the shining of His stars!

III

The second thought which we have been following leads us straight to the third and final one.

The worldly wisdom of Herod by itself ended only in defeat. The wisdom of this world is redeemed and made creative only when it is controlled by a high imagination. But what is the final standard by which imagination itself must be measured? What is the ultimate value toward which all other things lead on and without whose discovery they will be delusions? This was the question the Magi had to answer, and the answer to it they found in Bethlehem.

But what did they find in Bethlehem? They expected their star would lead them to the Redeemer. They believed that at the end of the road they should find some revelation of a power from God great enough to make this world new. Yet many would have said that what they found was far short of measuring up to that great expectation. They found nothing at all that this world would have recognized. All that they found was a man and

woman and a little child. The only light at the end of the road
of the star was the light in a mother's eyes as she looked into a
baby's face.

What was there in Bethlehem then which was great? The one
element was there upon which at last the transformation of our
life depends. Emotion was there. Without that all our shrewd
calculations end only in a barren hardness. Without that all our
imagination may be only a will-of-the-wisp. It is only when men
are led to the place where their emotions are moved that they
receive the heavenly fire which burns out their dross and forges
in them the strength of a new consecration.

For in Bethlehem love entered into life, and wherever the
divine love that was born there went, men's hearts were melted
with a new tenderness and understanding. The only power God
sent to earth in Jesus was the power of His love. The only weapon
Jesus ever used to win his way was love. He kindled men's emotions. He made them not ashamed to be deeply and instinctively
themselves. He helped them to be pitiful towards the suffering,
chivalrous to the weak, compassionate to every human need. He
made them know that as their lives reached out to touch and
help the lives of others, their own personalities began to touch
the greatness of God.

Certainly it is true that the men who, like Herod, harden
themselves into cruel and deadly worldliness have done so because
they have stifled the springs of their sweet emotions. For the
most part also it is true that those who have lost their imagination, or have been led by their imagination along false roads,
have suffered this result because they have cut themselves off
from their emotions. I do not say that there is no such thing as a
creative imagination which is emotionless. Perhaps there may be.
There are certain kinds of poetry and certain kinds of music
that seem to move in a realm which has very little to do with
the heart; but their light is a cold glitter, like the shining of the
aurora above the polar ice. The greatest splendors of imagination
in every realm have their roots in the emotions. Shakespeare is
the loftiest genius of our English poetry, and no one can read
Shakespeare without perceiving that here was a man whose warm
understanding went deep down into all the ground of human life.

And certainly the kind of imagination which carries the world forward into more generous and hopeful adventures for social betterment comes from those men and women who have emotions that make them care. Nobody can strive passionately for justice who has not first himself suffered in his sympathy. No one can have a flame of indignation against the cruel callousness of piled-up wealth nor devote himself with whole-souled power to the bringing in of a social order of more equal opportunity, unless he first, like Studdert Kennedy, has felt "a passion of pity for the poor." None of us can take our everyday business or profession and lift it up out of the arid dust of mean detail into something greatly inspired and inspiring unless the fire of human emotion is burning in our hearts—unless, that is to say, all that we do is warmed and made to glow by a sense of its reference to the things that really count for the sweetness and strength of life.

The greatest gift of Christianity is its power forever to kindle our emotions. One cannot go with an open mind and a sensitive heart into and through the Christmas and Epiphany seasons without feeling oneself breathed upon by an influence which makes one more tender and more gentle. We cannot think of the mother in Bethlehem and the child in her arms without being led back to all those springs in our own souls which the dust of the common days can never cover nor conceal—the springs of our instinctive understanding that it is only love entering into life which lifts this existence of ours into divineness. And whenever our thought in any fashion touches Christ, we know that he works a result upon our emotions. There may be a great deal about him which we do not understand. We may be only children in our theology. But that will not matter much if, nevertheless, we let our thoughts come within the range of his suggestions. We cannot remember him without finding it harder to be cruel or selfish or pitiless. We cannot remember him without having something in us warm toward him and make us more eager to be generous, understanding, compassionate, and kind. We cannot remember him without knowing that out of the heart are the issues of life. And some day, looking into our own heart and remembering him, we may be moved to cry: "O God, let the healing waters which may come from the fountain of cleansing tears, as well as from the fountain of a great rejoicing, begin to flow in me!"

Think again, therefore, of the scene with which we began; for that scene is typical of human life in the elements which meet and mingle in it always. There is the hard calculation of the Herods, and that may seem to promise life its swiftest and most conspicuous success; but in the long accounting, all it leads to is disillusionment and desolation. And there is the imagination that glowed in the story of the Magi, the imagination of the eager heart that believes in the shining stars of God's new suggestion for this earth—and, seeing those stars, will follow where they lead. But above and back of all, there is the remembrance of that which the Magi found: namely, that life begins to be redeemed by God only when there comes into it something which releases all its pure emotions. If any man is growing less sensitive to the quivering human implications involved in all his daily choices and his daily contacts, that man is drifting down to spiritual death. And wherever, on the other hand, there are those who are trying to keep their hearts alert to the subtle currents of human joy and pain, who are trying to be more quick in understanding, more wise in sympathy, and more alert to help, *there* are those who have learned the ultimate lesson of God. As the Magi found in Bethlehem, it is only when love is born into life that life begins to be redeemed.

XIV

MEN OF POWER

For thine is the kingdom . . .

THUS, since the first century, the Christian Church has been accustomed to conclude the Lord's Prayer. In the way that Jesus taught his first disciples, we lift up the hallowed name of God; we pray that His kingdom may come, His will be done on earth, as it is in heaven. And then at the end we say: "For thine *is* the kingdom, and the power, and the glory, for ever."

Those are short words and easy to say; but do we really believe that they are true? The world is filled with many kinds of power, the power of things, the power of human strategems, the power of evil. Often we are tempted to live as though the physical and tangible facts which press so close upon us were the only reality. These seem so near, and the invisible realities of God seem so hard to grasp. What do we mean, then, when we say, "Thine is the power"?

We may well try to imagine what the Lord's Prayer meant when it first fell from the lips of Jesus. That will give us a background of thought against which presently to measure our own. One day somewhere in Galilee the disciples asked him, "Master, teach us to pray," and then he began his immortal answer: "When ye pray, say 'Our Father.'" What were their surroundings then, we wonder. Perhaps Jesus had taken his disciples with him into the solitude of the hills, as we know that sometimes he did at the end of a crowded day. It may have been at evening with the shadows falling, and the tinkle of bells floating over quiet fields as the sheep went home to the folds. It may have been at night-time with white moonlight spreading its path across the waters of the Lake of Galilee, that same path of moonlight along which the eyes of men in every generation have gazed, and on which their dreams have followed as upon a misty way that leads beyond the stars. Or it may be that it was not at evening or in the night-time, but in the morning that he gave them the Lord's Prayer—

at morning when the dew was on the meadows and the fields, and the larks were singing, and on the horizon the snow-clad crest of Mount Hermon was blended with the colors of the dawn. At such a time, and in such a scene as one of these, perhaps, he taught them to say "Our Father," and helped them thus to put into expression that awe and wonder and hope and love of which every man is somehow conscious at certain moments when he feels the beauty of the world and the greatness of life, and senses through the things he sees a vaster Presence before which his soul bows down. "Thine is the power," their souls might well say when they had finished the prayer, echoing the great faith of its petitions thus as with a song. But were they so sure of it when they went back again among the rude and jostling facts of the human crowd? Their world, like ours, was filled with many competing kinds of power. Along the roads of Galilee they could see now and then a Roman legion marching, cleaving its arrogant way through the narrow streets of villages, and passing out again into the country-side, where the dust rose above the heavy rhythm of its feet. Rome had power, power that was often ruthless and sudden as lightning, power to carry men off and chain them as slaves to the oar-banks in the galleys, or to crucify them, as, more than once when rebellions had broken out in Galilee, they had been crucified for every passer-by to see. And in the larger towns there were men who were growing rich. They also had power, power to build their fine houses and to fill them with luxury, power to make the ordinary people servants to their pleasure. Up in Jerusalem, the capital, there were other men who had power, power of possession and authority. They governed the life of Israel both in its civil and ecclesiastical aspects. They were nominally the leaders of the Church; but they seemed more interested in the advantages of this world than in the ideals of a world unseen. In this nation of theirs as they actually knew it, the disciples saw many things flourishing which had in them no likeness of the divine. Yet Jesus had taught them to pray to "Our Father which art in heaven." He had bidden them believe in Him whose will is righteousness and whose spirit is redeeming love. It was possible to believe that way when under the spell of wonder they looked at the sunrise or the stars, or when in the stillness they listened to the voice of Jesus. But where were the signs of God's rule in the hurly-burly of everyday affairs? What did it mean to say *there* "Thine is the kingdom"?

As we go forward to seek an answer to that question, which is ours as it was also theirs, we shall first consider more particularly that which we have already hinted, namely, the contrary sorts of power which this world seems often to present. Then we shall go on to ask what it is that we most want power for, and then finally, we shall try to see how and where we do secure it.

I

The earliest sort of power which this world knew was the power of brute strength and violence. In the beginning the strong man was the man with a club. Physical stature and physical brawn were the things that mattered. If a man were big enough to beat others into submission, then he was master. The raw and rude conflict of the cave-man with his fellow-dwellers in the cave has passed on, in the course of human history, into forms of conflict less individualistic and less crude; but its essential nature has not vanished from our human race. We have measurably tamed the individual, but we have not tamed those aggregates which we call nations. We have put the mark of Cain upon the single murderer; but we can still glorify the mass-murder which we call war. Most of our public monuments in every country are to the warriors and the men of conquest—not to those who have created life, but to those who have destroyed it; not to those who have built up friendships, but to those who have battered down foes. We can exult in the messages of statesmen who rouse the enthusiasm of the crowd by the gospel of the big stick. We can still breed our militarists who genuinely believe that the only power is in guns, our generals and admirals who may be humble Christians in one aspect of their character and are unvarnished pagans in the wholly other aspect of their conviction. They may say the Lord's Prayer in church; but they do not believe it outside. If with half of themselves they say, "Trust God," with the other half they say, "and keep your powder dry"! And it is upon this latter emphasis that all their weight is cast. "Thine is the kingdom." Yes, that is all very well as a phrase in the sanctuary or as music to be chanted by a choir; but the real kingdom, they think, belongs not to the invisible potencies of righteousness and love; the real kingdom belongs to men who have in their hands the heaviest weapons with which to seize and hold it.

The second way to power in human experience has been through shrewdness. Little by little the plane of contact shifted. As men developed their brains, it was no longer the man of brawn who necessarily had the final advantage in the struggle for preëminence. The shrewder man could outwit his less nimble-minded neighbor. He could gradually so establish the rules of the accepted game that he could win. This is very obvious in the business world to which our modern thinking is accustomed. The prizes men struggle for are not determined in an arena where the winner is the heaviest gladiator. They are determined in the market place where the man of most foresight, of quickest initiative and of surest calculation will be the victor, even though physically he may be insignificant in comparison with others whom he defeats. It is this sort of power which the more recent generations in our Western world have pursued. In the glittering years preceding 1929, the tide of interest among the most ambitious young men was setting toward business. The majority of college men seemed to want to be stock-brokers, bankers and corporation lawyers. They wanted wealth, not only for the sake of wealth itself in its more tangible aspects of luxury and abundance, but wealth in its aspect of power. The dominant men in our civilization were more and more supposed to be the great financial executives. Religion was looked upon with a sort of inherited respect, and yet also with half-patronizing tolerance. The business world easily grew indignant if the Church meddled —for so the word was—in material affairs. The pulpit was to stick to "the simple gospel," by which was meant a gospel so mild, so lukewarm, and so remote, that it would never be disturbing. There was little consciousness that religion ought to be the pervasive power of a sovereign Spirit, power as Jesus himself said, like the leaven which should be kneaded into all the material of life until the whole is leavened. "No," thought the shrewd man into whose hands it appeared that our modern world had more and more put the scepter of authority, "let the Church teach our children with its decorous Sunday school, and be a place where our wives can go on Sunday, and where we may appear once a year at Easter or now and then as honorary pall-bearers at the funeral of a friend. Let the Church have its proper liturgies for the worship of God, but let it have no presumptions as to carrying the mention of God where this does not belong." In other words, religion was to be a pretty ornament, but not a thing of power. Power belonged to the men of affairs who played the practical game according to their own rules—rules, incidentally, which in recent years when they have been brought to light have shattered the reputations of more than one man of high financial rank who formerly had been supposed to be a citizen of integrity and honor. Theirs was the kingdom; theirs was the control—so our time thought—of the forces in this world which really mattered.

But latterly there is beginning to appear another mood. The collapse of material fortunes in the economic earthquake which has shaken all the ground of our Western life has set in motion processes of disillusionment. Men are beginning to wonder whether there is strength and ability enough anywhere to grapple with the dark facts which surround us. Nations are being driven in a world contagion of fear toward increased armaments, than which there could be no madder nor more ultimately suicidal policy; but even those who clamor most for armaments do not presume to suggest that anything constructive can be carried out through them. They are only the defenses which panic erects as the supposed bulwark against worse disaster. And certainly our time has lost confidence in the authority of shrewdness. If out of these hard years nothing else which was good had come, this at least is good: that we have been cured of our servile and almost superstitious awe of the supposed wizards of Wall Street. But there is a danger that our disillusionment will go too far. We may begin to think that only fate and chance are powerful, that men are only strutting puppets in a dark chaos of forces, material and moral, which move them here and there. The oncoming generation, and particularly the young men and women eager to find work and a place of usefulness, who find nothing but a

blank, are looking upon their world with sombre eyes. The
danger is that they may shrug their shoulders in hopelessness to
find a meaning anywhere. They conclude that our universe is
presided over by nothing but a senseless fate. Not God, not
Christ, but stupid chance, they think, is king.

II

We pass now to the second part of our consideration. In the
ultimate analysis, what do we want power for?

As we examine life and our estimates of it, I think we are
moved to confess that many of us instinctively have sought power
for the wrong ends, and therefore with the wrong interpretation.
We have wanted power for the sake of building up the outer
framework of our existence. We have too much ignored the fact
that life depends, not upon externals, but upon the spiritual
realities that are within.

The warrior has always made that blunder. He has thought
that if he could compel men to submission, he could cement an
empire that was proof against destruction. But all he could compel was the submission of men's bodies; and when his compulsion was withdrawn, then all the unwilling elements he had
brought together fell apart. The brutal conquerors of early
centuries—the Assyrians, the Babylonians, and their like—imagined that they could establish their dominance by ravaging cities,
desolating great areas of the earth, and bringing home multitudes
of captives; but one after another their empires crumbled, until
there are only a few mounds of dust in the midst of the desert
to tell where once they stood. The Romans had a glimmering
of a larger truth, and their empire had such relative permanence
as it attained through its cultivation of the willing allegiance
which by its relative good government it managed to enlist. The
British Commonwealth has embodied that truth more surely
perhaps than any great federation of peoples had embodied it
before, and its chances for security in the future are in exactly
inverse ratio to its compulsion and in direct ratio to the unforced
loyalty it can win among those who are partners in its spirit.
Little by little the world perceives that the only way power can

be won is not through outward duress but through the response
that arises from within.

We are perceiving also that the sort of power which we supposed that wealth could fashion is not lasting. Our illusion lay
in the supposition that, if men could build for themselves the
house of a material civilization which should be very large and
very glittering, then the gladness of those who lived in it would
be assured. But we have discovered that the kind of financial
power which can build up fortunes cannot build up the fabric
of anything beautiful in our human selves. What good does it
do to erect a palace if misery inhabits it? What have we achieved
if around us is the great structure of our material pride, and
within us is bewilderment, emptiness, and unrest. For the sort of
thing they have aimed at, our financial geniuses and our imperial men of affairs have had astonishing ability. But what they
did aim at was largely brittle and superficial, and what they have
been able to do has by itself had very little power to give men
the inspiration by which alone they can want to live.

The reason we have so often ignored God and imagined that
we could do without Him is that we have been obsessed with
the external show and blinded to the inward facts which matter.
We thought we did not need God in order to win dominance,
and indeed, that God was rather in our way. We could build our
empires, magnify our national advantages, increase our selfish
trade and commerce, without any reference to Him who is spirit
and whose will is righteousness and peace. The military boards
of strategy, the soldiers and the diplomats, could accomplish that.
We also thought we had no need of God to build our skyscrapers, to invent our machines, and to set our myriad factories
running. Inventors and executives could see to that. They had
the purpose, and they had the power, and no matters of the
spirit had to enter into their calculations. All that was true as far
as it went; but what we are learning now is that where it went
was nowhere at all when measured in terms of the final satisfaction of our minds and souls. What we are perceiving at least
dimly is that there is another sort of power, a power that may be
very silent, and that makes no vulgar show, and yet is the only
power which accomplishes the dearest ends we want.

When we say that in so many words, we may abstractly admit it. If we can see it in pictures, we can understand more vividly how true it is.

I remember once in another city happening to pass a large piece of open ground early on a certain morning when the circus had just come to town. There all its paraphernalia was being unloaded from a freight train backed into a railroad siding. The great cages which held the animals, heavy with their lumbering wheels, their thick wooden framework and their iron bars, were being taken from the train and rolled to their places in the circle over which would stand the circus tent. A herd of elephants was there already on the ground, and some of these elephants were being used to push the cages. One of them would be led to the back of a cage. He would put his great forehead against it, plant his feet in the ground, and shove; and the heavy truck would start rolling to where it was supposed to be. For that purpose the elephant was all-powerful; but it is obvious that the kind of power which the elephant had would be of no avail in different and more vital matters. Out in the grasses of a meadow is the nest of a skylark. In the nest are eggs that wait to be hatched. What power would an elephant have for that? But the tiny body and the fragile wings of the lark itself are powerful there. The elephant could destroy the nest, but only the lark could quicken the eggs to life.

Here is the keyboard of an organ, with all its delicate and subtle mechanism; or here might be a violin with its strings and bow. Down in the coal-mine somewhere is a man who physically may be a Hercules. With his pick-ax he can hew the coal out of its rocky seams; he could take an ordinary man and break him in two with the iron of his muscles; in anything which is measured physically, he is powerful. But what power would his great muscles and his gnarled hands have to call music from the keyboard of the organ, or to fret with delicate fingering the strings of a violin? For that, his power turns to weakness. The touch, not only of the great musicians, but of the least beginner in the world of music, has in these things a strength in comparison with which his untutored brawn is only weakness.

Here is a child. What is the power which can bring that

child to the fulness of its possibilities? The strength of the mason and the carpenter can build a house for it to live in. The huge forces moving in a locomotive may bring to the city the food by which that child is fed. The club of a policeman may keep the house he lives in from violence without. But all these things together, though they may safeguard existence, cannot give that child his highest life. In order for the house he lives in to be a home, there must be the wonder of a woman's love. For the child's full growth in happiness, in confidence, and in serenity of soul, the gentle spirit of his mother is more powerful than all the world beside.

What we believe in, therefore, will depend on what we are conscious that we want. If we want only the shell of things, we can build it out of crude energies; but if we want the power to bring the thing which is sterile into life, the power that wakes the world to song, the power that is sufficient for the unfolding of the miracle of the human soul, then we must go forward to understand what the faith of Christendom has always meant when it lifted up its eyes to God and said, "The power is thine."

III

As the climax of our thinking, we ask ourselves now what that power of God is which Jesus knew, and lived by, and on which he taught his disciples to depend.

We see the answer beginning to shape itself in the first days of Jesus' ministry. He goes into the wilderness, as the gospel puts it "to be tempted of the devil," or, in other words, to face the contrary alternatives of the spirit of God and the spirit of this world. The voice of the tempter bade him believe in the kind of power which our crude measurements are apt to value most. He should believe in miracles, and desire that his Father should intervene for him by miracles. He should believe in weapons of compulsion, and seek the world's successes by the world's means. But these temptations Jesus put behind him. He understood that because God is spirit His kingdom can be established only through the long ways of the spirit's working. He would dare to believe that one thing alone must be victorious, and that is the love of God embodied in the perfect obedience of a human life. Before that at last, though it might be a long last, he believed that all the barriers of ignorance, of hate, and of sin, would fall. Radiant, therefore, in his accepted choice, he came out of the wilderness to begin his public ministry. The love of God which he was permitted to express should be no sentimental thing. It could be relentless with God's unflinching pressure upon men to see and to be their best. He would make no compromise with deliberate sin, but he would be infinitely tender to the self-forgetting and the self-giving. Jesus did not ask for any of those accessories which men so often mistake for power. He did not covet rank nor wealth. He would simply be himself, a self of utter consecration, a self that was empty of self, in order that his Father's life might fill it. He knew that the choice he made might lead to crucifixion. Men are often afraid of the terrible power of the spirit, afraid of goodness in their midst, afraid of the white light of the heavenly truth, afraid of the heavenly love; and being afraid, they strike out passionately to shield themselves, killing the thing they fear. So from the beginning Jesus foresaw the possibility of his crucifixion. As the days went by, he saw that which had seemed possible becoming sure; but he never faltered in his belief. Whether death came soon or late to his human body did not so much matter. The victory of God in his triumphant soul did matter. Against every contradiction of sin and circumstance he still trusted that the Spirit of God, with which his soul was radiant, could build the only kingdom which was worth building on this earth.

Do you see what that means? It means a challenge to many of our crude estimates of power. It means that we, if we are Christians, are confronted with the question as to whether we will trust what Jesus trusted and believe that goodness and truth and loving-kindness are the only things which are strong enough to create the results which this world waits for. In the midst of that question, there is a cross. The real power may have to proceed to its unfolding through a crucifixion. It was so with the love of God as it was incarnated in Jesus. It is so with the love of God wherever it appears in this still imperfect and rebellious earth. The kingdom of the Spirit, the only kingdom which is worth winning, is to be won by long spiritual courage, and often at great cost. One of the spiritual warriors of our generation put the truth in his flaming way when he wrote:

I believe in God the Father Almighty is not a statement of fact but a confession of faith. It does not declare the existence of an absolute Almighty Monarch Who sits upon a throne and moves the world by His nod: it professes our faith in suffering, striving, but all-conquering spirit of perfect love, Who through pain and tribulation, which torture Him, now is working His purpose of perfection out. The first clause of the Creed is not a cold, theological statement of fact, it is a warrior's battle-cry. It is said by the soldiers of God, standing at attention with their faces turned towards God's altar and the dawn of better days.

"Standing at attention with their faces toward the dawn of better days!" That is what we do when we say the climactic words of the Lord's Prayer, "Thine is the kingdom." We believe in the possibility of better days, for one thing, for the relationships between the nations. It may be that we can awake from the long and bloody obsession of the centuries that power will ultimately come to a people through violence and war. For a little while, that specious delusion seems to be reality; but in a while—and no long while as measured by the ages—"they that take the sword perish by the sword." It is time for Christian people in every nation to begin to believe that the only enduring power anywhere is the power of integrity, justice, and good-will. The time has come when multitudes of Christian people in every land must make it plain that we will have no more to do with the old paganism which sets people periodically at one another's throats; that we will have no more war even if we have to go to prison for it; that we are going to dare the great conviction that, not through new armaments, but through a new spirit, must power come.

A parallel conviction is needed in the sphere of politics. Where is power here, men ask. And often their answer is that power is in an organization, even if the organization be corrupt; power is in the shrewd manipulation of greed for its own advantage; power is in the hands of the clever, the unscrupulous, and the conscienceless. But now and then, praise be to God, there rises a man who has the lonely courage to believe that there is another and a greater power. He comes to a city, as Samuel Seabury came to New York, at first like a prophet without honor. He comes to say that there is in the heart of the ordinary man a desire for decency and honor and righteousness that sooner or later will prevail; and when that conviction is let loose by some one who has held it, not as a tepid idea, but as a flaming passion, it is irresistible. Little by little, it may be by slow advances and through temporary defeats, our communities can and do move forward to higher planes as men carry into action the faith they profess when they look to God and say, "Thine is the power."

Believe that also in relation to the Church. What makes a parish powerful, you may ask. And some will give the answer in terms far short of truth. They will say that a parish is powerful because of its endowments, because of the number of its wealthy and well-known parishioners, because of the numbers on its rolls. But the real issue goes deeper than any of these things. Is a parish expressing in itself something of that redeeming love of God which Jesus carried through even to crucifixion? Is it creating men and women who are humble before the highest, penitent for their own sins and pitiful to the ignorance and sin of the world, ready to consecrate themselves to the service of Christ, not in mere convention, but in their offering up of what they have and what they are for him to use? God help us to look beyond the surface of things and see what is too often the invisible reality of the spirit. God help us to understand that our business here is not merely to make "church people" but Christed men and women, and to know that if really we have become Christians, then whether we be rich or poor, many or few, we shall be a part of Him in whom alone is power.

Finally and most intimately, believe this in your personal contacts with those individuals who are most near and dear to you. What do you think will avail to build a happy friendship or to make a happy home? Will it be money, social prominence, popularity, success? No, for all these things, glittering though they be, are too weak to satisfy the real hunger of the human heart. There is only one power which can build up the fabric of a life and of a love which will be proof against all change of circumstance, and that is the power of the spirit of God at work in us. Believe then in the value of all your unseen spiritual resources. Believe in sympathy and gentleness and kindness. Stop grieving too much over material losses or worrying over what you think you may lose tomorrow. Be glad in what life can never lose. Remember that if the greatness of God is working through your spirit then those who look to you will find such sufficiency that, whatever outward things may happen, they will still think that they have everything because they have you. Turn your eyes from the appearance to the reality, and dare to say to the near God, the true God, the God in your own soul, "The power is *thine*."

XV

THE OFFICIAL WHO WOULD NOT DARE

Pilate saith unto him, What is truth?

St. John xviii:38

PILATE. That is an old name, belonging to a figure who moved in a far-off world. At the first suggestion it seems remote from any modern interest of our own. We are preoccupied with a thousand instant things. We are involved in the living issues of our immediate time. What difference can there be to us in what a Roman official of nineteen hundred years ago thought, or did not think?

But the truth is that it does make a difference. There are certain great records of human life and literature which are never out of date. Shakespeare is never out of date. The men and women whom the genius of the great dramatist created reveal to us realities of human life which are independent of time. The Bible is never out of date. Its characters are involved in those webs of destiny which are woven of the same threads that constitute our own. When we ponder what a man like Pilate did or failed to do, being confronted with a crisis of his mind and spirit, we see exemplified the same eternal moral forces with which we also have to reckon.

I

The scene in which Pilate played a leading role was one of the supremely dramatic instances of history. All those who have ever seen the Passion Play in Oberammergau will have had this brought home to their imagination in a way which is thenceforth unforgettable. There on the great stage is visualized again the event in the court of the Roman procurator of Jerusalem, now more than nineteen hundred years ago. But the account in the Gospels is in itself sufficient to recreate the scene before the inward eye, if our imagination is at all alert. Jesus has been seized by the temple guard who with their torches had invaded the shadowed silence of the garden of Gethsemane, where he had gone to pray. He has been taken to the house of Caiaphas, the High Priest, examined by the hastily summoned and excited Sanhedrin, condemned to death—so far as they had the power of condemnation—for what they considered blasphemy. But any verdict of the Sanhedrin depended upon the consent of the Roman governor. Therefore, as soon as it was day, the priests, with a mob of the people at their heels, carried Jesus to Pilate. The procurator, as was his custom when Jerusalem was crowded for the great feasts, had come up from Caesarea, his usual residence, to his official seat at the Tower of Antonia on the height of Jerusalem, next to the temple. There into the open court of the Roman's house, the priests and their retainers come, leading Jesus bound in their midst. They send a message to Pilate, asking his appearance, and Pilate comes out upon the balcony overlooking the court. With half-contemptuous hostility he surveys the turbulent crowd. It is another instance, he thinks, of some fanatical excitement among these provincials, whom, as a Roman, he despises. He sees the prisoner in their midst. "What accusation do you bring against this man?" he says.

The priests knew quite well that their accusation would have no standing in a Roman court. As to Jesus' blasphemy, the procurator would be indifferent. They must build their complaint on other grounds. They must force Pilate into thinking that Jesus is dangerous, and compel Pilate to lay upon him the condemnation which Rome was certain to visit upon any one who could be tainted with the suggestion of sedition. But quickest of all it would be if they could force the procurator out of hand to agree to the verdict they themselves had rendered and endorse without further examination their demand for Jesus' death. "If he were not a malefactor," they replied, "we would not have brought him to you."

Pilate was angered by the effrontery of that. He said, "Take him then and judge him according to your law." There was veiled insult in his words. If the matter was so trivial that they could not give any specific accusation, their Jewish law was good enough to deal with it. Then the priests had to admit what they wanted. They wanted the death penalty, and they themselves were not allowed to inflict it.

Pilate then turns his back upon the crowd and goes from the balcony into his judgment hall, and has Jesus brought in where he may examine him alone. He looks with curiosity, and doubtless with some impatient bewilderment, upon this strange man of Nazareth who has somehow contrived to stir such passion in Jerusalem. "So you are a king!" he says. "Are you a king?"

"Do you say this of yourself, or did others tell you so?" Jesus asks him. Scornfully Pilate replies. "Am I a Jew? Your own nation and the chief priests have delivered you to me. What have you done?" "My kingdom is not of this world," Jesus answers. "If my kingdom were of this world, then would my followers fight, that I should not be delivered up, but my kingdom is not from hence." "Are you a king then?" Pilate persists, and Jesus answers, "You say that I am a king. To this end was I born, and for this cause came I into this world, that I should bear witness unto the truth. Every one that is of the truth heareth my voice."

The Roman looks at him incredulously. What bandying of words is this? A kingdom of the truth! He shrugs his shoulders. "What is truth?" he says.

Then he appears again upon the balcony, leading Jesus with him, and lifts his hand for silence. The clamor of the crowd ceases, waiting to see what he will say. He stands there, clothed with the tremendous consciousness of Roman power. In ample ways, his word is law. A garrison of the Roman legionaries is there to enforce his edicts. Morally, he can be authoritative too. He has the intuitive feeling that, whatever else this man of Nazareth may be, he is not guilty of any offense which makes him worthy of death. He sees and despises the ugly malignity of the crowd. If he will, he can settle the whole matter with a word. He can pronounce Jesus acquitted, order his legionaries to clear the court-yard, and have the matter at an end. This, if he be a brave man and a true man, he can do. But secretly Pilate nurses a fear. Beneath his cynical harshness, there is a calculating hesitation. One never knows what may happen with these unruly crowds. They may break into a tumult. They may do worse than that. They may send accusations against him to Rome. As an office-holder protecting his own interest, Pilate does not want to have his record questioned.

He points to Jesus. "I find in him no fault at all," he says, with a feigned decisiveness. But instantly the crowd breaks out into angry protest. "He stirs up the people," they cry, "teaching throughout all Jewry, beginning from Galilee to this place."

"From Galilee!" Ah, there is a happy possibility in that. Pilate's mind seizes instantly upon the suggestion which the words convey. So Jesus is from Galilee. Herod is tetrarch of Galilee, and Herod ought to have jurisdiction over Galileans. It happens luckily that Herod is in Jerusalem. Pilate determines that he will send Jesus to Herod and be rid of this highly disturbing matter.

So he does send Jesus to Herod; but Herod promptly sends him back again. He says that this case is no concern of his. Let Pilate see to it.

Again, therefore, Pilate is forced to confront the issue which he had sought to evade. He thinks of another stratagem. He wants to release Jesus; but he does not wish to take the responsibility of doing so. He will be safe if he can manoeuver the priests and the people into the position of asking his release. "You have a custom," he says, "that I should release to you some one prisoner at the time of the Passover. Do you want, therefore, that I release to you the king of the Jews?" Instantly they answer with fierce repudiation. There was a man in the Roman prison named Barabbas, a highwayman who was popular with the crowd just because he symbolized the hatred they had against the Roman authority. "Not this man," they cry, "but Barabbas. Release to us Barabbas!"

Pilate is being driven from one expedient to another in his shifty attempt to evade the positive decision which, now that he has once shown weakness, is becoming increasingly difficult. He has one more effort left to make. He hands Jesus over to the soldiers for the brutal preliminary punishment of scourging, and then presently he brings Jesus forth again, wounded and bleeding from the strokes of the scourge, and on his head a crown of thorns which the soldiers have woven and thrust there. "Behold the man," says Pilate.

But the priests and the people are in no mood for compassion.

Neither are they in any mood to stand in awe of Pilate now. They have seen the fact of his irresoluteness, and in pursuit of their purpose they have become like wolves, implacable. "Crucify him, crucify him!" they cry. With a last fading effort, Pilate tries to parley and persuade. To such an ignominious pass has he come, who began with every advantage of power on his side. But the crowd will not listen. "If you let this man go, you are not Caesar's friend," they cry. "Whoever makes himself a king, speaks against Caesar." At that implied threat, Pilate surrenders. With one angry gesture he thinks to close the matter. "Bring me a basin of water," he says to one of his servants. There on the praetorium in sight of the accusers of Jesus, he dramatically washes his hands of the whole question. "It is your affair," he says, "take him and crucify him if you choose. I am innocent of his blood."

But he was not innocent. Not so easily could he escape this critical relationship into which he had been brought. He could wash his hands, but he could not wash away the facts. His spiritual fate was tied with that of Jesus that day, and he could not disentangle it by words alone. He could not be innocent of what was going to happen by merely announcing that he preferred to be considered so.

For the truth was that Pilate could have protected Jesus if he had determined to. It was not that he willed evil, but that he hesitated and flinched at powerfully willing good. He did not desire that Jesus should die, but he let him die; and the inescapable reality of moral cause and effect made him none the less actually, even though less malevolently, guilty than those who forced what he through his compromise permitted.

Pilate is a symbol of an issue which will recur as long as life and time shall last. Always there comes to men the temptation to try to twist facts into some sort of appearance which will ease their conscience in some moral crisis which they have failed to meet. We do not like to feel guilty for results which we know are evil, and if we have not desired them we may piously protest that of course we are not guilty. But what of the evil which we may not have desired, but which we have done nothing to prevent? What of those crucifixions of the spirit of Christ in our world's actual life which we may not have deliberately promoted, but against which we have set up no barrier of an unflinching consecration?

To get the full force of this question, we must distinguish between the glorified Christ of our religious tradition and the spirit of Christ in the form in which it actually presents itself for our decision. We are prone to think that any condemnation of Christ by ourselves is not a live possibility. We honor him too much for that. How could we or any one else in his senses deliberately condemn Jesus Christ, the Saviour, and the revealer of God? But in the time of Pilate, the significant fact was that Jesus did not appear to men in any such convincing aspect as that, and he does not necessarily appear in that way now. Did the chief priests, or the crowd in Jerusalem, or Pilate, consider that they saw in him the Son of God? Emphatically they did not. They saw in him a troublesome and perplexing person, an insistent force pressing toward decisions which they did not want to make, a danger to their comfortable order of accepted things, one altogether too inconvenient to be suffered to exist. He had gone into the temple with no official authorization and had driven out the traders who filled its courts with their greedy traffic; and all those commercial interests which he invaded were filled with the same unreasoning anger with which men are always filled when their profits are attacked. He had challenged complacent leaders of the church by spiritual ideals which they knew they were not trying to maintain, and they resented his exposure of their worldly-minded compromise. He had disappointed the crowd which followed after him, as he said once, "for the loaves and fishes." The general feeling about him was that he made everybody uncomfortable. That was why one group condemned him, and why Pilate let him be condemned.

Consider how this same Jesus comes, as a great spiritual fact, into the midst of our living world. We imagine sometimes that we have dealt with him when we have come into the churches erected in his name, looked decorously at representations of him in stained glass windows, and confessed his name in ancient formularies that have no critical touch with modern life. But we cannot thus be quit of our reckoning with him. The real Jesus, the living and decisive expression of the reality of God, walks beside us in our everyday affairs, and in our vital choices we must decide what we will do with him. He is the challenge of the spirit as against the interests of the flesh; and in that distinction which he compels, we must determine whether or not, like the traders in the temple, we will cling to our questionable profits and our unscrupulous money-making and money-keeping when these do violence to God's spirit in our hearts. He is the challenge of that which is right against that which is merely popular; but when we refuse to stand by our ideals if our social set or the public opinion generally goes clamoring the other way, then we have turned the spirit of Jesus over to his new crucifixion. He is the challenge of the hazardous against the safe; and when in our private or our public lives we surrender to the tame little compromises which inwardly we despise, rather than hold to those things which will take much courage and much fortitude to prove, then again, like Pilate, we hand Jesus over to his enemies to be put to death. When we look deep into our hearts, we know well that by the judgments we instinctively pass in those moral discriminations which represent our actual estimate of Jesus, we ourselves are judged.

Jesus was on trial before Pilate for his life. But, meanwhile, before that quiet figure, Pilate had been on trial for his soul. We likewise may be on trial now.

II

"What is truth?" That was the half-indifferent, half-cynical question of the Roman. He knew the realities of the other world; but what reality was in this inner world which called itself *truth*?

"What is truth?" You did not know the answer to that question, Pilate. You doubted whether there was an answer; and whether there might be one or not, you did not care. But meanwhile the truth was working, and certain great aspects of it have registered in ways which are for ever plain.

1. In the first place, this was truth:—that in this life of ours there is an inexorable moral cause and effect by which small choices will come some day to their decisive climax. What a man

will be in the hour of unexpected destiny depends upon what he has been through the slow precedents of inconspicuous days.

Pontius Pilate came to Judaea as procurator in 26 A.D. to succeed Valerius Gratus. We do not know a great deal about his record; but we know enough to tell us what sort of man he was. During the early years he caused the standards of the Roman legionaries to be set up in the precincts of the temple. This outraged the sensibilities of the Jews, because to them it was blasphemy to allow any pagan symbols to be there. A delegation went down to Caesarea and besieged Pilate with their protests. He taunted them with a cruel malevolence. He kept them waiting, and then he refused to grant their petition. He had no insight into their feeling, no care for what to them was a matter of conscience. Nevertheless, at last he yielded; not because he wanted to, not because he was convinced, and not because he cared any more than he had cared in the beginning; but their determination wore him down. They threatened then to appeal to Rome against him, and he weakened before that danger. Time-server and opportunist, he could bluster when he seemed to have the advantage on his side, and surrender when his own lack of principle made him inwardly afraid.

There is one other reference to him in the Gospels. Jesus spoke once of certain Galileans whose blood Pilate mingled with their sacrifices. Apparently there had once been some disturbance in the temple and Pilate had suppressed it with a brutality that involved bloodshed. Evidently he was a man who had no ultimate conscience as to what he did. His last decision was always the thing which he thought was safest for himself.

Yet seemingly this man, evil in many aspects as he was, still had his points of sensitiveness. He seems to have been impressed by Jesus. He felt himself in contact with a greater spirit who made him uneasy. He discriminated between Jesus and the fanatical crowd clamoring for his crucifixion. If he could have had his own way without danger, he would have delivered this man of Nazareth; but he saw that that could not be. He could not save Jesus without risk to himself, and that kind of risk for the sake of conscience was the thing of which Pilate had become incapable.

Of course he did not know that day, nor had he known in the earlier days, that a time would ever come when his ability, or inability, to follow his better instincts would make so much difference. Most of his business had been about matters which had in them no inherent dignity, and Pilate had cultivated nothing in himself which gave dignity to them. He was giving orders to a soldiery accustomed to rough work. He was dealing with a machinery of taxation in which there was much greed and sordidness on the one hand and sullen resistance on the other. He was judging ordinary criminals whom he did not deign to try particularly to understand. In other words, he was doing what men in every age are tempted to do, and that is to treat common responsibilities as though there were nothing in them which is not common. It is easy to grow cynical about the ordinary affairs of life, easy to play the game in business or politics according to what seem the prevailing rules, to despise ideals as either unintelligible or impractical, and to let the ugly aspects of humanity breed a sort of slow contempt for the meaning of human life in general. Pilate little imagined that one day he should be confronted with life's supreme meaning focussed in one great witness who should test his recognition and test his ability to choose and to decide. But that is the way in which destiny may often work. If a man could see at the beginning, before his conscience has become indifferent, the great occasion which may test his soul, he might rise to it adequately; but he must learn little by little to be ready, or else never be ready at all. He must school himself to look beneath the surface of life with the sympathy and imagination which are seeking the finer values there. He must be giving a dignity of his own to occasions which have in themselves no dignity. He must bring pure motives, clean thoughts, and a generous desire to the everyday responsibilities which might be sordid unless they were spiritualized by him. If he does this, then in some sudden unheralded time, when he is confronted with the dangerous necessity of being true to a friend, or brave to defend at all costs some person unjustly maligned and assailed, or steady in championship of some cause against which the crowd is howling, he will rise to heroic stature. But if he has *not* done this, if into the ordinary days he has brought no extraordinary spirit, then in his hour of crisis he will learn the perilous truth of the moral cause and effect which he has ignored. Like Pilate he will surrender at his great point of opportunity, because he has never believed that all the little meannesses of everyday motives would ever be set in the blinding light of some great decision which would show how terribly they mattered.

2. And the second aspect of the truth made evident in Pilate was this: that there is a kingdom whose reality lies not in things seen but in the things unseen. Pilate believed definitely enough in one kind of kingdom. He believed in a kingdom which was represented in the iron rule of Rome. He believed in armies; he believed in tax-gatherers; he believed in all that machinery of material force by which Rome exacted the unwilling obedience of its subjects. But a kingdom whose realm is in the mind and heart, a kingdom whose resources are invisible—at the suggestion of this the hard lips of the Roman curled with incredulity. From the lips of Jesus these things had a momentary hypnotic sound; but Pilate, man of the world, would not take them seriously. Was it not plain that this was only so much empty chatter? Where was any power in Jesus? Listen to the crowd clamoring for his blood! Look at the crown of thorns set derisively on his head! Meanwhile, he, Pilate, had power which would still be power after this strange man had gone to his crucifixion. With a note of anger in his impatience, he said to Jesus, "So you will not answer me. Don't you know that I have power to crucify you, and power to release you?"

So it seemed. But what of the fact? The body of Jesus was crucified. But what then? Who has emerged victorious from that meeting of personalities in the Roman judgment hall? Well, look at the world and see—the real world, the world of ideas, thoughts, purposes, and great passions of men's souls which go flaming along the centuries past all the dust-heaps into which the proudest earthly empires crumble and go down. Jesus has emerged dominant. His spirit haunts the imagination of mankind. The sovereignty of his spirit lays hold of the noblest men and women in every generation. His head is crowned, not with thorns, but with the everlastingness of all the stars. And, meanwhile, what of Pilate? The fleeting authority of his procuratorship was like a feeble candle guttering into smoke. The empire which he represented is only the memory of an ancient grandeur long since dead. And the very name of Pilate is saved from oblivion only because of its tragic association with the name of Jesus. Like an uneasy ghost, he follows in the shadow of the man whom he thought that he could judge. There is a legend that Pilate's restless spirit, wandering the earth, came once to a company of people who were reciting some great proclamation which he could not understand, but in the midst of which, to his amazement, he caught the echo of his own name; and, drawing nearer and listening, he heard that this was what they said:

> I believe in him who died,
> By Pontius Pilate crucified.

And it is only because it is remembered that Jesus suffered under Pontius Pilate that the sinister figure of the Roman is prevented from being buried utterly in his forgotten grave.

Yes, Pilate; there are two kinds of kingdoms. There is the kind in which you believed and in which most men believe, the kingdom of riches, power, material achievements, greed and gain. That kingdom blinds and dazzles men for a little space of time, and then, together with its worshipers, it vanishes. But there is another kind of kingdom which you did not know, but which it is possible for all men to know and to inherit. It is the kingdom of high thoughts, great purposes, unselfish loyalties and exalted love. That kingdom every soul can possess inviolate, and in that kingdom the imperishable riches lie. Shakespeare understood the truth when in his *Henry the Eighth* he pictured Cardinal Wolsey, after he had been stripped of all the wealth and privilege which once he had thought to be the substance of his life. Cromwell, his follower says to him, "How goes your grace?" And Wolsey answers Cromwell:

> Never so truly happy, my good Cromwell.
> I know myself now; and I feel within me
> A peace above all earthly dignities;
> A still and quiet conscience.

3. The final aspect of the truth which is revealed in the history of Pilate is this: that truth ultimately is truth incarnate. There is no way of embodying truth in books of definitions. There is no way of putting it into a philosophy, or framing it into a creed. It can only be expressed through the flexibility of the fullest life. The disciples in Palestine could not have told what truth was; but they knew, nevertheless. Truth was the way of Jesus. To believe in truth was to live as he lived, for he had the secret of abundant living. And the same is true with us today. There is no such thing as setting down in formulas the whole meaning of the kingdom of Christian truth. It is a simpler matter than that, and more vital. To lay hold of truth is to enter into the mind of Jesus. It is to have that intuitive interpretation beween life's alternative values which comes to those whose minds and hearts are hid with Christ in God. Browning wrote in his *A Death in the Desert:*

> . . . the acknowledgment of God in Christ
> Accepted by the reason, solves for thee
> All questions in the earth and out of it.

Hardened into literalism, that is not true. Many questions in this world are not solved; many problems of understanding and of action still remain in shadow; but, nevertheless, it *is* true that when a man lays hold of the great conviction that an eternal reality shines through that quality of life which Jesus incarnated, then he knows the way ahead. In spite of many lesser uncertainties, of one thing he is certain, that whenever any word or deed is Christlike instead of un-Christlike, it has in it the heart of truth. Nothing else is ultimately real. Nothing else is lasting except that kind of life which is lived in companionship with the spirit of Jesus.

"What is truth?" You were very near it, Pilate; but you would not open your eyes to see. Many men are near it; but like Pilate, in uneasy fear of the consequences they avoid the intuition in themselves that almost makes them understand. But beside us all, as truly today as once long ago in the judgment hall of the Roman who himself was judged, there stands a quiet figure, looking at us with steady eyes and saying, *I am the truth.*

XVI

GREATNESS UNDER DIFFICULTIES

I know both how to be abased, and I know how to abound.

PHILIPPIANS IV:12

THAT is a great thing to say; and which one of us would not wish that he could say it? "There is that within my soul which is greater than all circumstances. Whatever happens, it is not the material fact but the spirit in me that is the master. Whether I go down to the depths of disappointment or be lifted up to the heights of my desire, I can keep my poise unshaken." This is what it would mean to declare, "I know both how to be abased, and I know how to abound."

James Moffatt in his translation of the New Testament gives to the familiar words a fresh vividness. He writes them thus: "I know how to live humbly; I also know how to live in prosperity." And then come these words following: "I have been initiated into the secret for all sorts and conditions of life, for plenty and for hunger, for prosperity and for privations."

Not in one sermon only, but in two, we shall consider this great theme.

The period of years beginning about 1930 has been a time of great and unusual difficulty for multitudes of people. It has had in it more of privation than of prosperity. There was an earlier period in America—and that period may return—when our temptations had to do with pride and success. But our recent danger has been that we may feel ourselves beaten down by fears which crush our spirits. In comparison with what we once enjoyed and hoped for, we may seem not to be exalted, but to be abased. But if we are so, the really crucial question still remains to be determined. It is not the fact of being abased, but how to be abased that matters. To know that there are great difficulties may be important; but it is more important to know whether we can meet them greatly.

I

Let us begin by examining those aspects of our life which might make us say in this or any other time that we are abased.

One obvious fact may be that many people may have lost their fortunes. There is a pathos in the poor. There is another and very real pathos in those persons who, having been rich, find themselves reduced to a scale of living which is relatively poor also. They may have been long accustomed both to spend generously and to give generously. They have many people who are dependent upon them—their families, the servants in houses which must be closed, the employees in businesses which must be cut down to skeletons of their former personnel. Material losses may alter the whole surroundings and associations of life. Men must change their occupations and take work which has in it none of the largeness of opportunity which used to be theirs. Women who never had to do so before may have to go out into the business world, with infinite shrinking because of their lack of preparation for it, to earn their livelihood as best they can. They may confess, as they look back on the privileges which formerly they enjoyed, that they lived then in ivory towers; but the towers have tumbled, and they move now on a level whose existence seems to have lost its height and spaciousness. It is unmistakable that their circumstances have been reduced. The danger is that they may begin to think that they, as men and women, also are reduced.

But there is another way in which there may come to many persons the feeling of having been brought down. We look back and see ambitions which have been defeated, or at least so halted that we are not sure that they will ever go forward again. When the year was new, there was some plan on which we had set our hearts. We believed that in the months which then were the future we should carry this through to fine fulfilment; but we have not done it. Always there are those in whose hearts disappointment is echoing like the strokes of an iron bell. Here is a man who launched some venture which he believed would succeed, and it has failed. Here is another who trusted, when the year was young, that the long hard effort to hold some old endangered business together would find at last more favorable auspices; but his hope has been frustrated, and the interests he was trying to safeguard for himself and for many others have gone down to disaster. And here are others, men or women, who in the church or settlement house or other agencies for helping human kind have set in motion eager plans and seen them fail. Such men and women come to the end of their reckoning scarred and wounded. They are like gladiators who have been beaten to their knees by the sword of circumstances which proved too strong for the utmost they could do.

Or again there is a more general way in which it is possible to feel abased—not *de*based, let us always note that the word is—but abased; not dishonored, but brought down from the heights to the flat ground. The influence which accomplishes this for innumerable people is simply the sense that life is passing. They may not have had any particular loss which stands out conspicuously. They may not even have had any specific ambitions set aside. But they are growing more and more acutely conscious of the shortness of time and of the evanescent quality of even their most ambitious efforts. When men and women are young, they feel that there is nothing too large for them to hope to do. The time ahead seems indefinitely long. But as the years go by, the perspective alters. They see how hard it is to point to any accomplishment and how little of what they do accomplish can by any stretch of the imagination be called great. Moreover, the dismaying moment arrives when they perceive that they are no longer the heirs of what once appeared to be an unlimited future. They have come in sight of the time when the span of human life is finished, and when the record of the much or the little which it has accomplished must be made up. Against the background of the past to which already too much of life belongs, and before the future which it will not share, the human spirit is apt to stand with a great sense of loneliness and isolation. The importance which it once took for granted that its career would have seems now to have been only an illusion. Beside the immense and impersonal passage of time, the significance of the one little individual life seems trivial. It dismays us to reflect how rapidly we have seen each year come and go. Presently in the same fashion years will begin and end which we shall not be here to number. Remembering that, we are prone to think that the utmost we can do is tragically small. It is not that by any particular defeat or disappointment we are abased. It is rather that by our whole consciousness of life's restrictions and relativities we are very much brought low.

II

Such then are some of the aspects of the reality. When we pass on to consider whether or not they can be met, it is good to remember that we do not have to begin in a vacuum. We can begin with the brave example of a man who met conditions more dispiriting than any we are ever likely to face. The words of the text are like a frame for an heroic face which the centuries have never been able to dim. Paul the Apostle looks at us with his steady eyes as he says: "I know how to be abased." And it is as though he added: "You can know as well."

Let us think, then, of what this man who lived long ago, but whose spirit is greater than any time or place, did experience, and how it was that he prevailed.

First and most obviously, he met the fact of material deprivation. From such fragmentary indications as we can gather, it would seem that Paul had been born into a life of relative abundance. He was not only a Roman citizen; but he had inherited citizenship; that is to say, his father before him was a man of consequence in Cilicia, the province from which he came. He was able to go as a young scholar to the rabbinical school of Gamaliel in Jerusalem, and there he studied for a considerable time. When he became a disciple of Christ, the old ties, of course, were broken. Henceforth, the well-to-do and privileged young scholar became the hated and ostracized representative of a sect which his former associates despised. We hear no more of any ties either with home or former friends. He goes about the world on his far-flung adventure of faith, trusting for the necessities of existence to such work as he himself could do, and to the free-will offerings of the little Christian communities which he formed. We see him in Corinth making tents. We hear him in his letters referring frequently to gifts which the different Christian congregations had sent him. But sometimes also nothing was sent. He knew what it was, he says, to be hungry. Privation was nothing strange to him. But he was not troubled, and above all, he was never bitter. When he wrote Timothy: "Thou therefore endure hardness as a good soldier of Jesus Christ," he was not writing theory, but he was sharing his own high-hearted experience. He was following the Master who had left behind him nothing but the clothes for which Roman legionaries gambled at the foot of the cross. He was following one who had the print of nails in his feet and hands. It did not seem strange to Paul that the *stigmata* of many iron sharpnesses should be in his flesh also. If he were poor, what did that matter? Still he had within him the unsearchable riches of Christ.

Furthermore, he had known the abasement of defeated ambitions. Often we think of Paul through our theological mists. We see him as a finished figure, sometimes almost legendary and non-human, and we do not perceive the poignant human struggles through which he arrived at his final greatness. We see him as a man caught up utterly into the glory of a selfless cause; but we forget the man who must have struggled with an inward agony to crucify all his earlier contrasting hopes. It was no small thing which he had abandoned to be a Christian. He had all the pride of his race and of his class. He had been, as he himself says, "a Pharisee of the Pharisees," born to all the immemorial traditions of Israel. There had been wide open before him the career of a great scholar and teacher, the career most honored and reverenced by those among his own people who had most influenced his thinking. But he had laid all this aside in order to choose something which was more authoritative for his soul. He had felt the overwhelming call to follow and to serve the Christ whose followers once he had persecuted. It was the last thing he had expected. It was in the beginning the last thing he could explain. He only knew that this was the vision his soul must obey. Then as the vision brightened and he went forward in the glory of his new surrender, there were doubtless moments when he saw the possibility of a great triumph for the gospel he was preaching. Perhaps it would kindle like a flame across the world, and innumerable souls would burn like torches to welcome Jesus Christ when he came back to earth again in glory, as Paul at first implicitly believed that he very soon would come. But what happened? The way of preaching and conversion was hard and slow. Here and there souls responded; but there was bitter and malignant opposition among great masses of people in general, and ignorance and human pettiness and much back-sliding even among those who listened to the word. And the glorious day which Paul had hoped for he came presently to understand would never dawn in his time. He had been mistaken in his first conception of an early second advent. The triumph of Christ would not come that way. Through long patience, by infinite faithfulness, and in a vista of time too far for his foreseeing, the Kingdom must be brought about.

So when all was said and done, what was left of his great ambitions? The career he had started on originally had come to its end and to its complete reversal. The second career upon which he had launched had proved very different from what he had expected. It seemed as though there were only a few fragments of his great dream out of which he must lay the foundations of what at best was a future that he should not inherit. And now, as he writes the letter to the Philippians from which the words of the text are taken, he is a prisoner in Rome. He is going to die there presently at the hands of Nero's executioner. It did not seem as though life which once had aspired to greatness could be more abased than that.

But the soul of Paul was not abased. There in the deepest valley he looked upward, and the sunlight of an eternal confidence was in his eyes. What did it matter that his first ambitions were set at naught? He would consider simply that the architecture of his mind had been too small. He would take the broken stones of his old imaginations and build them into the outlines of a mightier hope which God would bring to pass. If his ambitions had been defeated, it was only that God's infinite aims for him might be set free.

And, in the third place, Paul must have felt that general depression which accompanies the mood of every dying year. Paul was thinking, not only of the dying year, but of the dying moments of life itself. His time was short, and he knew it. How little of all that he had wanted to do had yet been done! How inadequate life seemed, and how short its horizon as compared with its range of hopes! It was not only that he himself seemed frustrated as an individual. Often he must have had dark moments of brooding as to whether humanity itself might not be frustrated in the conflict of its aspirations with all the heavy evil of the world. Was this all it meant for Christ to have died on the cross: that he himself, Christ's follower, must also die in the midst of a world that seemed as pagan as it had ever been? In thoughts like these, there was the possibility that his soul might have been brought altogether to humiliation. But here also he knew how to be abased. He had already learned how to conquer deprivation and disappointment. He could arm himself now at the last against despair. Past all the resources of his own life or the life of his generation, he relied upon the infinite reserves of God. "In all these things," he could cry, "we are more than conquerors through him that loved us." He trusted in Him with whom a day is as a thousand years and a thousand years as one day.

III

We have considered the facts by which lives in our time and in all times may be abased. We have considered one great figure who met his abasement in such fashion that the greatness of his soul was the more revealed. We pass on finally to consider the meaning of his secret as it applies to us.

Take first the fact of the loss of material things. It is possible, of course, for that to seem only a disaster. It may be like the crumbling of the structure which a man has laboriously built around and above himself, so that he himself is crushed and buried in its ruins. But if they are grandly treated, the same facts can present an altogether different picture. They can be the taking away of the ornate draperies which have been wrapped around a man, so that for the first time the nobility of his own simple and unadorned self may be revealed.

The only tragedy in loss of fortune, and even in great deprivation, is among those who show that they have not now, and perhaps have never had, any high belief in their own selves. They have thought they were important as long as they had an important place in the world of society, or could move with the freedom which much money gives. Now that suddenly they have become poor, or almost poor, they are sensitive to the point of mental agony. They feel as people feel sometimes in those strange nightmares when they dream that they are naked in the midst of a staring and deriding crowd. So men and women stripped of their wealth may feel embarrassed and humiliated. They want to hide the fact of it; and if they cannot hide that, they shrink away and hide themselves furtively from their former associations.

But what is there in poverty, either relative or absolute, to bring defeat upon any man or woman so long as the soul within is brave and true? Francis of Assisi, one of the most joyous and radiant figures that ever trod this earth, was known as "the little poor man of Assisi." Martin Luther, who shook a continent with his moral power, was born poor, and remained so all his life, and he gloried in it. "Poor men's sons," he said, "must labor to lift themselves out of the dust, and must endure greatly; and because they have nothing to boast about or pride themselves upon, they trust God, control themselves, and keep still." Paul the Apostle was poor; and yet he went about all his gallant business with a song. Jesus Christ was poor; and he could say of himself, with no hint of self-pity but with heroic freedom, "The foxes have holes, and the birds of the air have nests; but the Son of Man hath not where to lay his head." Why then should the mere loss of money dismay a man or make any man think that his life need for that fact have any less significance? God give us all, to begin with, a brave truthfulness! If any man has lost money, yes, if materially he has lost everything, let him not try to conceal it and torture himself either with pretense or with evasion. Let him be ready that everybody with whom he has had associations should know the facts simply and naturally, and without either apology or parade; and let him be sure that in the moment when he realizes that there is no longer any possibility of any one valuing him merely for what he has, then for the first time there may arise, both among his friends and within himself, a clear and virile new conception of what he *is*.

Have we not seen the reality of this all round us in these days? Every one of us can name friends who have endured loss of fortune and met that loss with a courage and constancy which has made them seem far bigger and more admirable people than we knew they were before. There are men who have had to give up great positions of leadership and abandon the benefactions which once they rejoiced in. A mean spirit put in that position would imagine that it could no longer live happily as it used to do before. But the big man shows within himself the kind of unabashed sincerity which burns like a flame that needs nothing beyond itself to make it into light and power. There are men today who, because of their own loss of opportunity, have come into inspiring new fellowship with other men. They have made those who used to be upon a lesser level of position, and were envious of what they thought was the great man's accidental greatness of opportunity, be envious no more. In place of envy, there is admiration, and a desire to learn what it is that can make the one who seemed a big man when he was exalted seem an even bigger man now, when, by the measurements of the world, he is abased. They love him for his self-reliance, his uncomplaining courage, and his steady willingness to give himself, and not to think that this self-giving is of any less worth now that he has no material things to give with it. And there are women too whose examples have had the same effect. Some of them have through all their lives been in positions of privilege. They have never done any hard work, even in their own households. But circumstances have changed now, and they have shown themselves surprisingly equipped to meet them. They have undertaken labors which they never would have thought they could accomplish, and in so doing they have revealed a humour, a good temper, and a cheerfulness which have given

to their families and to their friends something that no money
could ever conceivably have bought. Why then should any living persons today be unduly frightened lest materially they
should be abased? It is possible to learn how to be abased, and
out of abasement to rise with a grander and more evident integrity of soul—as the chiseled statue rises to its serene proportions the more the concealing marble is cut away.

But what shall we do when our abasement comes through
some defeated ambition and frustrated aim?

Well, we may rightly approach our answer here by considering what we must *not* do. We must not begin by blaming circumstances. It is possible that circumstances may be to blame,
but we can discover that later. The first thing we want is an
honest consideration of what measure of blame there may be
in us.

That was what Paul always did. He did not sit down and lay
his difficulties at the door of fate. He inquired first what there
was in himself to be set right. He examined his own soul to see if
there were any evil in him, and often he found that there was.
He said that there was a law in his members warring against
the law of his mind. There was that in his flesh which struggled
against the spirit. He did not spare these evils which he saw
in his own nature. He did not try to rationalize them nor to
deal with them by excuses and evasion. He confronted them with
honesty and called upon every resource in his own soul, and
cried out in his prayer upon all the resources of God, to help
him overcome them. He disciplined himself, that all his appetites
should be made subject to his aspirations. "So fight I, not as one
that beateth the air," he said. "But I keep under my body, and
bring it into subjection: lest that by any means, when I have
preached to others, I myself should be a castaway." He knew
that he had no right to blame circumstances until he had done
his best to see that his own soul was girded for effective action.

Surely there are many of us who can recognize the bearing
of that upon our own realities. We look back and see the things
in which we have more or less completely failed. Some of them
may have been good and great aims in which we think that
we ought to have succeeded. The world would have seemed

better, and the universe a place where it would have been easier to believe in the providence of God, if we had achieved those ends which appeared to be endued with the highest values that we knew. But we did not achieve them. And then what? Shall we stand and whimper before the face of fate? Shall we salve our vanity by saying that failure was due to the force of circumstances? Or shall we not better begin by being rigorous with ourselves? What flaws in our mental or moral forces may have been at least in part responsible? Where have we been secretly indolent even when we have appeared to be industrious; where have we dodged the difficult and important matters in order to be busy about secondary and more agreeable ones; where have we failed in the self-discipline which would have made us do the things which needed to be done, but which we pretended we were not equipped for and left to the chance that some one else would do them? These are the questions we need to answer, and upon the results of which we need to act. It may be too late to save the particular ambition or to carry through the particular plan on which we once adventured. But it is not too late to save the possibilities of ourselves for larger and better enterprise tomorrow. Some of life's greatest blessings come out of temporary defeat. One man by his reverses may be soured and halted; another will be corrected, made more clear in his perceptions, and more resolute in his will. The only real failures are among those who treat the obstacle as though it were the end of the road. When we find an obstacle, or when through our fault we know that we have created it, the thing to do is to set to work at the personal self-discipline which can make us able to surmount that obstacle and whatever others may lie beyond. There is one word which every single one should bar out of his or her vocabulary for ever, and that word is *discouraging*. A thing may be disturbing, yes; it may be disappointing, yes; but discouraging, no! No man ever can be abased as long as his courage burns; and no outward facts can quench his inner courage if to the flame of it he brings the fuel of his patience, his perseverance, and his prayer.

But what if it be true that after a man has examined himself and corrected himself, still beyond the utmost which he can accomplish the fact remains that his high desires are blocked and his plans defeated? Then let him put the issue up to God, and go on. It may be that some time tomorrow the gates in the iron wall which seems to hedge him round will suddenly open, and all his joyous desires will go forward into the spacious freedom he has longed for. But it may be that the gates through which he longed to go will remain barred, not because God does not mean him to go forward, but because He means him to go forward in another way. That happened more than once in the great career of Paul. Things which seemed at the moment to be the disintegration of his hopes were only the pressure of God's hands, withholding him from the smaller satisfaction, that he might be turned to the mightier purpose which otherwise he would not have seen. And in many of the experiences of our own time that same reality is evident. Surely there are few men and women who, looking back thoughtfully upon their own lives, can fail to know that many of the things which at the moment seemed cruel disappointments were, as one has put it, *His appointments*. Past their own blocked roadways, God has opened ascending paths to hilltops of accomplishment which else they never would have scaled.

Finally, we come again to that sort of abasement which is most sure at last to fall upon us, and ask ourselves how we shall deal also with that. When life seems short, and the years go fast, and our personal accomplishment seems so limited, how shall we still believe in the glory of life?

The way of the answer must lie through a transfer of our consideration from ourselves to that which is greater than ourselves. Paul was not concerned about his own record or about what his life amounted to, because his thought was merged in a loyalty which embraced in its great certainty all these lesser questionings. He had identified himself with the Kingdom of God as it was made beautiful to him in the spirit of his Master. He wrote for other men what he had proven true for himself: "Whether we live therefore, or die, we are the Lord's." He did not measure time by the span of his own existence. He did not measure results by what happened to him or through him. He was a part of something infinitely more grand, which gave stability and meaning to everything he might be or do, and which extended all the perspective of his hope. No matter how his present fortunes might seem to be abased, the real Paul could never be abased, because in his thought, in his love, and in his dedication, he was made one with the will of God.

What that means we have seen in many nearer instances. The beauty of the lives of the noblest women finds its interpretation here. The mother identifies herself with her husband, her children, and her home. She does not henceforth think of herself in a narrow and isolated way; and whether for the moment she gains what she might have desired does not greatly matter. The thing she lives for is the life of the larger group she loves. As long as that is being advanced, and she knows it is advanced in a thousand secret ways which the world can never measure, nothing which happens to her can ever quench her gladness. She will stoop to the royalty of the lowliest service in that same spirit with which Jesus on the last night in the upper room girded himself with a towel and washed the disciples' feet.

There are other figures also out in the wider life of human kind who have learned this identification of themselves with great loyalties which neither time nor fortune can affect. As Disraeli said of Richard Cobden when that great member of Parliament and leader of the public life of England died, "There are those who are independent of dissolutions, of the caprices of constituencies, and even of the course of time." Remember that whenever life's prospects seem to wane. There is forever a greatness of soul and a greatness of service which are independent of the course of time. The secret is in the immortal words of that great soul who has already furnished so much of the material of our thinking now. "I live," said Paul, "yet not I, but Christ liveth in me." All narrowness of personal self-seeking, all pettiness of concern for personal fortune and for personal praise, had been lifted upward and turned to brighter flame in the fire of his devotion to the purposes of God as these were revealed to him in Christ. When that had happened, nothing in him could really be a failure. All there was of him that was petty would fall away like ashes drifting to the ground. But all in him that was immortal would blend in joyous splendor with the blaze of the glory of God. Thus, and thus only, was he abased; and out of that abasement, he knew, and he can make us know, what it was triumphantly to abound.

XVII

THE MAN OF ABOUNDING LIFE

I know both how to be abased, and I know how to abound.

PHILIPPIANS IV:12

OUR thought now grows out of our foregoing theme. There we considered the first half of that great declaration of St. Paul: "I know both how to be abased, and I know how to abound." We thought of what it meant, and of what it can mean to all men in all times, to achieve greatness under difficulties. To be abased is the lot sometimes of almost every human soul; to learn how to be abased is the secret of the great ones. Paul knew that secret, and we were trying to listen, that he might pass the secret on to us.

Now we turn to the other half of this declaration. Superbly the clear words ring: "I know how to abound." No outward pressure of circumstances could thwart for long the expansive power of his soul. Even when to the eyes of the world his life seemed most certainly defeated, Paul was sure of his illimitable destiny.

Twice I have heard men describe their impressions of Mahatma Ghandi. He is, as every one knows, in physical proportions frail and unimposing. He dresses with the meagre simplicity of the Indian peasant. He has no surroundings of wealth or worldly dignity. Yet both these men who had seen him spoke of the indescribable sense of greatness which he produced. There was that in the ring of his voice and in the look of his eyes which created an instant sense as though all the horizons of reality had been pushed back, and as though one were suddenly inhabiting with him a larger world. It must have been such an impression as this that was made by the Apostle Paul. In his outward circumstances he was often abased. He went through persecutions which seem almost incredible as we read the record of them. The road of his journeyings led to a prison in Rome and out through the prison doors at last to execution.

Yet from beginning to end his career has about it a light of grandeur. His influence went out in immeasurable ways beyond the limits of the narrow fact. He who seemed abased, nevertheless beyond any other man of his generation has abounded.

Let us, therefore, recapture first of all the joyous suggestion of this fact: in the will of God for every human soul, abasement is not the end. When abasement comes, it is a descent into the valley, not that we may remain there, but that we may be forced to find the real way through. It is the confinement of our feet to the narrow pass, that along it we may discover the open spaces which lie beyond the hills. God means every life ultimately to emerge upon the uplands of bright experience which will justify all the cost of patience and of discipline.

Too often the familiar teaching of religion has forgotten this. It has talked too much of what it called the vale of misery and too little of the sunny spaces which in this life and in this world are meant to be the heritage of the children of God. The reason why Christian Science, in spite of all its crude associations and grotesque philosophy, has attracted so many people is because it did reassert this emphasis which traditional religion too largely had forgotten. It taught men to believe in the goodness of God and in gladness as our normal expectation. But this message is not the possession of any sect or modern movement. It is the eternal possession of the whole Christian gospel which we need to reassert. Paul, who knew how to be abased, knew also how to abound; and it was this latter which was the climax and the fulfilment of truth for him. So should we also as Christians lay claim for ourselves to this message of faith and hope and joy. Back of us may stretch the stony road of many disappointments. Back of us may lie the shadowed path of perplexities and doubts. But that is not all. Ahead of us lies the future. Ahead of us quivers the golden dawn of those new possibilities which wait within the wonder of each new day of God. Lift up your eyes then and face the sunrise! If you have walked as steadily and as bravely as you could along the roads of former days, be sure that those roads have already led you nearer to the place where great vistas of your soul's desire may come in view. Take as your own the singing words:

> I cannot in the valley stay;
> The great horizons stretch away.
> The very cliffs that wall me round
> Are ladders unto higher ground!

And now if we have listened to this prelude to the message, let us go forward to consider more fully its theme. We shall consider it in two aspects; first, the false way to abound; and second, the true way.

I

The false way to abound is to accumulate to ourselves those external facts and things which we imagine by their sheer increment will make us great. The false way is to suppose that abundance comes from without, and to forget that it will never come unless first it blossoms from within.

Think in this matter of Paul's experience. He lived in a world which was quite familiar, just as ours is, with the spectacle of men who thought they could be great by being rich. The Roman empire, together with some virtues, had the great vice of becoming often an instrument of exploitation. As Mark Antony said of Caesar:

> He hath brought many captives home to Rome
> Whose ransom did the general coffers fill.

The only difference between the oration and the fact was that more often the things brought back did not fill the general coffers, but men's own private chests. Roman governors in the provinces frequently enriched themselves at the expense of the subject peoples. The collection of taxes was farmed out to a ruthless and hated class of tax-gatherers, who made their living by extorting from people as much as they personally could above the appointed governmental dues. Great fortunes were being accumulated in the cities of the Roman world, and then, as now, there was the tendency to think that the men whose display of wealth was the envy of the crowd were the successful figures of the age.

But Paul had a different conviction. If he had ever had any desire to get wealth or keep it, he had abandoned it long ago. "What things were gain to me, those I counted loss for Christ," he said. "Yea doubtless, and I count all things but loss for the excellency of the knowledge of Christ Jesus my Lord: for whom I have suffered the loss of all things, and do count them but refuse, that I may win Christ." When he died in Rome, he had no material possessions. An old cloak and a few parchments were all the things that he ever asked his friends to bring him.

But what has become of the men in Paul's time who thought that they would abound by being rich? Where are their fortunes now? Where are their names now? What honor have they left behind, and who cares today to rescue the memory of them from the oblivion of the buried years? Concerning them, it is not difficult to arrive at our right estimate. Time sets perspectives straight. It is less easy sometimes to arrive at true judgments concerning the things close at hand. We are still tempted to believe, and young men and women are tempted to shape their own desires upon the imagination, that the rich men are those who have the abundant life. Yet even here we are beginning to see more clearly than we formerly did. Names of rich men in many American communities who, a few years ago, seemed masters of all they surveyed, have become names of reproach which serve as by-words for the betrayal of supposed integrity. A decade ago the mind of America paid its bankers almost superstitious respect. In the period of depression there have been many whom those same bankers have made poor, but there are few so poor to do them reverence. A while ago the word "businesslike" was like a potent charm. It was a symbol of value to be applied not only in the world of secular affairs, but as the first supposed requirement in church and spiritual matters. *Now* to "be businesslike" has a different connotation, from which the high-minded and idealistic men in business have the difficult task of delivering it. Notwithstanding shining individual exceptions, our personal or our corporate wealth in America has not sufficiently contributed to a life which in the finest sense abounded. People's souls have not ordinarily been made great by the fact that they may have made much money. Rich men's souls have sometimes been like huts which surrounded themselves with ornate structures branching out like the wings of a palace; but the very pretentious grandeurs of the added wings only made more mean by contrast the poor little centers from which they sprang. And though this, of course, is not always true, and though it is possible for a man to be great in and through his possessions when his soul enters these and uses them as the expression of himself, yet it remains a perilous thing, and it may be a fatal thing, for any man to imagine that because he has enlarged the boundaries of his possessions therefore in and by that fact he has himself abounded.

Consider also that aspect of a life's enlargement which has to do with its reputation. Many people seek abundance in the opinion of the crowd. They have no stability of conviction. They cannot trust the verdict of their own souls as to what they are and do. They want to be supported by the applause of others. If the majority is with them, then they are content. If the majority is against them, then they are not only fearful of their outward success, but they are doubtful as to what they themselves ought to think and to believe.

One of the significant instances in the life of the Apostle Paul was his visit to Athens. There on the Areopagus he found a group of men who liked to think of themselves as philosophers; but the comment in the Book of the Acts about them is that they "spent their time in nothing else, but either to tell or to hear some new thing." They were like those other people of whom Paul wrote that they were "carried about with every wind of doctrine." They liked to wear the new fashions in ideas. Like many of their descendants in our own time, they were much concerned with seeming to be up-to-date. They were not deeply and devotedly seeking after wisdom; but they were immensely anxious that the crowd should think them to be wise.

Now the temptation for people in all times and in all places is to set more value upon reputation than upon one's own reliance. We are sensitive to the pressure of the herd mind and the herd opinion. It is only the rare man or woman who for some sure principle's sake is willing to endure being called queer or unsafe or radical. We do not want to run counter to the prejudices of the unthinking, but instead to be in comfortable agreement with as many as we can. In many of our private adjustments, we may be like the politician who ended an impassioned speech with this declaration: "And so, my friends, those are my firm convictions; and if they don't suit—they can be changed."

There in the first century, Paul the Apostle was not immune from the suggestion of those same weak compromises which beset us all. He had begun as an "Hebrew of the Hebrews." He had gloried in that religious inheritance which meant to him what caste means to the Brahmin. He was proud of his orthodoxy: and when he suddenly made the great decision to enter the Christian fellowship, he knew that his step would be regarded with amazement and contempt by all his old associates. Henceforth to them he would be an outcast, a man despised for what they regarded as the failure of his intelligence, and hated for what they thought the betrayal of his faith. And within the Christian Church he still had often to go a lonely way. There was the party of those whose roots went back much farther than his did into the days of early discipleship. This party had the names of the apostles to give it dignity. If he, the newest, was to establish his reputation, it was important that he should do nothing that seemed disturbing. Theologically and practically, the way of wisdom might seem for him to play safe, and to preach the Gospel only in the way in which others preached it. But he had seen a new vision which the others had not seen. He believed that the Gospel which they had supposed was confined to one privileged nation must be carried to all the world, and in the face of prejudice and scandalized hostility he dared to follow his lonely but resplendent gleam. The result was that he was suspected within large circles of the Christian Church and assailed by the pagan world outside it. Like his Master, he deliberately accepted the necessity that he should be made of no reputation, in order that he might be loyal to God's revelation in his own soul. He could write to the Corinthians: ". . . with me it is a very small thing that I should be judged of you, or of man's judgment . . . he that judgeth me is the Lord." And he wrote to the Romans: "Let every man be fully persuaded in his own mind," and "who art thou that judgest another man's servant? to his own master he standeth or falleth; yea, he shall be holden up: for God is able to make him stand."

Against those words, set that pathetic utterance which Shakespeare puts into the mouth of Cardinal Wolsey:

> Had I but serv'd my God with half the zeal
> I serv'd my king, he would not in mine age
> Have left me naked to mine enemies.

There are many men who serve a king who is not competent for their ultimate support. Their king may be the feared authority of the crowd. They truckle to the ideas and passions of the multitude. But these ideas and passions have in them no stability, and therefore can give no final safety; and the man who tries to build his abounding life on the smooth extent of his reputation will leave himself some day naked to enemies of contradiction which there is nothing in his own soul to resist.

I think today of a certain man who in his bearing and in his personal charm used to seem to hosts of people as a sort of paladin. He was sensitive to all fine ideals of honor. His inclinations and his natural associations were of the highest. He went into political life. Many rejoiced in the confident prospect of what such a man would stand for, and of what his personality might achieve. But he was snared by a subtle force. Politicians of longer experience came to him and persuaded him that he must be what they called "practical." With all his good intentions, he must not show helpless innocence. He must prove that he was not "a mere idealist," upon whom men who knew the ropes of real affairs would look with amused contempt. He must show that he could be as much a force as the different sort of man could be. He must play the game according to its necessary rules, always with the admitted end of reaching thus his high purpose, of course—and so on—and of course. He listened, and followed the advice by which so artfully he was meant to be ensnared. He did "play the game according to the rules." He did make his alliances with what seemed the dominant political group, in order that through that alliance he could, as he thought, advance his ends. And the result was only that he was caught in toils too strong for his breaking. He accomplished nothing that was conspicuous, while all his disillusioned friends were sad. Presently he was defeated for re-election to the office he had held. He might have been defeated in any case even if he had been fully and uncompromisingly himself. But he was defeated now without the glamor which would have come with great adventure. Consciously or unconsciously he had sought for reputation. He had not won it, and meanwhile he had lost his own great chance.

God help us all in our own choices to be more surely wise! If any young man is going into politics, let him not suppose that the way of real success lies along the seductive paths of easy reputation. Let him fashion in his own mind and soul the convictions to which through success or failure he is determined to be loyal; and then if he does succeed, there will be grandeur in his accomplishment; and if outwardly he fails, still his failure will have round it the halo of an undying honor. And for those other young people who go out into the mêlée of our modern life, once again may there be the strength to know that it is not reputation which will tell them the way of truth. What they need is reliance upon the light of God in their own souls; and if they follow that brightness, they need not fear but that somehow and somewhere their lives will move forward into real abundance.

II

We come thus to the more positive aspect of our thinking. We have thought of the wrong way of trying to abound. We have already seen grow out of it a suggestion of the true way. We cannot abound through accretions; we must abound through the quality of a new life whose increase begins within the soul.

That is why abounding must often grow out of abasement. It was so with Paul. It is so with many another man or woman, great or small. When a life is abased, it may be emptied of its little self-sufficiency. It is like a room swept and cleared, perhaps by painful processes, but nevertheless made ready thereby for a greater guest. The trouble with many of us is that we are so full of our little plans and satisfactions, so occupied with our inadequate conceptions of life's significance, that the greater purposes of God find no entrance and no welcome there. Then comes some experience which at the moment we interpret as failure and disaster. The things we trusted in have given way. The vanities, the adulations, and the self-satisfactions which used to sit down with us at the table of our pride have turned their backs and vanished. Life seems lonely and discredited. We are in part ashamed of the things in which we used to find our satisfaction, and in part we are humiliated because we can have them no more. But out of that experience may grow a finer consciousness. The empty soul may cry out now for the God whom once it thought it did not need. It knows that the old thoughts and emotions have played it false, and it seeks for a companionship now that will not fail.

Remember that this was true of Paul. In the earlier years of his life he had been confident that the things which he had would give him fulfilment of all his desires. He had material sufficiency. He had position and prestige. He had strong friends and powerful connections. Every one who knew him would have predicted for Paul a prosperous and distinguished future. But, nevertheless, he had been secretly unhappy. His persecution of the Christians, though started in an honest fanaticism, gradually became an effort to drown by its vehemence the protest rising in his soul. He saw that the loyalty to Christ which he had tried to crush was claiming him. Then one day the slow shifting of the weight of his subconscious motives came to the critical point, and in one tremendous moment the whole center of gravity of his nature was overturned. The restraints which had held him to his old career were broken. New impulses, drawn to a new loyalty, were set free. His personality moved out into a spontaneous power such as he had never known before. *Abundare,* to rise in waves, to overflow, that is the root derivation and the original meaning of abound; and Paul in his experience became a witness to this vital and resistless meaning of the word. Like waves of a river now for the first time released, his energies flowed out in an exultant stream.

We can see in our own contemporary experience how lives may again and again abound in some such way as this. A new impulse may come through love. Here is the boy who has been going along his more or less careless way, attractive, debonair, but vagrant as the wind. He will follow the breeze of any passing interest with all sails set, and then turn round tomorrow and steer in a new direction. But then he falls in love; and if he has real stuff in him, something decisive happens. Deeper resources of energies than he had ever revealed before begin to be tapped. He wants to make a place in the world now for himself and for the girl he means to marry. There is the port of a new desire which he seeks to reach, and his hand is laid upon the rudder of his life's direction with a firmness which he never showed before. He steers toward his one purpose whether the wind blow this way or that. And in the same fashion a girl, who previously had seemed ease-loving and careless, or if not that, yet nevertheless unawakened to any full interest in her life, is transformed when love comes. She may have appeared before to be leading a cheerful and satisfied existence; but as a matter of fact, she was not satisfied. Down underneath the surface of her nature lay something which was unawakened, the breathing of which now and then in the silences of her soul she heard, but the face of which she had never seen. Then when love comes to her, this more eager and abundant self arises. She becomes capable of activities, emotions, and sacrifices which have been beyond her ken before. Now perhaps for the first time she knows what it is to be through and through alive.

Some other great loyalty may have the same effect as love. In one of the essays of Dean Briggs of Harvard, he tells of a freshman whose aimless drifting and incorrigible indolence had brought him to the point of being dropped from college. As a last resort, the dean turned for help to a very able and inspiring senior. He asked him to go to this freshman and see what he could do to wake him. The first question the senior asked when he went to see the boy was this: "Jack, did you ever in your life do anything as well as you could?" He had put his finger upon the central fact. The boy had never learned to do anything or to be anything with his complete self; and the one essential was to create for him some loyalty big enough to rouse him and to call out the utmost resources at his command. The pity is that many young people do drift through the crucial years of their existence without ever finding anything which stirs their banked fires and sets the engines of their spiritual energies throbbing with a full head of steam. When no such loyalty arises, a life is apt to end in a frustration which is all the more pathetic because of the contrast with what ideally it might have done. It goes by fits and starts along its way. Half its cylinders are missing fire, and the wheels drag. And, on the other hand, there are those young people who take time to think and ponder and decide, and for whom some clear loyalty has become compelling. It is not native gifts of ability which usually make the difference between failure and success. It is not often genius, or the lack of it. It is not the accidents of opportunity. No, but what makes the difference between the life which will do great things and the life which will do little (and do that little in a half-hearted way) is the fact of whether or not some one interest has ever seemed clear and thrilling enough to magnetize the whole desire. The first and most essential prayer which every one of us needs to make at the beginning of life, and at the beginning of each new year or chapter in it, is this: "O God, give me so unmistakably to see what I want to do that the utmost there is in me may be on fire for its doing!"

It should be plain also that the fulness of life in us will never be called forth if the ends we aim at are narrow. A person may be loyal to the interests of his family, and may call out thereby a certain thrift and energy; but he will not tap the profounder and more generous fountains of his nature. He may be loyal to some business venture which he shares with other men, and he may thus develop in himself initiative and sagacity; but if all his ends are expressed in business values, he will never call out the wider human sympathies which might flow through him. He may be a public servant, loyal to his party, or even to his nation; but unless his loyalty extends to something greater even than these, he will fail to discover those unlimited possibilities which might be the gift to him from God. It is only religion which will call out in any human being his utmost and his best.

The gates of his soul must be so widely opened that an imagination and sympathy as far-reaching as the will of God may go forth from him. It is not, perhaps, the wicked souls which constitute the most frequent tragedy of our human failures; it is rather the wizened souls. It is not those which are sinful; it is those which are shrunken. It is not those who have in themselves gateways of wrong desire which encourage the world's evil to come in; it is those whose gateways of good desire are so cramped that no generous emotions can go out. Our greatest need for religion is not that it may protect us. It is that it may attract us. God help us to see life in the real perspective of its diviner spaciousness, and beyond the little walls of our selfishness and our personal and group advantage to seek the great fields of service into which a consecrated spirit ought to move; for only when we feel the impelling beauty of these so fully that we will move out into them shall we find there our abundant life.

Some years ago there were excavated in Northern Africa the noble ruins of a once great city. Its name was *Leptis Magna*, and it was the birthplace of the Emperor Septimius Severus. For a time it was an important center of Roman power on the African coast and a port from which the galleys went to other harbors near and far. At length the city vanished from the earth; and its destruction was not due to fire or to flood, to earthquake or to any such catastrophe. It was not due to invasion or to war. It was due simply to the fact that its harbor was allowed to be blocked with silt, so that its commerce with the great world was destroyed. Little by little then its people abandoned it, and as the years went by the sands of the desert drifted in and buried it from sight. There are human souls which may be like that city. If the gateways of our imagination and our sympathy are silted up, so that we have no vital contact any more with the great world of human needs which God means us to be in touch with, then gradually the desert sands of dryness and desolation drift in to bury the nobility which once was ours. Only as long as our harbors are open to the sea, and as long as the vessels of our desires are not dropping anchor in our own land-locked concerns but going on adventures as wide as life itself, can we inherit life abundant.

Ask then that your horizons may be made wide. Guard your soul against the peril of that insidious complacency which is like the silt that blocks the channels to the ocean. Pray God to keep you from ever being smug or satisfied. Ask Him to make you faithful in your home and honorable in your business, but not to stop with this respectability. Be worth something to the larger life of your country and your time. Do not count it as enough for you that you should maintain your own position, but go and take position there where the strength of a man or woman such as you is needed. Value your life's work not by what you get, but by what God makes you glad to try to give. So shall you be made free from littleness, and all your mind and heart shall be enlarged. So shall you be able to say with the great Apostle, "I know how to abound!"

XVIII

MEN WHO ENDURED AND TRIUMPHED

And others had trial of bonds and imprisonment.
HEBREWS XI:36

THESE words come near the end of one of the most triumphant chapters of all the New Testament. *Now faith is the substance of things hoped for, the evidence of things not seen,* it begins. Then follows the roll-call of those heroic figures in the history of Israel who by faith dared, endured, and triumphed. By faith Abel—by faith Enoch—by faith Abraham—by faith Joseph—by faith Moses—so one by one with the increasing marching rhythm of this majestic heralding the great souls in the history of the chosen people are marshalled as witnesses to that sufficiency of God on which they had laid hold. Then the long chant of spiritual victory sweeps up to its climax:

What shall I more say? for the time would fail me to tell of Gideon, and of Barak, and of Samson, and of Jephthah; of David also, and Samuel, and of the prophets; who through faith subdued kingdoms, wrought righteousness, obtained promises, stopped the mouths of lions, quenched the violence of fire, escaped the edge of the sword, out of weakness were made strong.

Here then, it would seem, is the praise of overcoming lives. Religion is glorified in that which it is has enabled men to do. Here is the high progress of the victors, with palms strewn upon their highroad and exultant trumpets sounding for their coming home.

But that is not all. Follow the chapter to its end. Suddenly its music takes another note. There is no longer triumph now, but tragedy.

Others were tortured, not accepting deliverance, that they might obtain a better resurrection. And others had trial of cruel mockings and scourgings, yea, moreover of bonds and imprisonment. They were stoned, they were sawn asunder, were tempted, were slain with the sword: they wandered about in sheepskins and goatskins; being desti-

*tute, afflicted, tormented; (of whom the world was not worthy:)
they wandered in deserts, and in mountains, and in dens and caves
of the earth.*

Where are the trumpets now? What palms are on these roads
that lead to dens and caves and hunted wilderness? What glory
of religious vindication is there in these struggling ones whose
record ends not in victory, but in defeat?

Nevertheless, they do have their place in the spiritual paean
of overcoming. They stand not at the beginning, but at the
climax of it all. These are the men who are great not through
what they did, but through what they endured. Here is the victory of the vanquished, the life won through the valor of the
life laid down.

Any one of the descriptions of those who proved their faith by
their endurance might occupy our thought, but I have chosen
this one—as it might seem the least thrilling, the least romantic
of them all—*Others had trial of bonds and imprisonment.*

That is a hard trial to bear. The man who by his lonely self
might be tempted to play the coward may be brave in the heat
of action when the flags go on before and the drums quicken
what otherwise would be his lagging steps. It is possible to be
noble when all the surroundings seem to provoke nobility. But
bonds and imprisonment! What is there in these to lift or inspire
the soul? Could anything be more sure to bruise its wings, to
fetter and stifle every aspiration that would soar?

Yet it is out of bonds and imprisonment that souls have been
called upon in God's strange providence to find the way to
glorify Him. From iron chains of their humiliation they have
been bidden to fashion the crown of the highest victory they
might wear. And they have done it. I would have you think of
those circumstances which for everyday lives, in this time of ours,
may bring that dread yet glorious testing. *Yea, moreover, of
bonds and imprisonment.* Some of you face and will face these
things.

I

To begin with, there is the bondage of temperament. We may
be conscious of a shrivelled something in our own inner selves.

We are shy when we should like to be outgoing, apprehensive when we should like to be brave, grudging and cautious when we covet the abandon of the eager soul, self-distrustful and ineffective in the very moments when we most need high-hearted freedom. Do we not know what a galling imprisonment those bindings and crampings of our own personality can be? They shut us in upon ourselves in what may become a morbid feebleness.

What attitude ought we to take toward this bondage of our inferior selves? Certainly there are times when for the glory of God we must break these prisons. There are many lives today which are hindered by a bondage which God never intended— men and women inhibited from their finer self-expression by all sorts of imagined bars through which a will that is quickened by a right self-reliance can instantly break its way. It is pitiful to see in our modern civilization people who are in bondage to their fears. They are afraid of losing their money, afraid even of having less money than they have now; and so they let the fetters of stinginess hold back their hands from generous devotion. They are afraid of diseases for themselves and for their children; so they walk in a timorous round of feeble, so-called prudence. They are afraid of any change in the social and economic order, lest they may be disturbed in their own privilege; and so they remain in willing bondage to false ideas and to a cruel callousness. They are afraid of having their ecclesiastical preferences disturbed; and so they imprison themselves and the Church with their own traditions and formulas, while the thrilling opportunities of the living world that needs to be won for Christ go by unregarded outside their dusty windows. Concerning such prisons as these false prisons of mood, or habit, or tradition, which our own indolence or selfishness has created, the great challenge is not that we endure them, but that we destroy them. To us, as to Peter in prison, God's message comes like the angel to open the prison doors and set us free.

It is a wonderful thing to behold any fine example of a life which has deliberately and successfully broken the fetters of its own littleness and gone out into the wideness of life. Theodore Roosevelt in our own time was such a one. Whatever differences of judgment concerning him in other aspects there may be, all men can find inspiration in *this* fact. Here was a college lad, shy, perhaps not extraordinarily prepossessing, with poor physique and indifferent health, who broke through all those limitations and made himself in body, mind, and spirit the very type of vital, forth-giving strength. No better gift could come from him to America than the impulse to men and women to stop being fearful, distrustful, cowardly, and cautious, and to sally out in the strength which God meant to belong to them into the joy of full living with a bold body, an open mind to meet truth unafraid, and a spirit ready to play its part in service for the general good.

Yet when this has been said, there remains another side to the reality. There are some restrictions of temperament from which we may never finally escape. The very fact of our different temperaments makes it inevitable that we cannot all be like each other. One of us may look at some other person greatly admired and loved, and wish that one could be as large-hearted, as able, as effective, as that other person is; and yet nothing is more sure than that this may never be. We see our own shortcomings, and some of them we are not able to transcend. It may be that neither by inheritance nor by instinct do we possess those outgoing and ardent qualities which enable another man so instantly and surely to make friends. It may be that we are too contemplative to be temperamentally suited as leaders in action. We may lack the talents for art, for music, or even for the swift human interest and the brilliant conversation which another has; and sometimes the aptitude that might perhaps have been set free has been held back by lack of education, until now it is too late for it ever to catch the pace of others. To many spirits there is constant sadness in these facts. They cannot help feeling the contrast between what they are and what, as they look at other lives which excite their admiration, they dream that they might have been. They think that they must plod along within a narrow circumference. They will do the best they can, but that best does not seem very inspiring or worth-while. Temperament and circumstance combined have laid upon them the trial of bonds and imprisonment.

Is there no glory for men and women such as these? A thousand times, yes! That which seems to be the prison can be made the place from which the glory of God in a faithful life may shine. The true values are not concerned most of all with the size of the room we live in, but with the quality of beauty with which the spirit may invest it. Fra Angelico, whose name is immortal among the painters of Italy, spent most of his life in a monastery. The most beautiful work that he has left is on the walls, not only of the chapel, but of the dining-room and cells and common corridors of the old monastery of San Marco in Florence. He peopled those narrow spaces with the faces of saints and angels. He brought under those low roofs the glory of heavenly wings. And what he did with his brush is a parable of what the true imagination of the soul can do. It can glorify what we suppose to be the small spaces of our unsatisfied personalities with the colors of the immediate meaning of God. Because there are certain activities which a life is not fitted to carry on does not mean that it need fail to serve nobly in that sphere where it does move. St. Francis of Assisi recognized, when the Order which he had founded began to grow, that he had no aptitude for organizing so large a matter, and he gave its control into other hands. He himself was content with that which he had been doing, namely, to go about among the poor and the needy with his unostentatious ministry of love; but that which seemed so small he made the supreme witness of the glory of life, and his gifts and his temperament were great enough to give space for the presence of God. Oh, you who are shy or self-distrustful, limited in talent or in opportunity, shrinking by comparison with some more brilliant friend, or sensitive perhaps from some old wound to the affections, nevertheless to you also the message comes. You too may be enrolled in the company of those who have borne high witness to God, if in the midst of the prison of your seeming limitation you will set up the shrine of your dedication of such as you have to Him.

II

There is the bondage of poverty. Perhaps to the mind of many of our generation this would seem to be the most galling imprisonment of all.

And it is true that poverty can mean the straitening of life. It may hold one back from many generous adventures both in service and in friendship. Among the multitudes of the people it may even mean the bitter chains of want and suffering and of frustrated affection. The poor man may see his wife dying of tuberculosis and know that he has no money to send her away to where she might find a cure. He may see his children forced to go to work and denied the broader education which other men's children so carelessly take. He may be haunted by the dread possibilities which sickness or unemployment or old age bring. That sort of poverty may be terrible, and altogether apart from the purposes of God. It is the business of individuals to try to escape from it and of society to destroy the vicious conditions of injustice and selfishness which allow its stifling walls needlessly to be built around any life.

But there is a relative poverty, a noble and refining poverty, in which high souls can be shut without dismay. It was said of Martin Luther that, when he died, he "left no ready money, no treasure of coin of any description." All through his life he never had anything of consequence in the way of worldly goods, yet he, in his virile poverty, was mightier in his world than such an emperor as Charles the Fifth with the treasure of kingdoms in his hands. Martin Luther accepted his poverty not as a calamity, but as a discipline out of which strength could come. There is an enfeeblement which often comes to men and women too luxuriously protected against the shocks and necessities of the world, and, on the other hand, a disciplined vigor to those who by necessity have been forced to learn the hardihood which meets the straitening facts with mastery. "He who has had to battle," wrote Carlyle, "were it only with poverty and hard trial, will be found stronger and more expert than he who could stay at home, concealed among the provision wagons, or even rest unwatchfully and 'abiding by the stuff.'" The willingness to be poor for the sake of some great loyalty which is costly of material things can lift the soul up into a courageous independence, in comparison with which the mere clinging to wealth is cowardly impotence.

Yet it is true that there are few things which the spirit of our time dreads so much as poverty. There are men and women who are afraid, not indeed of being poor in any real sense, for that hardly enters into the imagination of their complacent privilege, but even of *seeming* poorer than their neighbors. They dare not appear to fall short of the maximum success which money can measure. Though they are already rich, they hold it as a point of necessary distinction that their sons and daughters should marry heiresses and heirs. They do not want their sons to go into a profession where they will not amass a fortune. One of the reasons why the ministry and the work of missions and teaching and the poorly remunerative posts in organizations for social welfare are so seldom turned to by the children of the rich is because of this enervating and ignoble reluctance at not keeping pace with the wealthy. No finer message has come to our generation that these clean-cut words of William James:

It is certain that the prevalent fear of poverty among the educated classes is the worst moral disease from which our civilization suffers. . . . Among us English-speaking peoples especially do the praises of poverty need once more to be boldly sung. We have grown literally afraid to be poor. We despise any one who elects to be poor in order to simplify and save his inner life. If he does not join the general scramble and pant with the money-making street, we deem him spiritless and lacking in ambition. We have lost the power even of imagining what the ancient idealization of poverty could have meant: the liberation from material attachments, the unbribed soul, the manlier indifference, the paying our way by what we are or do and not by what we have, the right to fling away our life at any moment irresponsibly,—the more athletic trim, in short, the moral fighting shape. . . . What we now need to discover in the social realm is the moral equivalent of war: something heroic that will speak to men as universally as war does, and yet will be as compatible with their spiritual selves as war has proved itself to be incompatible. I have often thought that in the old monkish poverty-worship, in spite of the pedantry which infested it, there might be something like that moral equivalent of war which we are seeking. May not voluntarily accepted poverty be "the strenuous life," without the need of crushing weaker peoples?

Others have trial of bonds and imprisonment. Which are they today who, for the sake of what James calls "the unbribed soul, the manlier indifference" will dare to enter, if need be, into what others might call the prison of self-denial and voluntary poverty? Certain it is that our civilization will not be made better by those who have no courage for that sort of limitation. It is not going to be made better by young men who come out of college with no other notion than that of getting into their father's profitable business or of entering, through some other avenue, as quickly as they can, into the position where with least inconvenience of public service they can most easily and quickly get money for themselves. It is not going to be made better by the girls whose only ambition is a round of extravagant amusement, followed by a marriage in which their own self-indulgence is still so controlling that they never face seriously the ideal of a consecrated wifehood and motherhood, nor ever faithfully assume their spiritual responsibility to bring the highest that life has to their husband, their children, and their home. But it can be made better, and will be made better, by those who have in their nature the moral hardihood which is not afraid of self-abnegation, and, for the sake of conscience, or for a happier chance to serve where they know they ought to be, will go deliberately into what the unknowing consider to be the bonds and imprisonment of comparative poverty, and will find God there.

III

In the third place, there is the imprisonment of seeming failure and repudiation to which the hostility of men may condemn those who have espoused an unpopular righteousness. Sometimes there is an actual imprisonment. This has been true of many martyrs in the long story of human warfare for the higher things. More often nowadays it is the moral imprisonment of unpopularity, ostracism, the desertion of friends, the suspicious aloofness of the crowd. Condemned to this invisible punishment, it is possible for the human spirit to have the same sense of loneliness and of alienation from its kind which is visited on one who is shut within the actual prison cell. A man rebels against some corrupt practice in the corporation to which he belongs, or challenges some iniquity in the political party with which he has been allied, and presently in social and in business estrangement he will be made to feel that he is under sentence. Some prophet arises in the Church, speaking the brave new truth that needs to be proclaimed, and the whispering forces of reaction gather instantly to shut him, if they can, into the imprisonment of silence. A man or woman challenges some unworthy social practice, the gambling, the flaunting of liquor, the loose talk and practice of divorce, and that man or woman may be condemned at once to isolation. Sometimes the stout-hearted can laugh at the ineffective malignities which are directed against the courageous speaker of the unpopular truth; but there are the times when the consequences of obeying conscience may be more grave. They put the most eager desires and energies in bonds. They cripple the would-be ways of influence, block up the natural roads of human relationships, and stifle the spirit with the sense that, for the time at least, it is helpless to do what it most wants to do. Sometimes for long years a life may seem to itself to be shut up into rejection and defeat. It is condemned and ignored. It is fenced about with such denials that its utmost desires for usefulness seem to be in vain.

Yet there is no higher test of moral heroism than the willingness thus to seem defeated rather than to purchase popularity and success by compromising the loyalty which men and women know they ought to proclaim. "I had rather suffer," said John Pym in the days of the Commonwealth in England, "for speaking the truth than that the truth should suffer for want of my speaking." There is witness that needs to be borne to truths which are not popular in America—truths of discipline and refinement in our society, of a more imaginative justice in economic matters which may bear harder on the classes of privilege, of a new crusade against the iniquity of war. Often in small matters or in great, it seems as though the loyalty of one individual to what he or she believes is right makes little impression. Apparently the individual is thrown aside, and the evil thing goes on. A man endures the bondage of dislike or even apparent hatred for no apparent gain. But that is not true. No word of moral truthfulness is ever spoken, no brave stand for fine ideals is ever taken, no willing imprisonment of ostracism undergone, but that the ultimate triumph of right and truth is brought more near. Catherine Breshkovsky enduring the grim punishment of exile in Siberia for her fight against the old tyranny of Czarist Russia, said once to George Kennan, the journalist, "Mr. Kennan, we may die in exile, and our children may die in exile, and our children's children may die in exile; but something will come of it at last." And commenting on those words, he says: "I have never seen or heard of her since that day; but I cannot recall her last words to me without feeling conscious that all my standards of courage, of fortitude, and of heroic self-sacrifice have been raised for all time, and raised by a woman's hand."

IV

Thus far we have considered three ways in which the trial of bonds and imprisonment may come. There is that bondage of temperament which arises from the strange necessities of our inner selves, and there is the bondage of poverty, and the bondage of ill-will laid upon us by circumstances without. Then at last there is another bondage which may seem laid upon us most mysteriously of all directly by the hands of God.

It is the bondage of illness, or some other crippling limitation of the body. Are there not many who know what this means? Life in its normal years walked on all wide ways of happy self-expression, eager, unhampered, strong. Then at some turn of the road, before eyes that looked aghast to see it, the grey doors of some prison-house of infirmity threw their fell shadow across the way. Silently, yet inexorably, they waited there while the spirit, with all the music of its singing hushed, passed with slow steps into the vacant corridors and heard the grey doors shut behind. No longer should there be for it the sunshine and the blue sky of exultant days. Rather it must know that for the years to come it should move within the cramping walls of its bodily limitation; or, going painfully out to attempt the old roads of service, drag a weight of crippling weariness behind it like a chain. Nothing in all the experience of St. Paul seems to have caused him deeper bitterness of spirit than that strange infirmity—whatever it was

—under which he suffered. Pathetically he speaks of it when his spirit had humbled itself to bear his humiliation. *There was given to me a thorn in the flesh, lest I should be exalted above measure.* Thrice, he says, he besought the Lord that it might depart from him; but this was not so to be, and his spirit rose at length to his supreme comprehension of the purpose of God: *And he said unto me, my grace is sufficient for thee: for my strength is made perfect in weakness. Most gladly therefore will I rather glory in my infirmities, that the power of Christ may rest upon me.*

I glory in my infirmities—that is a strong saying. It may seem as if it took a soul of such heroic proportions as the soul of Paul to rise to such a height as that. Nevertheless, our human experience makes it plain that many in all times, through gallantry and patience, can make that trial of bonds and imprisonment which sickness brings a thing of glory, and this they may do in one of two ways.

It is possible sometimes for sickness to become the spur to some definite new development of one's capacities. It may close the former roads, but only to direct the spirit to a different and more intensive exercise. A young doctor in New York is stricken with tuberculosis. Apparently his career, if not his life itself, is at an end. But Edward L. Trudeau goes to the Adirondacks to begin his own lonely struggle for some measure of health, and presently to build up that great institution at Saranac which became the haven of multitudes of men and women who flocked to him for encouragement and hope. The shadow of the dread disease was on him always, as it was on those to whom his own brave adventure with the out-of-doors had given new courage to fight for life. The colony that grew up round him was full of human gallantry, yet of human tragedy too; but his spirit lightened it then, and his memory lightens it today. He took the fetters that sickness had put upon his hands and transmuted them, till they were like the ropes which the Alpine guide binds between himself and his fellow-travellers, that he may help them up the precipices and along the climbing way. He ennobled his necessity, and the spirit in which he did so is expressed in his own words:

My sympathies are naturally in the world with the vanquished. My favorite statue is that great one of Victory carrying the dying gladiator, his broken sword in hand. The world applauds and bows before success and achievement; it has little thought for those who fall by the way, sword in hand; and yet it takes most courage to fight a losing fight!

For sometimes the fight does seem to be a losing fight. Then it is not true that sickness opens the way, as it opened it for Trudeau, to new achievement. The duress is too strait for that. The tides are ebbing too fast for the ships to be launched in any new channel. There is not to be any question of *doing* any more.

What then? What, when this most extreme and relentless trial of the bonds and imprisonment has shut in? The faint-hearted imagine that all things are at an end. There is no use in trying to make life glorious.

But they are wrong, and the valiant-spirited everywhere reveal it. There was a man in one of these United States who was broken by illness in the prime of his strength. He was a lawyer of brilliant ability, widely beloved in the community where he lived. He had, as few men have, a civic patriotism not to be described by any common phrase, a devotion to his state, her traditions and her people, which had in it all the exaltation of a lover. He already held honorable office by the election of the people. He could have climbed to almost any place of public authority in the gift of his state. But the illness which came to him cut all that short. Every unfolding of the future to which he might have looked forward was blighted as completely as fruit buds are blighted when the killing frost comes. It was as though, in the moment of his life's full career, a sword had struck home to the heart of all his hopes. But not for a moment did he capitulate before disaster. There was no bowing of his head. No wry lines twisted the corners of that mouth which still could smile before the Shadow. It was not that he was resigned only. Rather he was redemptive through the transfiguration of his loss. He permitted round himself no atmosphere of brooding wistfulness, but filled it instead with gallant gaiety. Out of the fagots of his daily weariness he lit the fires to illumine other hearts. Within the prison of his limitation his spirit shone so grandly that men who looked toward its windows saw it as a palace where a king kept festival. And when the doors opened, and his spirit went on the eternal highways, all the word and thought and spirit of him floated back to those who listened like a song.

Is there not something in that experience which the spirit of us all can echo? Have we not all known some who thus have turned the iron into gold, the dark to light, the limitation into infinite enlargement? Are there not some whom we remember afresh and thank God for today who are making their sick-rooms centers of inspiration, and who by their example teach us what we in our time may yet need to remember, that sickness and limitation may be part of God's method for creating life?

When one of the great saints of another century lay dying he cried to God, *Bring my soul out of prison, that I may give thanks unto thy name*. Ultimately God will bring every soul which has been faithful out of any prison which it has dared to enter for Him. But more glorious than coming out of prison may be the courage that dares to go in. From the midst of our modern life, as from the record of ancient Israel, the roll of the heroes may be assembled. Now, as then, that roll will include not only those who subdued kingdoms, stopped the mouths of lions, and escaped the edge of the sword, not only those who have achieved, but those who valiantly endure. Oh, for those today who will add to the company of the mighty ones who, when visited with the bonds and imprisonment of imperfect temperament, of poverty, of ill-will, or sickness, will not flinch before the necessity of that trial! Oh, for those who through all this shall prove their faith in God, their trust in things as yet not seen, and their heroic confidence in the victorious outcome of every faithful life!